JAN RICHARDSON

THE NEXT STEP FORWARD
IN GUIDED READING

An Assess-Decide-Guide Framework for Supporting Every Reader | GRADES K–8

To my six favorite readers:

Caleb, Jacob, Josh, Luke, Anna, and Ryan

Credits

Animals! Animals! by Kate Sinclair. Copyright © 2010 by Scholastic Inc. Published by Scholastic Inc. *Let's Eat!* by Margaret Bellings, illustrated by Amy Lam. Copyright © 2010 by Scholastic Inc. Published by Scholastic Inc. "Alphabet Chart" from *The Next Step in Guided Reading* by Jan Richardson. Illustrations by Maxie Chambliss, copyright © 2009 by Scholastic Inc. "From Seed to Sunflower" by Angela Kaplan from *Next Step Guided Reading Assessment: Grades 3–6*, copyright © 2013 by Scholastic Inc. "Domingo's Cat" from *Guided Reading Short Reads Fiction*, copyright © 2014 by Scholastic Inc. Illustration © Yurchak Alevtina/Shutterstock, Inc. Published by Scholastic Inc. "Landslide Disaster!" from *Superscience* magazine, October 2001. Copyright © 2001 by Scholastic Inc. "Thank You, Ma'm" featured in *Spotlight on . . . Point of View*, compilation copyright © 2004 by Scholastic Inc. Published by Scholastic Inc. First published in *The Langston Hughes Reader* by Langston Hughes. Copyright © 1958 by Langston Hughes. Published by George Braziller, Inc., New York. *Buddy: The First Seeing Eye Dog* by Eva Moore, illustrated by Don Bolognese. Text copyright © 1996 by Eva Moore. Illustrations copyright © 1996 by Don Bolognese. Published by Scholastic Inc. Used by permission. *Hatching Chicks* by Michèle Dufresne. Copyright © 2007 by Michèle Dufresne. Published by Pioneer Valley Educational Press, Inc. Used by permission. *Gorillas* by Ruth Mattison. Copyright © 2011 by Michèle Dufresne. Published by Pioneer Valley Educational Press, Inc. Used by permission. "Just How Smart Are Animals?" from *Guided Reading Short Reads: Nonfiction*, copyright © 2014 by Scholastic Inc. Published by Scholastic Inc. *Jellyfish: Mysterious Creatures From the Sea* by Michèle Dufresne. Copyright © 2013 by Michèle Dufresne. Published by Pioneer Valley Educational Press, Inc. Used by permission. All rights reserved.

Cover Design: Eliza Cerdeiros
Interior Design: Sarah Morrow
Cover Photography: Bob Leverone
Interior Photography: Kevin Carlson/Seed Multimedia LLC, Bob Leverone, and Ellen O. Lewis
Publisher/Acquiring Editor: Lois Bridges
Editor-in-Chief/Development Editor: Raymond Coutu
Editorial Director: Sarah Longhi
Copy Editor/Production Editor: Shelley Griffin

Portions previously published in *The Next Step in Guided Reading*, copyright © 2009 by Jan Richardson.

Excepting those parts intended for classroom use, no part of this publication may be reproduced in whole or in part, or stored in a retrieval system, or transmitted in any form or by any means, electronic, mechanical, photocopying, recording, or otherwise, without written permission of the publisher. For information regarding permission, write to Scholastic Inc., 557 Broadway, New York, NY 10012. Scholastic Inc. grants teachers who have purchased *The Next Step Forward in Guided Reading* permission to reproduce from this book those pages intended for use in their classrooms. Notice of copyright must appear on all copies of copyrighted materials.

Copyright © 2016 by Jan Richardson.
All rights reserved. Published by Scholastic Inc.
Printed in the U.S.A.
ISBN-13: 978-1-338-16111-3

SCHOLASTIC and associated logos are trademarks and/or registered trademarks of Scholastic Inc.
Other company names, brand names, and product names are the property and/or trademarks of their respective owners.
Scholastic does not endorse any product or business entity mentioned herein.

CONTENTS

Acknowledgments 6

Introduction How Can We Move Forward in Guided Reading? 7

Chapter 1 • Guided Reading Essentials 13

Chapter 2 • The Pre-A Reader 26

Chapter 3 • The Emergent Reader: Levels A–C 53

Chapter 4 • The Early Reader: Levels D–I 106

Chapter 5 • The Transitional Reader: Levels J–P 159

Chapter 6 • The Fluent Reader: Levels N and Higher 219

Chapter 7 • Moving Forward With Comprehension 255
    Instruction: Pre-A to Fluent

References 287

Appendices 288

Index 333

Videos

Go to scholastic.com/NSFresources to access this book's full menu of professional videos. Watch Jan teach key parts of lessons with readers at each stage.

Pre-A Video Links

1. Tracing an alphabet book 31
2. Working with names 36
3. Working with letters 37
4. Working with sounds: Picture sorting 39
5. Working with books: Shared reading 40
6. Interactive writing 42
7. Checking letter knowledge 46

Emergent Video Links

1. Sight word review 70
2. Introducing a new book 73
3. Prompting for cross-checking 74
4. Reading the book with prompting 75
5. Selecting a teaching point 77
6. Teaching a new sight word 79
7. Word study: Picture sorting with medial vowels 82
8. Word study: Making words 83
9. Guided writing 90

Early Video Links

1. Sight word review 121
2. Reading the book with prompting 125
3. Retelling 128
4. Selecting a teaching point 129
5. Word study: Making words 134
6. Word study: Sound boxes 136
7. Guided writing 142

Transitional Video Links

1	Using assessment data to guide teaching	163
2	Introducing new vocabulary in four steps	177
3	Reading the book with prompting	178
4	Prompting for phrasing and fluency: Finger sliding	179
5	Discussing a nonfiction text	182
6	Word study: Teaching vowel patterns with an analogy chart	186
7	Word study: Make and break a big word	188
8	Guided writing	197

Fluent Video Links

1	Reading the book with prompting	238
2	Discussing the text: Shared questions	240
3	Discussing the text: Identifying important events that support the central message	240
4	Adding words to the New Word List	242

Comprehension Modules Video Links

Module 1	Comprehension Monitoring: Stop and Use Fix-Up Strategies	258
Module 2	Retelling: Stop, Think, Paraphrase (STP)	259
Module 6	Retelling: Who-What	263
Module 7	Developing Vocabulary: Strategies to Explain New Words	264
Modules 8 and 9	Asking and Answering Questions: Green and Red Questions	265, 266
Module 10	Identifying Main Idea and Details: Very Important Part (V.I.P.) Fiction	267
Module 11	Discussing Main Idea and Details: Very Important Part (V.I.P.) Nonfiction	268
Module 12	Discussing Main Idea and Details: Turning Headings Into Questions	269
Module 13	Analyzing Characters: Track a Character's Feelings	270
Module 15	Analyzing Characters: Who-What-Why	272
Module 18	Analyzing Relationships: Compare and Contrast With Yellow Questions	275
Module 19	Analyzing Relationships: Cause-Effect Questions	276
Module 24	Summarizing: Somebody-Wanted-But-So (Then)	281

Acknowledgments

My list of acknowledgments must begin with Dr. Marie Clay, author of the Reading Recovery® program, who taught me about the reading process and the importance of searching for strengths in struggling readers.

This book is supported with video clips that demonstrate guided reading procedures. I deeply appreciate the teachers and children at Springfield Estates Elementary School, Springfield, Virginia, who joyfully participated in producing the guided reading lessons and teacher interviews.

I owe a profound debt of gratitude to my special friend Ellen Lewis, who wrote the online materials for professional learning. Her expertise and passion for teaching shine through each staff development module.

Sheer courtesy also demands that I thank my dear friends and colleagues Deb Rosenow, Sunday Cummins, Heather Micheli, Sandra Weaver, Julie Allsworth, Carolyn Gwinn, and Karen Cangemi for testing my procedures with children in classrooms throughout America. Their critically important work ensures this book is grounded in sound practice.

I cannot thank my friend Dr. Michèle Dufresne enough for her suggestions and advice. I especially appreciate her generous gift of allowing us to use materials from Pioneer Valley Books in this book and in the accompanying video clips. I also thank C. C. Bates of Clemson University for her deep read of Chapters 3 and 4, and the extremely helpful feedback she provided.

No author could have received better support from her editors. I appreciate the extensive editorial assistance from Ray Coutu, Lois Bridges, and Sarah Longhi, whose attention to detail has provided a much more polished work.

Copy editor/production editor Shelley Griffin made many sound suggestions for improving the book, and Sarah Morrow created a beautiful, easy-to-navigate interior design. I am most grateful to both of them.

My thanks to the many teachers and administrators who have invited me into their schools and classrooms to conduct workshops and give presentations. These exceptional educators inspire me with their uncompromising commitment to teaching excellence. To each of them I owe a deep debt of gratitude.

Last, but certainly not least, I thank my husband, Cecil, for his patience and support during the countless hours of research, traveling, and writing. His ideas and suggestions were invaluable.

Introduction

I love guided reading! It makes me smile to see children lean over a table, dig into a book, solve problems, and construct meaning. Why? Because these precious children are experiencing a wonderful feeling of accomplishment. They know they are becoming better readers, and they're excited about it. I'm convinced that there is no instructional approach more powerful than guided reading. What an honor it is to see lives changed forever by the simple yet profound joy of learning to read!

Let me share a story from Allyson DeYoung, a former fifth-grade teacher who is now a principal in Chattanooga, Tennessee. Allyson witnessed a complete transformation in Deshaun, a struggling, angry, reluctant reader who came to her school reading on a second-grade level.

> Deshaun, a fifth grader who lived with his mother and grandfather, rode a school bus every morning from the inner city to our school in the suburbs. As one of the very few African American children in our school of 500, Deshaun was extremely self-conscious. He was quiet, distant, and at times volatile. At the beginning of the school year, he was reading at a second-grade level, far below where he needed to be as a fifth grader.
>
> One day, Dr. Jan Richardson visited our school and modeled guided reading instruction with our below-grade-level students. I shared with her that I didn't think Deshaun would be able to catch up by the end of the year.
>
> I'll never forget Dr. Richardson's response. After giving me some instructional advice on how to meet Deshaun's needs, she said, "Allyson, you are Deshaun's Obi-Wan Kenobi." In other words, I was his only hope for success. (Star Wars fans will understand.) If I couldn't teach Deshaun to read, he would suffer his entire life. That conversation left me with a profound sense of urgency.
>
> I decided to meet with him every day for a ten-minute, one-on-one transitional guided reading lesson. After identifying his areas of strength, I began to work with

Deshaun using texts he liked and could read successfully. It was fascinating to see the change in him as we consistently met for daily reading instruction. By January, Deshaun had made enough progress to join a guided reading group, but I continued the daily one-on-one lessons.

At the end of the year, Deshaun was reading at grade level. In fact, he performed "proficient" on the state assessments in reading, writing, science, and social studies, and "advanced" in math. He was so proud! As for me, his Obi-Wan Kenobi, I was beyond words, completely overwhelmed with joy.

Deshaun continued to excel in middle school and high school. He played football and was on the honor roll almost every semester. He received a football scholarship, and today he's in his third year of college. Deshaun's future is bright!

Oh, how I love being an Obi-Wan Kenobi!

UNDERSTANDING GUIDED READING

Heartwarming stories like Deshaun's are not uncommon in a guided reading classroom. Guided reading is strategic, differentiated small-group reading instruction. Its aim is clear: to help readers confidently, proficiently, and independently process increasingly challenging texts.

Based on 40 years of irrefutable research drawing from cognitive science and the linguistic principles that inform our understanding of language and literacy development (Clay, 1975; Richardson, 2009; Richardson & Walther, 2013; Fountas & Pinnell, 2016), guided reading supports all readers: striving, advanced, and dual language learners (DLLs).

Regardless of the grade level you teach or your students' reading stages, the basic tenets of guided reading remain constant:

- Teachers match students with challenging books that are at their instructional reading level and support their next reading goal.

- Students become better readers by reading, self-monitoring, and problem solving their way through text, rereading as needed to check understanding.

- Teachers are intentional in their instruction and responsive to the specific needs of their students.

- Teachers know when to step in and scaffold and when to reduce support, enabling students to move forward as independent readers.

Researcher Anita Iaquinta describes guided reading as one of the "most important contemporary reading instructional practices in the United States" (Fawson & Reutzel, 2000). Simply stated, guided reading has propelled millions of children into successful independent reading.

HOW CAN WE MOVE FORWARD IN GUIDED READING?

Whether you are brand new to guided reading or have been teaching it for years, this book will help you move forward in your instruction by using the Assess-Decide-Guide framework. These three basic steps simplify the guided reading process while they ratchet up each lesson's effectiveness.

Assess

Assessment is not a popular word in America's schools. Because districts and states are requiring more and more testing, teachers are being deprived of valuable time for instruction. This is especially sad because most of the mandated assessments have little or no instructional value. They don't help children become better readers, nor do they assist teachers in deciding how to meet the needs of students who struggle. Guided reading, on the other hand, utilizes formative assessments that help teachers make instructional decisions about grouping and text selection. Teachers conduct systematic assessments to determine student strengths and needs (Richardson & Walther, 2013) so they can place students in flexible groups for efficient reading instruction. While every child has unique strengths and challenges, students in a guided reading group are enough alike that they can be taught together. Teachers select slightly challenging texts for each group—books students will be able to process successfully with instruction (Richardson, 2009). Other assessment goals include the following:

- Know each student's reading habits and preferences.
- Pinpoint each child's developmental word knowledge.
- Understand a learner's ability to comprehend in various reading (or listening) situations.

- Determine a child's instructional reading level.
- Identify the skills and strategies a student needs to learn in order to become a proficient reader.

Decide

Because they reveal a student's strengths and needs, assessments have tremendous value when they're used to make instructional decisions. With assessment information in hand, we can

- Form flexible, needs-based groups
- Pinpoint an instructional focus
- Select texts that will compel readers to think and problem-solve
- Differentiate and evaluate reading instruction
- Monitor progress

Guide

The framework shows you how to use your assessment to plan and teach powerful guided reading lessons. As you work with students, you will uncover the optimal instructional area, also known as the Zone of Proximal Development (Vygotsky, 1978). Stay in this zone as you

- Introduce the text and state the learning target
- Scaffold and teach for strategies
- Incorporate word study and vocabulary instruction

- Connect reading and writing
- Engage readers!

The "Guide" sections in each chapter describe in detail the lesson plan for each level. Each lesson plan is divided into three broad categories: reading, word study, and writing. By integrating reading, word study, and writing, students are able to make connections between these reciprocal processes. The errors you notice as students read reveal what they need to learn about words and how words work. Armed with this information, you can then provide explicit instruction during guided word study on the necessary phonemic awareness and phonic elements. During the guided writing component, students have the opportunity to apply what you have taught them. For example, if students struggle to read words that contain digraphs or blends, you would have them sort pictures or make words with digraphs and blends during word study. During guided writing, you would look for opportunities to reinforce those same skills as students write about the book they just read.

How This Book Is Organized

Chapter 1 provides a general overview of how guided reading fits into a balanced reading program. It includes ideas for fostering student independence and setting up independent literacy activities.

Chapters 2 through 6 each focus on a level of reader (i.e., pre-A, emergent, early, transitional, and fluent). I have used the alphabetic reading levels created by Fountas and Pinnell (2008) to help you pinpoint the stage that best matches your students' reading abilities.

Reading Stage	Alphabetic Level	Approximate Grade Range
Pre-A	—	Pre-K
Emergent	A–C	K
Early	D–I	1
Transitional	J–P	2–3
Fluent	N and Higher	3–5

Each chapter is organized around an Assess-Decide-Guide framework that will guide your assessment process and inform your instruction.

Chapter 7 focuses on reading comprehension. It contains 29 easy-to-follow modules that address as least one of 12 essential comprehension strategies. I label these strategies "essential" because children cannot move forward as readers until they fully comprehend what they read. Each of the 29 modules showcases one of my favorite scaffolds for teaching comprehension. After a brief description of the scaffold, you'll find step-by-step guidelines for teaching the strategy across a series of lessons.

All Appendix items can be downloaded from scholastic.com/NSFresources.

The Appendices contain essential tools you'll use practically every day in your teaching: detailed lists of strategies and skills by level, word lists by level, an illustrated alphabet chart, the Letter/Sound Checklist, lesson plan templates for all five stages, Sight Word Charts, cards for shared retelling, sound box and analogy chart templates, a sample Word Knowledge Inventory, New Word List template, a list of character feelings and traits, comprehension cards, and more.

Targeted and intentional instruction characterizes the daily routine of a guided reading teacher (Richardson & Walther, 2013). The teacher continuously monitors progress: Are students developing efficient processing systems? Are they engaged with the text and using strategies that enhance their comprehension? Are they ready to read more challenging texts? Guided reading calls for hard work from the teacher and students, but it's the best guarantee we have that our precious students will hit their stride and become proficient readers who gain maximum insight, knowledge, and enjoyment from the texts they read. That's why we became teachers in the first place—and that's where we get our joy!

Professional Study Guide

Go to scholastic.com/NSFresources for a downloadable professional study guide written just for this book. This guide will help you understand and apply to your teaching the information and ideas presented in this book. Use its chapter-specific questions and activities on your own or with your colleagues in a study group or professional learning community to realize the full benefits of The Next Step Forward in Guided Reading.

CHAPTER 1

Guided Reading Essentials

This chapter explains the essential elements of guided reading and how guided reading complements yet differs from other approaches to reading instruction. You will also find steps and guidelines for fostering independence and establishing literacy routines for reading workshop so you can teach guided reading without interruptions.

A DEFINITION

Guided reading is small-group differentiated instruction that supports students in developing reading proficiency. It acknowledges that children bring different backgrounds and instructional experiences to the reading process and therefore move forward at different rates. The small-group model allows teachers to target specific learning needs, provide appropriate scaffolding, and gradually reduce support to promote independence. Guided reading essentials include small groups, instructional-leveled texts, and targeted teaching.

Small-Group Instruction

The teacher conducts guided reading in small groups (four to six students), based on each student's individual needs. Groups are flexible. Configurations change as students progress and as the teacher identifies new learning goals. These small groups allow children to feel supported as they take risks to problem-solve texts and construct meaning.

Slightly Challenging Text

Texts are chosen at the group members' instructional reading level, not at their independent level. In other words, the text should be a tad too hard. As students read, they should encounter challenges that require them to problem-solve and practice strategies that help them comprehend and discuss the passage. Celebrate errors as opportunities for teaching and learning.

Targeted Teaching

Assessments are critical to guided reading lessons. Use assessments to group students and pinpoint specific skills and strategies students need to learn next. As students read, you will observe, listen, question, prompt, and coach. The interactions between students and the teacher help students internalize the strategy focus so they can apply the skill independently. Teacher involvement is key to acceleration.

BALANCING THE READING PROGRAM

Guided reading does not stand alone. Each guided reading lesson should build on the lessons you teach the whole class. During whole-class instruction use read-aloud and shared reading experiences to teach state standards. Then, while you teach a guided lesson, other students can practice the state standard and other strategies on texts at their independent level. Guided reading is the scaffold between modeling and independence.

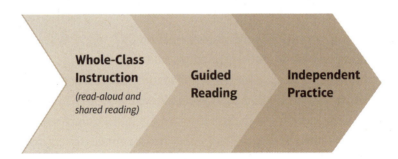

Read-Aloud

Reading aloud to students is an important component of a reading program at any grade level. It provides opportunities to foster interest and motivation, model fluent reading, engage students in discussing and analyzing a text, and demonstrate comprehension strategies. An interactive read-aloud (Fountas & Pinnell, 2001; Hoyt,

2009) is a slightly different approach. Its purpose is to encourage reflective thinking and enhance comprehension by guiding students in discussing the text. During an interactive read-aloud, you read a text to students and stop two or three times during the reading to pose questions that encourage deeper thinking. As students turn to a neighbor to talk about the book, they share their thinking and listen to and value the opinions of their classmates. Employ a variety of genres, including nonfiction and poetry, so children can apply comprehension strategies and standards to different kinds of texts.

Shared Reading

Shared reading, conducted with the whole class, is often used for focus lessons (also called mini-lessons). Select a grade-level text that supports a specific instructional focus or reading standard. Primary-grade teachers commonly use big books, charts, or a text displayed on an interactive whiteboard. With intermediate students, shared reading can be done with poetry charts, content area textbooks, novels, anthologies, or short passages. Give students a copy of the text or display it on an interactive whiteboard so they can follow along. As with read-alouds, you should use a variety of genres.

The purposes of shared reading is to teach skills and strategies, increase reading fluency, and support developing readers. The challenge of shared reading is keeping students engaged and focused. To help them stay on task, I suggest limiting shared reading to 10–15 minutes.

Independent, Self-Selected Reading

Create a love for reading by knowing your students' reading interests. Students should have an opportunity each day to read books they select themselves. Allowing them to choose the books they read boosts their reading motivation, but you should monitor the texts to ensure they are not too difficult. I have found that some intermediate students will select texts that are too challenging because they see someone else reading them. The problem is, students will lose interest if they encounter too many unknown words. Teach students how to choose books they will like and are able to read. Independent reading improves automaticity with sight words, increases fluency, and gives students an opportunity to practice the strategies you have taught. During individual reading conferences, you can discuss book selection, teach needed skills or strategies, evaluate progress, and identify the next learning goal. To assess comprehension and monitor accountability, you might want to require a weekly written response related to the student's independent reading notebook.

Summary of Balanced Reading Approaches

Approach	Grouping	Text Level	How Text Is Read	Purpose
Guided reading	Small group	Student's instructional level	By students while the teacher coaches	Practice reading strategies with teacher support Differentiate instruction based on need
Read-aloud	Whole class	Above grade level	By the teacher	Model fluent reading and reading strategies Support comprehension Expand vocabulary Motivate students to read
Shared reading	Whole class	On grade level	By students and the teacher	Teach strategies and standards Support oral language
Independent, self-selected reading	Individual	Student's independent level (varies by student)	By the student	Promote enjoyment, fluency, and comprehension Practice strategies that have been internalized

Teaching Independence

As you prepare your students for guided reading, you will need to establish firm routines for working independently or in small groups. Explicitly teach procedures for the literacy activities they will be doing while you teach a guided reading lesson. Students will need to solve problems without asking for your help.

Cathy, a dear friend of mine, attended a guided reading workshop years ago and went back to her classroom thrilled about what guided reading could do for her kindergarten students. The next day she taught her class six literacy centers and a guided reading lesson! What a disaster! She almost quit teaching. When she contacted me, I gave her tips on how to engage children independently in literacy activities so she could teach guided reading lessons without interruption. Cathy is now one of the most polished and effective guided reading teachers I know, but she learned the hard way that children must be taught independence for guided reading to work.

The following six-week schedule for primary grades gradually releases responsibility from the teacher to the students and teaches classroom routines and procedures. If students have worked in stations or centers in previous grades, you may not need the full six weeks; however, I strongly recommend you follow this plan if you teach kindergarten.

The First Six Weeks, K–1: Teaching Routines and Procedures for Reading Workshop

Week 1: Prepare for reading workshop by building community and collaboration. Have students work in small groups for ten minutes each day doing activities they can manage with little direction from you. I call these activities "tub activities" because you can place easy, independent activities in separate plastic or rubber tubs. For example, you might have tubs of nonfiction books, puzzles, blank writing journals, Legos®, coloring books, etc. Tub activities will eventually be replaced by literacy activities as you teach students to be independent learners.

Week 2: Introduce a literacy activity to one of the groups each day while the other groups work on tub activities. Literacy activities will vary by grade level, but they should always be authentic reading and writing experiences that build on the whole-class instruction you've provided. Examples include reading books, listening to recorded books, and retelling familiar stories.

Week 3: Introduce a second literacy activity and lengthen the reading workshop time to 15 minutes.

Week 4: Lengthen the reading workshop to 20 minutes and introduce a new literacy activity to one of the groups each day.

Week 5: Introduce another literacy activity while other groups work on tub activities or on previously introduced literacy activities. By the end of the fifth week, students should be able to work 30–45 minutes without direct supervision. Continue to assess students, adjust practices, and clarify expectations for each independent literacy activity.

Week 6: All students should be working independently with purposeful literacy experiences. The tubs should no longer be required.

After Week 6, as you gradually lengthen the time for reading workshops, teach two or three guided reading groups each day. To maximize engagement, alternate whole-class and small-group instruction. On the next page is a sample schedule based on a 90–100 minute literacy block. Your schedule will reflect the requirements from your district and the needs of your students.

Sample Reading Workshop Schedule	
Time	Instruction
10–15 minutes	Whole-Class Focus Lesson—Read-Aloud (comprehension)
20 minutes	Guided Reading/Independent Literacy Activities
10–15 minutes	Whole-Class Focus Lesson—Shared Reading (poetry, informational text, big book)
20 minutes	Guided Reading/Independent Literacy Activities
10–15 minutes	Whole-Class Focus Lesson—Word Study, Vocabulary, Phonics
20 minutes	Guided Reading/Independent Literacy Activities

Literacy Activities

The most common question I get from teachers who are new to guided reading is, "What are the other children doing while I'm teaching a small group?" My answer is always, "Keep it simple. They should be reading, writing, listening, and speaking (softly)."

A first-grade teacher in Tampa, Florida, invited me to visit her classroom and offer advice on her guided reading instruction. The only day I had available was the day after winter break, and the only time I had free was the last 30 minutes of the day. (Not the most ideal time for reading lessons!) When I walked into her classroom, I saw six children sitting or standing around a table totally engrossed in writing stories. As soon as they saw me, they asked if they could read their stories to me. (I've never had a student ask to read a worksheet to me!) I also saw three children sitting at computers. They were wearing headphones and listening to stories. On the floor were three small circles of four to six students. In the middle of each circle was a stack of guided reading books. One student passed out the books and then said, "Let's read." All the children in that circle read the story together. When they finished the book, the leader passed out another. I was amazed at how softly they read with everyone on task. Then in the far corner of the room, I saw the teacher working with a guided reading group. How many "centers" did she have? Only three: reading, writing, and listening. It was simple and it worked!

Independent literacy activities provide an opportunity for students at every grade to engage in purposeful practice while you work with individuals or a small group. When possible, connect the independent activities to the whole-class lesson. If you did an interactive read-aloud, students can write about the book during independent practice. Primary students might draw pictures and write a few sentences that describe important events that happened in the beginning, middle, and end of the story. Intermediate students might compare the story elements or themes of two picture books you read to them. No matter what students are doing during reading workshop, it is important they understand the procedures and expectations for each activity.

Gail Boushey and Joan Moser (2014) have developed a simple framework for their literacy block. Students not meeting with the teacher for reading instruction do one of the following activities: read to self, read to someone, listen to reading, work on writing, or do word work. The beauty of this approach is that it is easy to manage. Students choose three or four of those activities each day.

You can find plenty of ideas in books and on the Internet about independent literacy activities. Find the activities that work for your students and explicitly teach the routines. Following are some activities I have used. They can be adapted for any grade level.

Book boxes

Students have a personal box or bag that contains a variety of books for independent reading. Include books students have read during guided reading and other easy books they can read without support. This activity gives students an opportunity to develop fluency and practice strategies on easy, familiar texts. At the beginning of kindergarten, include alphabet books, easy nonfiction books, and traditional tales. Although kindergartners will probably not be able to read these books, they can look at the pictures and practice book-handling skills. When you begin guided reading sessions, include books they have read with you so they can increase reading fluency and automaticity with sight words.

Buddy reading

Students choose a book from their book box to read with another student. The children often sit next to each other so they can see the text at the same time. Buddy reading can be done in several ways: Students can share one book and take turns reading a page; they can take turns reading an entire book from their box; or they can share a book and read chorally. After students read a book, they should briefly retell what they read or heard. You must, of course, teach children how to whisper-read.

Writing

Students write individually or with a partner and usually continue the work they are doing during writing workshop. Motivation increases if children are allowed to choose their own topics. Some teachers set up a writing corner that includes special writing tools (colored pens, markers, stamps, stickers, sticky notes, colored paper, fancy stationery, etc.). You could establish a message board or post office for students to leave messages for friends and teachers, and have covers of used greeting cards available so students can use them for a personal message.

Readers Theater

This is a highly motivating way to get students to reread a text. While you teach guided reading, students prepare for a Readers Theater performance by reading and rereading a script. They are not required to memorize or act out the play but are encouraged to use their voices, facial expressions, and hand gestures to interpret the dialogue. Scripts for Readers Theater are available in books and on the Internet. Teachers and students may also adapt favorite stories through collaborative script-writing activities. If you schedule a performance time every Friday, all you have to do to maintain this activity is make new scripts available on Monday. You could assign a script to each group or allow the groups to choose the script they want to perform that week. Obviously, each group should have a different script.

Poems and songs

Poetry books are a favorite for children of all ages. Each week, teach a new poem to the whole class. Then give each student a copy of the poem to put in their personal poetry notebook. Primary students can illustrate the poem and reread it to themselves or with a buddy. Intermediate students can write about the poems (make connections, expand on the theme, describe figurative language) or use the weekly poem as a mentor text to write their own poem.

Angela Kheradmand from Fairfax County, Virginia, uses poetry notebooks to facilitate cross-age tutoring in her Title I school. Each first-grade student reading below grade level is paired with a sixth grader who has applied to be a reading coach. These partnerships meet every morning during the first 20 minutes of the day to reread the first-grade poetry notebooks. The first graders love the personal attention of the "reading coach," and the sixth graders enjoy interacting with and helping the lower-grade students. Although any sixth grader can apply to be a reading coach, Angela was surprised that several struggling readers applied for the position. The 20 minutes of extra reading increased their fluency, too!

ABCs, word study, and spelling

Kindergartners can match magnetic letters to an alphabet chart, match uppercase and lowercase letters, make classmates' names, or practice easy sight words you have introduced to the class. To practice letter formation, they can trace their names with colored dry-erase markers. Once you begin word study lessons, students can sort words or make spelling words out of magnetic letters.

Word wall

If you have a classroom word wall, students can use special materials such as glitter markers, magnetic letters, or Magna Doodles™ to copy the wall words. Any phonics skill that has been taught to the whole group can be practiced using the words on the word wall. Students can find words with short or long vowel sounds, silent *e*, initial or final consonant blends, words within a word, inflectional endings, etc.

Listening to recorded stories

Students listen to recorded stories and follow along with copies of the text. After the reading, they can respond to the story by softly retelling it with a partner, drawing a picture of their favorite part, writing three sentences that retell the beginning, middle, and end (B-M-E), writing a Five-Finger Retell (second or third grade), or doing a story map.

Oral retelling

Every primary classroom should have a retelling corner. Once you read a book to the class, place it in the retelling corner. Include some retelling props such as three paper plates that have the words *beginning*, *middle*, and *end* (B-M-E) written on them. Or you can take a new garden glove and write a story element on each finger: characters, setting, problem, events, and solution. This becomes the Five-Finger Retell.
Students can practice the comprehension strategies described in Chapter 7 of this book with familiar stories. They can ask and answer questions, compare and contrast the settings or characters from two different books, identify the main idea, etc. Whatever comprehension strategy you have taught during whole-class instruction can be practiced using familiar stories.

Computer

Use software that reinforces skills you have already taught the class. Never expect computers to teach new skills or strategies. Computers cannot take the place of teachers, but they can be useful in reinforcing learning. Students can sort words by their spelling features, write stories, or use educational software that focuses on phonemic awareness.

Research related to content areas

Students work on projects related to content areas. They can work individually or in small groups to research a topic and prepare a presentation that summarizes their learning.

Literacy Activities for the Intermediate Grades

Although many of the activities described above can be adapted for intermediate students, I prefer that those students read self-selected books and write about them while the teacher does guided reading.

MOVING FORWARD

The chapters that follow focus on guided reading lessons at a specific stage of reading (i.e., pre-A, emergent, early, transitional, and fluent). The procedures are organized around an Assess-Decide-Guide framework to help you take the next step forward in guided reading instruction.

QUESTIONS TEACHERS ASK ABOUT GUIDED READING

How is guided reading different from literature circles?

In literature circles (also called book clubs), students read the same book and meet in small groups a few times a week to discuss it. They are taught to express their opinions, predictions, and questions. Some teachers ask students to take on specific roles, such as summarizer, director, and investigator, to provide more structure for the discussion. As students become more skilled in literature circle conversations, they move beyond those roles.

Guided reading and literature circles can coexist in the intermediate classroom. In guided reading, the teacher uses assessment results to form groups and select a challenging text that meets a specific comprehension focus. While he or she is working with the group, other students can be reading their literature circle novel and preparing for the discussion.

	Guided Reading	**Literature Circles**
Groups	Needs-based by teacher	Student-selected by interest
Text level	Students' instructional level	Students' independent level
Genre	Short texts or selected excerpts: fiction, informational, poetry	Mostly fiction/novels
How the text is read	With teacher prompting and scaffolding	Independently
How the text is discussed	With teacher scaffolding and guidance	Without teacher support
Primary purpose	Improve strategic processing	Encourage thoughtful discussion and a love of reading

How do I get everything done in the allotted time?

If you truly want to get everything in, you need to keep to your schedule. Use a timer for guided reading and whole-class lessons. See the suggested reading workshop schedule on page 18.

How do I know students are actually reading their self-selected books?

You can monitor self-selected reading in a variety of ways:

- *Reading conference.* Schedule a short weekly conference with students who are not engaged during independent reading. Check the text level. Help them find books they like and can read.
- *Written responses.* Have students write a one-page response to the book they are reading, possibly connecting the response to your whole-class instruction. For example, if your focus lessons have been about making inferences based on a character's actions, have students write about three places in their book where they made that type of inference.
- *Reading logs.* Ask students to keep a log of the books they have read.
- *Impromptu book talks.* Each day ask a few students to talk briefly about their independent reading books.

How can I keep children from interrupting me while I teach guided reading?

- Demonstrate and practice routines so students know exactly what to do during all parts of reading workshop, including guided reading.
- Do not respond to children who interrupt you during guided reading. If you do, they will continue interrupting.
- Place a couple of chairs on either side of the guided reading table. If students become disruptive, ask them to sit in the chairs and read from their book boxes while you teach your lesson to the other students. When the lesson is over, you can deal with the problem.

What should the reading notebook look like for intermediate readers?

A reading notebook is a tool for monitoring and assessing independent reading and guided reading. Students can take a composition notebook and create dividers for each section, or you can have your district print notebooks for your students. Here are my recommendations for sections of the notebook:

Part 1: Independent Reading Record. Reserve the first five pages of the notebook for students to record the title, author, and genre of books they read.

Part 2: Independent Reading Responses. Each week, have students write a one-page response to their independent reading book. If they use both sides of the page, they need only about 20 pages for this section.

Part 3: Guided Reading Notes. Delegate the next 30 pages for students to use during guided reading. They can jot down their thinking, record questions, write summaries, and create graphic organizers that relate to the comprehension strategy focus. They can also use this section to write longer responses during guided writing lessons.

Part 4: New Word List. Save the last seven to ten pages for students to record vocabulary they learned during guided reading and whole-class instruction. Students write the new word in the first column and a synonym for it in the second. Every week or so, test students on words they learned most recently.

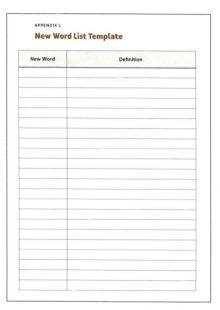

Appendix L

Professional Study Guide

Go to scholastic.com/NSFresources for a downloadable professional study guide written just for this book. In it, you'll find questions and activities about guided reading to use on your own or with your colleagues in a study group or PLC.

CHAPTER 2

The Pre-A Reader

William knew he couldn't read. He told me so as he walked through my door. The only letter he knew was the *W* in his name. After our first Reading Recovery® lesson, I gave him one of the easy books we had read together. He bolted out of my room to the principal's office, waved the little book in the principal's face, and said, "Mrs. Jones, I can read!"

PROFILE OF A PRE-A READER

Children enter school with different literacy experiences. Some know all their letters and sounds on the first day of kindergarten, but others know only a few letters and no sounds. Research shows that students who enter school with a meager knowledge of letters and sounds are seriously at risk (Allington, 2011). The good news is we can change the literacy course for these readers by providing developmentally appropriate, small-group instruction.

Pre-A readers know fewer than 40 upper- and lowercase letters. These children often lack concepts of print, such as left-to-right tracking and the difference between a letter and a word. Most pre-A readers need help learning how to write their first name, especially with correct letter formation. Many educators think that students need to learn all their letters and sounds before they can read a book. The truth is, much can be learned about letters, sounds, and words by reading and writing. The pre-A teaching procedures contained in this chapter are highly contextualized to engage students in literacy learning while they read and write. During pre-A lessons, students learn the following foundational skills:

- Letter names and sounds
- Letter formation

- Phonological awareness, including hearing syllables, rhymes, and initial consonant sounds
- Concepts of print
- Oral language

ASSESS

The letter/sound assessment is the only assessment you need for planning pre-A lessons. This assessment will tell you which letters and sounds students know and which ones you need to teach. Show each student an alphabet chart in which the letters are out of sequence. Point to each letter and ask the student to say the letter name. Highlight the letters the student identifies on the Letter/Sound Checklist and update weekly until he or she knows all the letters and sounds.

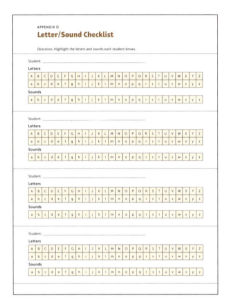

Appendix D

DECIDE

Keep the Letter/Sound Checklist handy. You will use it to determine which letters and sounds to teach in your pre-A lesson. You can also use the checklist during the lesson to record new letters and sounds students are beginning to recognize.

Form Groups

Use the results of the letter/sound assessment to form groups of three or four students. For example, children who know the fewest letters will be in the same group so you can better target their needs. At the beginning of kindergarten, you may have several pre-A groups. You will see substantial progress within four to six weeks of instruction. It's common to have only one pre-A group left after two months of school.

Select a Text and Materials

During the pre-A lesson, children chorally read a book with you. Use a simple, Level A book that has engaging pictures and one line of text per page.

Since young children learn best with kinesthetic-tactile experiences, you will use a variety of materials. During every lesson component, children should have something in their hands, such as magnetic letters, picture cards, markers, pointers, and books. Here is a list of materials you will need:

- Alphabet books (one per student)
- Alphabet charts in plastic sheet protectors (Appendix C)
- Name templates
- Name puzzles
- 6–8 sets of lowercase magnetic letters
- Dry-erase markers
- Pictures for sorting by initial consonant
- Sentence strips
- Pair of scissors
- Level A books
- Timer

Prepare and Organize Materials

Before the lesson, prepare the following materials for each student and place them in a plastic tub. To keep materials organized, use a different tub for each pre-A group.

Name template

Print the first name of each student on a sheet of white paper and place it inside the plastic sheet protector that contains the alphabet chart so that the alphabet chart is visible on one side and the name template on the other.

Name puzzle

Write each student's first name on a strip of tag board. Cut into two pieces and place in an envelope. Print the student's name on the front of the envelope.

Magnetic letters in personal letter bag

Label each quart-size plastic bag with the student's name. Insert the lowercase magnetic letters the student knows and the letters in his or her first name even if the student doesn't know them. If the student knows fewer than ten letters, include two of each letter. Assess students' letter knowledge every week, and add new letters they have learned. Once the student knows at least ten lowercase letters, remove the duplicate letters from the bag.

Pictures for sorting

Label 20 envelopes with the consonants (excluding the letter *x*). In each envelope insert six to eight pictures that begin with each consonant. Avoid pictures with beginning blends.

GUIDE

All students benefit from whole-group activities such as read-alouds, shared reading, and shared writing. The specific needs of pre-A students are best addressed with individual and small-group lessons. The two procedures described in this chapter, tracing an alphabet book with a tutor and using the pre-A lesson framework, quickly teach letter names and sounds, phonemic awareness, concepts of print, and oral language. My research has shown that the sooner you begin these lessons, the better chance these students have to catch up with their peers. To achieve the best results, do both procedures every day.

Tracing an Alphabet Book

It is important for these children to learn the entire set of letters as soon as possible. Students should trace an alphabet book with a tutor every day. You can use any simple alphabet book, but the process works best if the pictures in the student's ABC book are the same pictures on your classroom alphabet chart or frieze. Each page of the alphabet book should have the uppercase and lowercase letter along with a picture. Do not include the word for the picture, as it can be confusing.

The goal of the tracing is for the student to learn the name of each letter, correct letter formation, and a picture link for the letter sound. The tracing occurs outside the pre-A small-group lesson and is usually done by a teaching assistant, a volunteer, or an upper-grade student. Be sure to train tutors in the following procedures:

Tracing procedures

The tutor and student sit next to each other with the tutor sitting on the student's dominant side so he or she can guide the student's hand when necessary.

The student uses his or her pointing finger to trace each uppercase and lowercase letter in the ABC book, saying the name of the letter each time. Then the student points to the picture and names it (e.g., *A, a, apple*). Do not allow students to trace with a pencil or marker. The tactile experience is essential for building a memory trace for the letter (Fernald, 1943). The tutor observes the student trace each letter and helps if the student struggles with remembering the name of the letter, using correct letter formation, or identifying the picture concept.

- If the student does not know the name of the letter, the tutor says the letter name. Then the student should repeat the name of the letter while tracing it with his or her finger.
- If the student does not know how to form a letter correctly, the tutor lightly holds the student's hand and helps trace the letter. Always have the student trace the letter from top to bottom.
- If the student does not know the concept in the picture, the tutor should explain the concept and have the student repeat the picture.
- If the student knows fewer than ten letters, have the student trace only the letters he or she knows and the letters in his or her first name for one month. For example, if Isaiah can only identify the letters *x* and *o* by name, he should trace

the letters *a, h, i,* and *s* (because they are in his name) and the letters *x* and *o*. If after four weeks the child still knows fewer than ten letters, have the student trace every letter in the book. Sometimes the letters in the child's name are not the easiest to learn. You can never predict which letters the student will learn first. (At age three, my son learned the letter *M* first because of McDonald's!)

Assess letter knowledge each week and track progress on the Letter/Sound Checklist. Discontinue the tracing when the student identifies at least 40 letters.

Watch Jan guiding a student to trace an alphabet book.

Research on tracing

For 20 years I have been collecting data on tracing the alphabet book. Tracing is by far the fastest and easiest way for children to learn their letters, even if they are learning English. Rates will vary, but most students learn about five to ten letters a week. Some who begin the year knowing fewer than ten letters progress at a slower rate and may take up to 12 weeks to learn all 52. It is extremely rare to take longer than 12 weeks if the tracing is done consistently.

For the past several years, I've worked with a rural North Carolina Title I school that has 91 percent qualifying for free or reduced lunch and 32 percent dual language learners (DLLs). In 2015 (a typical year), 40 out of 62 kindergartners (65 percent) entered school knowing fewer than 40 letters. After four weeks of tracing, only four (6 percent) were still pre-A, knowing fewer than 40 letters.

Progress of Pre-A Students Who Knew Fewer Than 40 Letters			
Total Students Entry to K	Total Pre-A Entry to K	Total Pre-A After 4 Weeks of Tracing	Total Pre-A After 8 Weeks of Tracing
62	40 (65%)	25 (40%)	4 (6%)

As I was writing this chapter, I asked the kindergarten teachers from this school to send me their midyear reading levels as measured by their state's (North Carolina) Reading 3D assessment. The 3D assessment uses PC to identify pre-A readers and RB for Level A. The chart below demonstrates what is possible for a high-poverty school after only one semester of instruction. I can't wait to see their data at the end of the year! These teachers have altered the future for the children in their classrooms. They're definitely on a pathway to success.

Midyear Reading Levels for Kindergarten (N=59)					
Pre-A* (PC)	A (RB)	B	C	D	E
1	10	15	17	11	5

This pre-A student is classified with a developmental delay.

A Title I school in Virginia sent me data on their pre-A students. They have 92 percent DLL (no, that's not a typo!), and 86 percent of their students qualify for free or reduced lunch. At the beginning of the school year, only 31 of their 107 kindergarten students (29 percent) knew 40 letters or more. After three months of using pre-A lessons and letter tracing, 88 percent knew their letters (94 percent after four months).

Progress of Pre-A Students in Kindergarten (Title 1 School, 86% Poverty)				
	Sep 3	Nov 1	Dec 17	Jan 15
# of pre-A students	76	49	13	6
% of kindergarten who were pre-A	71%	46%	12%	6%

What effect does learning letters as soon as possible have on a student's reading progress? I asked this school to send me their end-of-year data. The chart below again demonstrates the impressive impact of tracing the alphabet book and pre-A lessons. Eighty-six percent read Level C or higher, which was the end-of-year benchmark.

End-of-Year Reading Levels for Kindergarten (Title 1 School, 86% Poverty)				
	Level A	Level B	Level C	Level D+
Percent of students at this reading level	1%	13%	35%	51%

The Pre-A Lesson

In addition to tracing an alphabet book every day, students who know fewer than 40 letters should receive small-group instruction that targets foundational skills. The pre-A lesson has four distinct components designed to improve alphabet knowledge, visual processing, rapid naming of letters, writing one's own name, phonological awareness, oral language, and concepts of print. These are the building blocks of emergent literacy and strong predictors of reading success (Shanahan, et al., 2008).

Overview of the Pre-A Lesson

Working With Names and Letters
Working With Sounds
Working With Books
Interactive Writing

Pre-A Lesson Plan (< 40 letters)

Students: _____ Date: _____

COMPONENTS AND ACTIVITIES	OBSERVATIONS/NOTES
Working With Names *(2–3 minutes)* Choose one. Omit once child can write first name without a model (using correct letter formation).	
☐ Name puzzle ☐ Magnetic letters ☐ Rainbow writing	
Working With Letters *(2–3 minutes)* Choose one per day. Activities 5, 6, and 7 are for children who know at least 30 letters.	
☐ 1. Match the letters in the bag ☐ 2. Match letters to an ABC chart ☐ 3. Name letters left to right ☐ 4. Find the letter on an ABC chart ☐ 5. Name a word that begins with that letter ☐ 6. Find the letter that makes that sound ☐ 7. Name the letter that begins that word	
Working With Sounds *(2–3 minutes)* Choose one per day.	
☐ Clapping syllables 1 2 3 ☐ Hearing rhymes ☐ Sorting pictures	
Working With Books *(5 minutes)* Shared reading with Level A book; teach print concepts.	
Title:	
Choose one or two: ☐ One-to-one matching ☐ Concept of a word ☐ Identify first/last word ☐ Concept of a letter ☐ Identify first/last letter ☐ Identify period ☐ Locate upper/lowercase letters	
Interactive Writing and Cut-Up Sentence *(5 minutes)*	
Dictated sentence:	
Letter formation:	

Letters and Names Next Steps:	Sounds Next Steps:	Books Next Steps:	Writing Next Steps:

Appendix E

Understand the purpose and procedures for each lesson component

Each component in a pre-A lesson supports one or more reading skills and standards. The following chart summarizes procedures and purposes of each component.

Pre-A Lesson Procedures and Purposes		
Component	**Procedures**	**Purposes**
Working With Names and Letters	• Use magnetic letters and alphabet charts to firm up and expand letter/sound knowledge. • Use magnetic letters, name puzzles, and rainbow writing to teach first names.	• Alphabet knowledge • Visual processing • Rapid naming of letters • Letter formation • Letter-picture links • Left-to-right directionality • Writing first name
Working With Sounds	• Clap syllables. • Work with rhymes. • Sort pictures by first letter.	• Phonological and phonemic awareness
Working With Books	• Do a picture preview. • Conduct shared reading. • Teach concepts of print.	• Oral language • Use picture clues • Concepts of print
Interactive Writing	• Students write a simple sentence with teacher scaffolding. • Students remake a cut-up sentence.	• Alphabet knowledge • Phonemic awareness • Link sounds to letters • Oral language • Print concepts • Letter formation

The pre-A lesson lasts about 20 minutes and should include one activity from all four components. To ensure that you can complete the lesson in the time allotted, spend only three to five minutes with each component. Changing the activity every few minutes keeps students engaged and focused. I have two suggestions for keeping the quick pace—use a timer and limit teacher talk. Remember, the student is also tracing an alphabet book every day outside the pre-A lesson time.

For a two-day lesson, do Working With Names and Letters and Working With Books on Day 1. On Day 2, do Working With Sounds, Working With Books, and Interactive Writing.

DESCRIPTION OF THE PRE-A LESSON

Each day students work with one letter activity, one name activity, and one sound activity. Then they read a book together and write a sentence interactively.

Working With Names and Letters (2–6 minutes)

Working with names

Phonetic writing often starts with letters from a child's first name (Both-deVries & Bus, 2008). So each day spend one to two minutes doing *one* of the following name activities. This component can be omitted once children know the letters in their first name and can write their first name without a model.

Name puzzles. Each student receives a name puzzle (see page 28). Begin by cutting the name into two pieces. Have students put the pieces together using the front of the envelope as a model. Then turn the envelope over and have students remake the puzzle without looking at the model. When a child is successful rebuilding the name puzzle from memory, make an additional cut. Gradually cut the name into individual letters. This usually takes several days, since you are spending only a minute or two on this activity. As students put their puzzles together, work with individuals on the letters in their names. Possible prompts:

- *Show me the letter* a.
- *How many* a*'s are in your name?*

> **Tip**
> *Do not let students build their name incorrectly. Let them use a model until they can make their name from memory.*

> **Tip**
> *If a student goes by initials, such as A. J., use the complete first name (e.g., Andrew) in the name activities.*

> **Tip**
> *Once students can make their name puzzle with each letter cut apart, choose a different name activity.*

- *What is this letter?* (Point to a letter the student knows.)
- *Let's say the letters in your name.* (Help the student spell his or her name.)

Magnetic letters. Students remove the magnetic letters from their personal letter bag (see page 29) to make their first name. If necessary, students can use the name template as a model. Insist on left-to-right sequential construction of the name. Repeat the process until each student constructs his or her name without support.

> **Tip**
> Provide a starting place, such as a sticker on the dry-erase board, so students always make their name left to right.

> **Tip**
> Writing on the sheet protector allows students to erase their writing and reuse the template for another lesson.

Rainbow writing. Students use the name template in a plastic sheet protector (see page 28) to trace their first name with a dry-erase marker. Once they trace their name with one color, they can trace their name with another color. Work with individuals on letter formation, reminding them to start at the top.

Pre-A Video Link 2

Watch Jan conducting a name activity.

Working with letters

Do *one* of the following letter activities for two to three minutes. The purpose of these activities is to build automaticity with known letters. The activities mentioned first are easier. Use one of the final three activities with students who know about 30 letters and are beginning to hear sounds.

Match the letters in the bag. This activity is for children who know fewer than ten letters. Their personal letter bag should have two sets of the letters they know and the letters in their name. Children empty their letter bag and match the letters that are the same. Help students say the name of each letter.

Match letters to an alphabet chart. Students match the letters in their letter bag to the letters on the alphabet chart. Teach them to say the name of the letter and the picture as they place the letter on the chart. Ask students to give the letter sound if they know it.

Name letters left to right. Children randomly choose letters from their bag as they place the letters in a line. Have them name the letters as they line them up. Encourage speedy recall. "Let's see how fast you can do it."

Find the letter on an alphabet chart. Distribute an alphabet chart to each student. Name a letter in the first row and ask students to point to it. For example, say, "Find the letter *D*." Students should say the letter name and the picture (e.g., *D, dog*). Continue naming a letter in each row for children to find. This is an excellent activity for students who have difficulty recalling the names of letters.

Name a word that begins with that letter. Name a letter and have students find it on the alphabet chart. Then ask students to think of a word that begins with that letter. If they have difficulty thinking of a word, use the pictures on the alphabet chart or give them clues, such as, "I'm thinking of an animal that begins with the letter *p* and says, '*Oink*.'"

Find the letter that makes that sound. Ask students to find a letter on the alphabet chart that makes a particular sound. For example, "Find the letter in the first row that says /b/." Students say the sound, the letter, and the picture (e.g., /b/, *B, bear*). Repeat with other letter sounds.

Name the letter that begins that word. Say a word and ask children to find the letter on the alphabet chart that makes the sound at the beginning of the word. For example, "Find the letter that you hear at the beginning of *book*." Children point to the *B* and say, "*B*, /b/, *book*."

> **Tip**
> *Watch your timer. If you spend more than four minutes on letter activities, you won't have time for reading and writing.*

> **Tip**
> *Children use their personal letter bags for the first three activities and the alphabet chart for the last four activities.*

> **Tip**
> *Vary the letter activity each day so children learn different ways of working with letters.*

Pre-A Video Link 3 ▶▶▶

Watch Jan teaching letter activities.

Working With Sounds (2–3 minutes)

Do *one* sound activity each day to teach phonological awareness.

Clapping syllables. Say a picture on the alphabet chart and have students clap the syllables as they say the parts of the word (e.g., *mon-key*). Work with words that have one or two syllables before you use words with three syllables. At first you will have to clap with students, but the goal is for students to clap the syllables without your support. Discontinue this activity when students are able to clap three syllables in a word without your support.

> **Tip**
>
> Teach children to clap syllables before you teach them to segment phonemes.

Hearing rhymes. Say two words and have students repeat them. If the words rhyme, students should put their thumb up. If the words do not rhyme, they should put their thumb down. For example, if you say "*pig, wig,*" students say "*pig, wig*" and put their thumb up. If you say "*pig, table,*" students say the words and put their thumb down. Teach them to listen to the ends of the words to determine if they rhyme. Segment a few words at the onset and rime to illustrate the process. Say, "*C-at* and *b-at* rhyme because they both have *at* in them."

> **Tip**
>
> To teach children to hear rhymes, use words that are distinctly different (table/desk) before you use words that share the same beginning sound (turtle, top).

Sorting pictures. Choose two consonant sounds for students to sort. When possible, begin with letters students already know by name but not sound. Also consider the names of students in your pre-A group or classroom. If you have a Kaitlyn and a Zack in the group, sort pictures that begin with a *k* and a *z*. Children who know few letters and sounds often make connections to the names of their classmates. Begin with distinctly different letter sounds (such as /t/ and /m/) and eventually sort sounds that are often confused (such as /b/ and /d/ or /r/ and /w/). Follow these steps:

1. Distribute picture cards for two consonant sounds. Tell students the name of the picture as you pass it out. Do not waste time having children figure out the pictures.

> **Tip**
>
> The following letter sounds are the easiest to learn because they have the sound in their letter name: b, d, f, j, k, l, m, n, p, r, s, t, v, z. There is no sequence for learning these sounds. Use the Letter/Sound Checklist to choose two sounds to sort.

2. Write the two consonants on a dry-erase board and review the sound each letter makes. "If your picture begins with the /m/ sound, it will go under the *M*. If your picture begins with the /t/ sound, it will go under the *T*."

3. Have students take turns saying the picture, saying the beginning sound, saying the letter name, and putting the picture under the correct letter (e.g., *moon*, /m/, *M*; put the card under the letter *M*).

By teaching children these procedures, you ensure they will not only learn the letter sounds, but also they will hear and record sounds when they write.

> **Tip**
>
> *Do not let students put their pictures under one of the letters too quickly. They have a 50 percent chance of guessing the correct sound.*

Pre-A Video Link 4

Watch Jan leading picture sorts.

> **Tip**
>
> *Do not use big books for the Working With Books component. Children are more engaged and learn print concepts as they hold a little book in their hands.*

Working With Books (5 minutes)

Select a very simple Level A book for guided reading. It should have one line of print per page and clear spaces between words. For DLLs, choose books that have familiar concepts. Then follow these steps:

1. **Picture preview.** First, guide students through the book and have them take turns discussing the pictures. Encourage them to use complete sentences as they describe what is happening in the picture. Avoid asking students a question that requires a one-word answer, such as, "What is the boy eating in this picture?" Instead, say, "Talk about the picture. What's happening?" Model by saying, "On this page, the boy is eating a red apple. Now tell me about the picture on the next page." If students have trouble giving a complete sentence or responding with standard English structure, model a simple sentence about the picture and ask students to repeat it.

2. **Shared reading.** Next, read the book with students. This is choral reading, not guided reading. Students should point with their finger or a small stick. As

> **Tip**
>
> *During shared reading, don't allow students to cover the word with their finger. Say, "Point under the word." Be insistent.*

students read the book with you, circulate and help those who need support with one-to-one matching. After students have read the book with you, they may read it on their own. During the second independent read, work with individual students and differentiate your prompting based on need. Some students may need your help with one-to-one matching; others may need to be reminded to use the pictures; some may be ready to show you a specific letter or word.

3. **Concepts of print.** After students have had the opportunity to read the book on their own, teach them *one* or *two* of the following print concepts, demonstrating as you go.

- *Concept of a word:* "Put your fingers around each word on the page. How many words are on that page? Let's do it again on a different page."

- *First/last word:* "Point to the first word on the page. Point to the last word. Let's do it again on another page."

- *Concept of a letter:* "Show me one letter. Show me two letters. Show me the biggest word. It has the most letters. Let's count the letters in that word. Find the smallest word. How many letters does it have?"

- *First/last letter:* "Show me the first word on that page. Now frame the first *letter* of that word. Frame the last letter. Let's try this on the next word."

- *Punctuation:* "Show me a period. Find the period on another page."

- *Upper/lowercase letters:* "Find a capital *T*. Show me a lowercase *o*."

> **Tip**
> *Diminish your voice as you progress through the book. Since these books use repetitive patterns, students should need less support as they remember the pattern.*

> **Tip**
> *Teach one concept at a time. Model it on one page before you have students practice it on another.*

> **Tip**
> *Show students how to use their index fingers to frame a word or letter.*

Pre-A Video Link 5
Watch Jan doing a shared reading.

Interactive Writing (5 minutes)

During interactive writing, students help the teacher write a simple message by sharing the pen or marker (McCarrier, Pinnell, & Fountas, 2000). This activity builds oral language and provides the opportunity to teach phonemic awareness, letter-sound links, print concepts, and letter formation. Follow these steps:

1. Dictate a simple sentence containing four to six words. Most often the sentence will relate to the book students just read, but it doesn't have to be an exact sentence from the book. Carefully construct the sentence to include letters and sounds you have been teaching. If you sorted pictures that begin with /m/ and /s/, you might write, I made a snowman.

2. As children slowly repeat the sentence, draw a line for each word on a strip of tag board.

___ _____ ___ _____

3. Have students help you write the dominant sounds in each word. Once students isolate a sound, use the alphabet chart to link the sound to a letter. "Let's write *made* together. Say *made*. What do you hear first? /m/ What letter says /m/? It starts just like *moon* on your chart. Find the moon. What letter do you see? M. Who'd like to write the M in our sentence?"

4. While one student is writing on the sentence strip, the others should practice writing the letter on their alphabet chart, which has been inserted into a heavy plastic sheet protector. Teach correct letter formation at this time.

5. Select one or two letters for teaching letter formation. Teach students to say the verbal directions as they write the letter in the air with big movements before they practice it several times on the bottom of the alphabet chart. For more information on teaching letter formation, see page 43.

> **Tip**
> All students should point to the target letter on their alphabet chart before they write it on the sentence strip or at the bottom of their chart.

> **Tip**
> Don't worry about students using uppercase letters when they write on the sentence strip. These students usually learn how to form the uppercase letters first because they are distinctly different from each other. Many lowercase letters look similar.

6. After you write a sentence with students, cut it into parts. Students then work together to remake it. At the end of the lesson, put a paper clip around the cut-up sentence and give it to one of the children to take home.

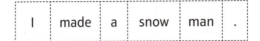

Students' contributions will vary depending on their phonemic awareness skills. Some are able to hear long vowels easily; others are not. Tailor your instruction so that you are constantly teaching what they are ready to learn. For example, in the sentence *I made a snowman*, some groups would only write the capital *I*, *m*, and *s*. The teacher would need to write the other letters. Students who know more letters and sounds might be able to write more of the sentence. Since this is interactive writing, use conventional spelling, not invented spelling.

> **Pre-A Video Link 6** ▶▶▶
> *Watch Jan teaching interactive writing.*

Letter Formation

Although word-processing programs and assistive technology are advantageous to children with handwriting problems, technological advances do not eliminate the need for explicit teaching of handwriting. Children who struggle with letter formation are usually less motivated to write, leading to future problems with taking notes, doing homework, and writing essays. Research has shown that children with good handwriting skills produce more writing and higher-quality writing than those who have poor handwriting (Reutzel, 2015).

Teach correct letter formation when children are learning the letters. If they internalize bad habits, such as poor pencil grips, writing a letter from bottom to top, or drawing the letter from right to left using separate strokes, those habits can be difficult to break. Tracing the alphabet book will help with letter formation, but you should also teach letter formation during the pre-A lesson. You can monitor and scaffold letter formation in a small-group setting more effectively than you can during whole-group instruction.

In the following chart, I offer "verbal pathways": letters are grouped according to how they are formed. Teach similarly formed letters together. For instance, the letters *c, o,* and *d* all begin with the same loop. When children are learning to form a letter, begin with large movements such as forming the letter in the air using the entire arm. Each time students form the letter, they should say the motor pathway. For example, when children learn to write the lowercase *d*, they should say, "Around like a *c*, up, down—*d*." Insist on one continuous stroke. Although the ultimate goal is for children to quickly form the letter, speed should not be emphasized until they have memorized the correct formation. In this case, fast is last.

Verbal Pathways for Teaching Letter Formation			
Start with a loop		**Start with a stick**	
c	around like a *c*	l	start at the top, down
o	around like a *c*, close	i	down, dot
a	around like a *c*, close, down	t	down, cross
d	around like a *c*, up, down	j	down, hook left, dot
g	around like a *c*, down, hook left	b	down and around
q	around like a *c*, down, hook right	p	down, up, and around
s	around like a snake	k	down, in, out

Start with a stick, hump		Start with a slant		Unique formation	
r	down, up, over	v	down, up	e	across, around
n	down, hump	w	down, up, down, up	f	around, down, cross
m	down, hump, hump	x	down, cross	u	down, up
h	down, hump	y	down, down	z	across, down, across

SAMPLE FILLED-IN LESSON PLAN

Pre-A Lesson Plan (< 40 letters)

Students: Jaxson, Jose, Ariel, Arianna **Date:** 9/23

COMPONENTS AND ACTIVITIES	OBSERVATIONS/NOTES

Working With Names *(2–3 minutes)*
Choose one. Omit once child can write first name without a model (using correct letter formation).

- [x] Name puzzle
- [ ] Magnetic letters
- [ ] Rainbow writing

Work on naming the letters in their first name.

Working With Letters *(2–3 minutes)*
Choose one per day. Activities 5, 6, and 7 are for children who know at least 30 letters.

- [ ] 1. Match the letters in the bag
- [ ] 2. Match letters to an ABC chart
- [ ] 3. Name letters left to right
- [x] 4. Find the letter on an ABC chart
- [ ] 5. Name a word that begins with that letter
- [ ] 6. Find the letter that makes that sound
- [ ] 7. Name the letter that begins that word

It was easier for the children to find a letter than to name a letter.

Working With Sounds *(2–3 minutes)* Choose one per day.

- [ ] Clapping syllables   1 2 3
- [ ] Hearing rhymes
- [x] Sorting pictures   p and l

Some students struggled to hear the initial sound. Use a mirror to show them their mouth formation for sounds.

Working With Books *(5 minutes)* Shared reading with Level A book; teach print concepts.

Title: Rosie's Pink Friends

Choose one or two:
- [x] One-to-one matching
- [ ] Concept of a word
- [ ] Identify first/last word
- [ ] Concept of a letter
- [ ] Identify first/last letter
- [ ] Identify period
- [ ] Locate upper/lowercase letters

Students did a good job pointing to each word.

Work on the difference between a word and a letter.

Interactive Writing and Cut-Up Sentence *(5 minutes)*

Dictated sentence: We like the pig.

Letter formation: p and l

Used ABC chart to locate letters

Letters and Names Next Steps:	Sounds Next Steps:	Books Next Steps:	Writing Next Steps:
Say letters in 1st name	Segment 1st sound	Choose familiar concepts	Top to bottom formation

Examples of "Next Steps"

Next Steps: Carlos

Letters and Names Next Steps: Say letters in first name.	Sounds Next Steps: Segment first sound.	Books Next Steps: Choose familiar concepts.	Writing Next Steps: Encourage top-to-bottom formation.

Next Steps: Samantha

Letters and Names Next Steps: Link letter names to letter sounds.	Sounds Next Steps: Sort initial sounds of known consonants.	Books Next Steps: Use a pointer to help her control one-to-one matching.	Writing Next Steps: Send the ABC book home so parents can help her trace letters.

Accelerating Pre-A Readers

The key to accelerating pre-A readers is consistency. Last year I tracked the progress of pre-A students from eight classrooms at two different schools (both Title 1). They traced the alphabet book with a tutor and received daily pre-A lessons as described above. Notice the rapid progress students made in letter identification.

Number of Pre-A Students at Weeks 1, 3, 6, and 10				
Classroom	Week 1	Week 3	Week 6	Week 10
A	15	3	0	0
B	8	2	2	1
C	13	3	3	0
D	14	10	3	2
E	11	7	3	0
F	12	7	2	0
G	7	6	0	0
H	12	5	2	0
Total	92	43	15	3

If you still have pre-A students after 12 weeks of *consistent* individual and small-group instruction, the student is usually a dual language learner or has special learning needs. These children can still learn to read. Here are a few suggestions for accelerating them.

Faithfully follow procedures

Make certain you have taught the framework with fidelity. Do not omit any component. If you have the support of an intervention teacher or assistant, have him or her do a second pre-A lesson later in the day. He or she can repeat the lesson you taught earlier.

Individualize instruction

If you notice a student is distracted, even in a small group, teach that student individually. If the child can only stay focused for ten minutes, do the first two components one day and the final two the next. Keep the lesson fast-paced and limit your talking. I've seen children who stay on task when they are reading books or writing with the teacher, but stare off in space as soon as the teacher starts talking.

Check letter knowledge

Some children can find a specific letter when asked to do so but struggle to name the letter. Try the following assessment to get a clearer picture of what the student knows. Line up three random magnetic letters and ask the student to show you one of the letters. If the student points to the correct letter, place it in the "known" pile. If the student points to the wrong letter, remove both the letter you asked for and the letter the student pointed to and place them in the "unknown" pile. Continue adding more letters (never showing more than three) until you've assessed the entire alphabet. Assess the uppercase letters one day and the lowercase another. You will learn which letters are partially known (the student can identify them but not name them) and which are unknown.

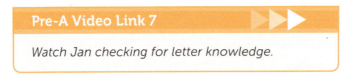

Pre-A Video Link 7

Watch Jan checking for letter knowledge.

Analyzing Problem Areas for Pre-A Readers

Use the following chart to identify each student's strengths and needs. Meet with other teachers who have observed or taught that child. Discuss each area on the chart and record a few comments. Is the area a strength or a need? What are you noticing?

Name: _____

Directions: Mark strengths with a plus (+) and needs with a minus (-).

\	Problem-Solving Chart for Pre-A		
Uses Oral Language Skills	Writes Name	Identifies Letters	Forms Letters
Knows Letter Sounds	Claps Syllables	Hears Rhymes	Hears Beginning Sounds
Uses Pictures	Applies One-to-One Matching	Understands Concepts of Print	Other

NEXT STEP FOR STRUGGLING PRE-A READERS

Each area on the Problem-Solving Chart is addressed during the pre-A lesson. Communicate with other teachers, specialists, or teaching assistants who are instructing the child. As you plan your lessons, select the options that best address the student's needs. Work together to create a plan that helps *this* student accelerate. In the following chart, I offer suggestions for each focus area. Use these ideas to plan your next steps for small-group and individual lessons.

Focus	Suggestions for Intervention

Uses oral language skills	• Make a special effort to engage the student in conversations throughout the day. Encourage "turn and talk" during whole-group instruction. Seek the advice of the DLL teacher, if your school has one.
	
	• During the shared reading component, model a simple sentence about a picture and have the student repeat it. If he or she can't repeat the sentence, shorten it.
	
	• Encourage quiet talking during independent learning centers. Create a "play center" where students reenact a fairy tale or nursery rhyme you have read to the class. Include simple props, such as a red hood and basket (*Little Red Riding Hood*), mixing bowls and spoons (*Goldilocks*), or a stool and a fake spider (*Little Miss Muffet*). All children will enjoy this center, but it is especially beneficial to those learning English.
	
	• Use gestures and props to explain unfamiliar concepts in books.
	
	• Technology tip: As an independent activity, have students listen to stories on an app.
	  » The Farfaria app offers thousands of picture books that children can listen to. The stories are leveled so you can match them to your readers. www.farfaria.com
	  » Create personalized books with student names in them at www.bookbuilder.com. These books are perfect for beginning readers because one of the first words they will recognize is their own first name.

Writes name	• As an independent practice activity, have the student do rainbow writing with his or her first name. You could have a rainbow-writing center with every student's name written on a sheet of paper. The student can use different colored markers to practice writing his or her name and classmates' names. • Technology tip: Use an app that helps the child trace his or her name.

Focus	Suggestions for Intervention
Identifies letters	• Do the alphabet tracing twice a day. Send an alphabet book home with a letter of explanation. If the parents don't speak English, try to find someone who can help you make a CD or DVD of the directions in their language. • Check letter knowledge by doing the activity described on page 46.
Forms letters	• Teach one letter formation every day during the pre-A lesson. Use the verbal pathway for each letter, and have the child say the phrase as he or she writes the letter. • Research handwriting programs (e.g., Handwriting Without Tears) that target letter formation. • Experiment with different writing tools such as markers, gel pens, and special pencils to find one the student likes. • Have the student try different pencil grips and see if he or she produces a firmer grip. • Technology tip: Use a handwriting app to support letter formation (e.g., iTrace).
Knows letter sounds	• Use hand gestures or picture links to teach letter sounds. • If the student knows most of the letters but very few sounds, continue the tracing of the alphabet book with a tutor. Have the student say the name and sound while tracing the letters.
Claps syllables	• Use picture cards that have one syllable. Then do one and two syllables. Clap with the student and gradually release your support.
Hears rhymes	• Use picture cards for the rhyming activity. Show two cards. Say the words and have the student repeat the words. Segment the onset and rime (e.g., *t-op, m-op*) to emphasize the rhyming portion of the word. • Teach the child to memorize nursery rhymes. • Read rhyming books (Dr. Seuss) and chants ("Teddy bear, Teddy bear, turn around") during whole-class instruction. Emphasize the rhyming words.

Focus	Suggestions for Intervention
Hears beginning sounds	• Use the student's Letter/Sound Checklist to select sounds for picture sorts. Always begin with the letters the student knows and the ones that have the sound in the letter name. Choose one known sound and one new sound for picture sorts. Follow the procedures on pages 38–39. The student must say the word and initial sound before he or she places the picture under the correct letter. If the student has trouble saying the initial sound, sit next to the student and use a mirror to show how your mouth makes the first sound. Have the student mimic your mouth formation while he or she looks in the mirror.
Uses pictures	• For the pre-A lesson, choose books that have familiar concepts. • Prompt the student to check the picture during shared reading.
Applies one-to-one matching	• Have the student read with a pointer, such as a craft stick, during shared reading. • Model how to read a page by framing each word with two index fingers. Have the student practice framing each word on several pages. • When remaking the cut-up sentence, point out the space between each word.
Understands concepts of print	• During the pre-A lesson, teach one print concept each day. Teach the concept of a "word" before you teach the concept of "first word." Model, if necessary, but give the student the opportunity to show you the concept on several pages. Don't assume the student understands the concept until he or she can demonstrate it without your help. • Make connections throughout the lesson. Emphasize the same print concept taught during shared reading and interactive writing. If you taught "first word" during the reading, ask the student to find the first word on the sentence strip and when you cut the words apart.

MONITORING PROGRESS

Check on letter/sound knowledge each week until the student identifies 40 letters by name. Usually by the time the student knows 40 letters, he or she also knows most of the letter sounds. There are advantages to doing a weekly letter check. You know which letters to add to the child's personal letter bag for the pre-A lessons, and you are communicating to the student that letter knowledge matters. Remember, once the student identifies at least 40 letters and knows some sounds, discontinue the pre-A lessons and the alphabet tracing. The student is now ready for emergent guided reading lessons.

MOVING TO THE EMERGENT LESSON PLAN

Consider moving students to the Emergent Guided Reading Plan when they can

- Write their first name without a model
- Identify about 40 uppercase and lowercase letters
- Demonstrate left-to-right directionality across one line of print
- Understand enough English to follow simple directions
- Hear some letter sounds (at least eight)

QUESTIONS TEACHERS ASK ABOUT PRE-A READERS

When should we start the tracing of the alphabet book with pre-A students?

Start the second week of school. Use the first week to assess students' letter knowledge and train tutors. After four weeks most of the students will no longer need to trace the alphabet book.

Can instructional assistants be trained to do guided reading groups?

I have trained assistants to deliver the pre-A and emergent lessons. However, it works best if I plan and teach the lesson first and the assistant repeats the lesson on the following day. I suggest you do the same.

What can I do if a student is making slow progress?

Use the Problem-Solving Chart on page 47 to identify specific needs and intervention procedures. Most pre-A readers who make slow progress began the year being able to identify fewer than ten letters. It may take several months for them to learn all the letters (and their sounds). Be consistent with daily tracing of the alphabet book and pre-A lessons.

What if my pre-A students don't have the stamina for a 20-minute lesson?

Do half the lesson to start and the other half later in the same day or on the following day.

> **Professional Study Guide**
>
> *Go to scholastic.com/NSFresources for a downloadable professional study guide written just for this book. In it, you'll find questions and activities about teaching pre-A readers to use on your own or with your colleagues in a study group or PLC.*

CHAPTER 3

The Emergent Reader: Levels A–C

The "*b* and *d* struggle" for many kids can be exasperating. Without sentence context, emergent readers often stumble over words that begin with *b* or *d*. One of my favorite true anecdotes is of the kindergartner who said, "Mrs. Lewis, *b* and *d* are so hard. Why did the alphabet people make them look so much the same? Were they too lazy to make them different?"

PROFILE OF AN EMERGENT READER

Reading is more than blending sounds together to make words. It is a complex network of strategies and behaviors the brain uses to make sense of print. Children who develop strong skills at the emergent stage establish a rock-solid foundation for future reading success.

The emergent guided reading lesson is designed for students reading texts at Levels A–C. The activities and prompts are also appropriate for children at higher grade levels who are learning to speak English or have experienced challenges in learning to read. The emergent lesson framework helps young children build a foundation with letters and sounds, strategic actions, phonemic awareness, phonics, sight words, word solving, comprehension, and writing.

Emergent readers at Level A can write their first name without a model, identify at least 40 uppercase and lowercase letters by name, demonstrate left-to-right directionality, understand enough English to follow simple directions, and know at least eight sounds. By the time children successfully read texts at Level C they typically

- Know all the letters and sounds

- Match one-to-one (What they say matches what they point to as they read.)
- Control left-to-right directionality across several lines of print
- Use meaning, structure, and initial letters to figure out unknown words
- Form letters correctly
- Hear and record consonant-vowel-consonant (CVC) sounds in sequence
- Monitor for meaning
- Reread a sentence to correct errors or confirm predictions
- Read and write about 30 sight words
- Discuss a story with teacher prompting
- Write a simple message about the book with teacher scaffolding

ASSESS

Each of the following four assessments is necessary to identify an emergent reader's strengths and needs so you can select appropriate texts and plan effective guided reading lessons.

Assessments for Emergent Readers		
Assessment	How is it administered?	What does it tell you?
Letters and sounds	Individual	Letters and sounds the student knows
Running record	Individual	Instructional text level range Strategic actions to teach
Dictated sentence	Small group	How the student hears and records sounds in words
Sight words	Small group	Sight words the student can write

Letters and Sounds

Students should already know most of their letters and sounds from the pre-A lessons and the tracing of the alphabet book. However, there could be a few you need to teach. Show students an alphabet chart in which the letters are out of sequence. Point to each letter and ask students to say the letter name and sound. Use the Letter/Sound Checklist (Appendix D) to summarize your students' letter/sound knowledge. (See page 27 for details.) Each week check on the letters and sounds you have taught during guided reading and update your chart. Discontinue this assessment when the student knows all the letters and sounds.

Running Record

Running records (Clay, 2000) are valuable assessments for emergent readers, but don't put too much emphasis on the text level. Most emergent texts are patterned and predictable. Once children recognize the sentence structure in the story, they might read the entire text accurately but not really attend to the print. Often a single error on the text will tell you a great deal about which strategic actions the student uses and which ones you should teach next.

It's easy to take a running record on an emergent reader. As the student reads aloud, mark his or her errors and reading behaviors on a recording sheet. Also record the child's comments, eye movements, and facial expressions to learn if the child is monitoring and interacting with the story. The most valuable information from a running record is gained when the emergent reader makes an error or stops to figure out a word. Does the child look at the pictures to figure out unknown words? Does the student notice when something he or she says doesn't make sense? Record those behaviors on the running record sheet. When you find a text the student can read with 90–94 percent accuracy, you have identified the student's instructional text level range.

Now that you have taken a running record, you can get a glimpse of the child's reading process. Notice whether the student

- Matches one-to-one
- Uses picture clues
- Uses visual information
- Uses known words
- Makes multiple attempts on an unknown word
- Rereads
- Self-corrects

Analyze errors for meaning, structure, and visual information

Take a close look at the errors the student made. There won't be many, as these passages are so short, but you only need one or two errors to understand the child's processing system. There are three information systems to consider (Clay, 2006):

Meaning (M): Does the student's error make sense? At the emergent stage, this means the reader is using picture clues and the meaning of the story. For example, the child says *fly* for *bug*.

Structure (S): Does the student's error follow the rules of grammar in standard English? If so, the student is using structure (also called *syntax*). Most of the time, if the error makes sense it also matches structure. For example, the child says *skips* for *skipped*.

Visual Information (V): Is the error visually similar to the word in the text? For example, if the book says, "Mom took the dog for a walk" and the child substitutes *day* for *dog,* he or she is using visual information because both words begin with the same letter.

It is common for emergent readers to use more than one source of information. In the above example, if the child had read, "Mom took the *doggy* for a walk," the error (*doggy*) would be coded M, S, and V because *doggy* makes sense, fits the grammatical structure of the sentence, and is visually similar to the word *dog*.

Assess comprehension

Although there isn't much to retell in an emergent text, you can ask the student to tell you what he or she read. To assess comprehension beyond retelling, use a listening comprehension assessment such as the one in *Next Step Guided Reading Assessment: Grades K–2*.

Dictated Sentence

For emergent readers, a dictated sentence is a quick and effective way to assess whether a child hears and records sounds in words. You will also learn whether the child has other emergent skills such as directionality, return sweep, and letter formation. You can save time by administering this assessment to a group of four or five students. Encourage children to stretch out each word as they write the sounds they hear in one of the following sentences. Be careful not to say the words slowly for them.

Dictated Sentences for Emergent Readers	
Sentence	Skills Assessed
I like to eat oatmeal.	Consonants and long vowels
I can sit on the rug and not get up.	Consonants and all short vowels
My mom is going to get me ice cream at the park.	Sight words, long vowels, and endings

Analyze each child's written response to determine if the student is hearing sounds in words. Does the child hear and record beginning consonants, medial vowels, and/or ending consonants? Are there confusions with letter sounds? Does the child struggle with letter formation? Record the child's pencil grip and how he or she forms the letters. This information will guide you in selecting appropriate word study and guided writing activities.

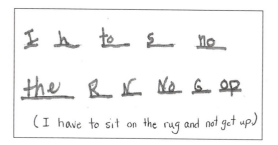

Example of a dictated sentence: This student hears initial consonants and is ready to learn how to hear and record final consonants.

Sight Words

Students write sight words that match their instructional text level. Administer the Sight Word Chart (Appendix F). This will tell you which sight words students know well and which you should target in your lessons. The following chart contains sight words that appear frequently in emergent texts. Words at Levels A and B are mostly phonetic, since these are easier for beginning readers to learn. This assessment is quick, easy, and useful. Assess students at their instructional level, indicated by the running record, and one level below.

Recommended Sight Words for Levels A–C		
Level A	Level B	Level C
am	dad	and
at	he	are
can	in	come
go	it	for
is	look	got
like	mom	here
me	my	not
see	on	play
the	up	said
to	we	you

Determine an instructional reading level

Use the instructional level identified by the running record as a starting place, but be prepared to make adjustments. Several factors, including learning sight words, hearing and using sounds, and developing strategic actions for reading more complex texts, will affect the rate of progress.

DECIDE

Now that you have assessed and analyzed your emergent readers, you are ready to summarize the assessments to help you form your groups, pinpoint a focus for instruction, and select a text.

Summarize the Assessments

Summarize the results of the four assessments on the Assessment Summary Chart (page 61 and scholastic.com/NSFresources).

Directions for completing the Assessment Summary Chart

Columns 1 and 2: Name and Level Range. Record the student's name and instructional level range.

Column 3: Knows Letters and Sounds. Write the number of letters (uppercase and lowercase combined) and the sounds the student identified on the Letter/Sound Checklist. For example, if the student knows 43 letters and 8 sounds, write 43/8.

Column 4: Identifies Sight Words. Record the number of sight words the student wrote correctly. Update monthly and use the information to regroup students and plan instruction.

Column 5: Hears Sounds in Words. Use the dictated sentence to analyze how the student hears and records sounds in words. Put a B if the student hears and records initial consonant sounds, an M if the student correctly records medial vowels, and an E if the student hears final consonant sounds.

Column 6: Uses MSV (Meaning, Structure, and Visual Information). Analyze the errors and self-corrections on the running record to identify the information systems the student uses. Put an M if most errors are meaningful and the child uses picture clues, an S if the student's errors match the grammatical structure of the text, and a V if the errors are visually similar to the word in the text or the student tries to sound out an unknown word. Most emergent readers reading at text Levels A and B will have MS in this column.

Column 7: Matches One-to-One. Put a plus (+) if the student is looking at the print, points to the words as he or she reads, and doesn't insert or omit words. Put a check (√) if the student appears to be looking at the print but occasionally says extra words or leaves out words. Put a minus (-)

if the student does not appear to be looking at the print. For example, the student might be adding extra words or using only the sentence pattern and the pictures.

Column 8: Uses Pictures. Put a plus (+) if the student consistently searches the picture when encountering an unknown word, a check (√) if the student occasionally searches the picture, or a minus (-) if the student does not use picture clues.

Column 9: Uses First Letters. Put a plus (+) if the student consistently uses initial letter sounds at difficulty, a check (√) if the student occasionally uses initial letters, or a minus (-) if the student ignores first letters at difficulty.

Column 10: Cross-checks. This is a highly important strategy for emergent readers. It is the action of checking one source of information against another. For example, emergent readers who use meaning and initial letters to figure out an unknown word are cross-checking. Put a plus (+) if the student consistently cross-checks, a check (√) if the student occasionally cross-checks, or a minus (-) if the student shows no evidence of cross-checking. Children reading at Levels A and B rarely cross-check without prompting. However, they should be cross-checking without teacher prompting before they are moved to text Level D.

Column 11: Other. Use this column to record information relevant for teaching emergent readers. For example, you might indicate whether the student is learning English as a second language or receiving services from a specialist.

Assessment Summary Chart for Emergent Readers, Levels A–C

Name	Level Range	Knows Letters and Sounds Record #/#	Identifies Sight Words Record #	Hears Sounds in Words B M E	Uses M S V	Matches One-to-One + √ -	Uses Pictures + √ -	Uses First Letters + √ -	Cross-checks + √ -	Other

Emergent

Form Groups

Use the information on the Assessment Summary Chart to form guided reading groups. Consider multiple factors beyond the text level. Give priority to the number of sight words students can write and whether they hear sounds in words. The other columns (Uses MSV, Matches One-to-One, Uses Pictures, Uses First Letters, and Cross-checks) will help you pinpoint a focus for your lessons and shape your prompting and scaffolding during reading and writing.

Place students together if they are close to the same reading level (not more than one level apart) and have similar needs. For example, you may form a group of students reading at text Levels A and B who know very few sight words and are just learning consonant sounds. Another group reading at the same levels may be able to write 8–12 sight words and know most of their consonant sounds, but only in isolation. This other group needs to focus on using the known words and sounds when reading text.

If you teach first or second grade, you may have only a handful of emergent readers. Should you put them together in one group? The answer is yes, if they are reading at adjacent text levels. If you have one student reading at Level A and another at Level C, you shouldn't put them in the same group. They will have distinctly different needs that would be difficult to address in the same lesson. It would be best to teach them individually for ten minutes a day. Follow the ten-minute lessons on page 102.

Pinpoint Your Focus

Use the Assessment Summary Chart as well as the anecdotal observations you've made during whole- and small-group instruction to help you pinpoint a strategy focus for each group. Write the focus on your lesson plan. Teach one-to-one matching and using pictures to reinforce meaning before you teach cross-checking. Ideally, you want emergent readers to check the picture before they begin to read the words on the page. Children who constantly check the picture often avoid going back to look at the print.

Emergent Guided Reading Plan (Levels A–C)

Students: _____   Dates: _____

Title/Level	Strategy Focus	Comprehension Focus
DAY 1		DAY 2

Select a Text

Book selection plays a critical role in supporting beginning readers as they navigate their first experiences with print. Beginning readers need text with good spacing between the words, useful sight words, and illustrations that clearly support the text. I recommend patterned text for Levels A and B. (See example of a Level A text below.) Because the same words are usually repeated on every page, the repetitive pattern helps students learn sight words. The downside of using patterned texts is that they can lead children toward thinking reading is only about memorizing a pattern and looking at the pictures. Once students have mastered one-to-one matching and learned 15–20 sight words, move them to less patterned text at Level C. (See example below.)

A Level A book should have only one line per page and a patterned text.

Use less patterned texts once students control one-to-one matching and have a small bank of sight words they recognize.

Consider your focus when you select the book. If you are teaching children to match one-to-one, select a book with a single line of text on each page. If learning to use picture clues is your focus, choose texts with supportive illustrations and mostly familiar concepts. When children are ready to use letters and sounds to solve words, choose books with concepts that could have two labels, such as horse/pony, doctor/nurse, bird/robin, and flower/rose. Now the student must use both the picture *and* the initial letter to solve the word. This strategic action, called cross-checking (Clay, 2005), is a critically important strategy for emergent readers to learn. The new book should have some known sight words students can use to monitor their reading, but the text should also include at least one new sight word you can teach.

When selecting a text for dual language learners (DLLs), choose a patterned text with mostly familiar concepts. Repetitive sentences will help these children learn English sentence structures, and the pictures will support vocabulary development. There's no problem with having a few new concepts as long as the pictures provide support. For example, don't choose a book about the solar system when children have no understanding of planets, moons, and stars. This just makes the task of learning to read more difficult for them.

Selecting Texts That Match Your Focus	
Focus	Text Features
Identifying sight words	Some familiar sight words and one new sight word to teach
Matching one-to-one	One line of print per page. Easy-to-read font and extra space between words
Using meaning	Strong picture support
Using first letters and cross-checking	A few pictures that elicit two labels/concepts such as *dog/puppy*
Reaching dual language learners	Some repetitive phrases and mostly familiar picture concepts

Gather Other Materials

Organize the following materials and place them within reach:

- Alphabet charts in plastic sheet protectors (Appendix C)
- Letter/Sound Checklist (Appendix D)
- Sound box templates in plastic sheet protectors (Appendix H)
- Pictures for sorting by initial consonants and medial vowels
- Sight Word Chart (Appendix F)
- Dry-erase boards, markers, and erasers
- 6–8 sets of lowercase magnetic letters
- Guided writing journals
- Leveled books
- Timer

GUIDE

You've assessed your students, analyzed the assessments, formed your groups, and selected the text. Now you are ready to prepare for your guided reading lesson.

The Emergent Guided Reading Lesson

The emergent lesson takes place over two days, about 20 minutes each day. The same book is read and discussed on both days. Each lesson component covers one or more strategic actions and skills that are developmentally appropriate for students reading at text Levels A–C.

Overview of the Emergent Guided Reading Lesson	
Day 1	Day 2
Sight Word Review	Sight Word Review
Introduce a New Book	
Read the Book With Prompting	Reread Books With Prompting
Discuss and Teach	Discuss and Teach
Teach a New Sight Word	Reteach the New Sight Word From Day 1
Word Study Activity	Guided Writing

TEACHING COMPREHENSION

Although comprehension is the goal of every guided reading lesson, the short, simple stories written at the emergent levels will not always lend themselves to deep discussions. Retelling is appropriate, but you might also discuss story elements or have students compare and contrast ideas. Read the book first to see if any of the following comprehension strategies are appropriate to teach. Write your comprehension focus on the lesson plan, and weave it into your discussion. See Chapter 7 for more ideas.

Comprehension Strategies for Emergent Readers

Narrative/Fiction Strategies	Informational/Nonfiction Strategies
• Retell the story • Make connections • Ask and answer questions • Identify the characters, setting, problem, and solution	• Ask and answer questions • Identify main topic • Recall key details • Make connections • Compare and contrast concepts

Emergent Guided Reading Plan (Levels A–C)

Students:		Dates:	
Title/Level		Strategy Focus	Comprehension Focus
DAY 1			DAY 2

Understand the purpose and procedures for each lesson component

Each component in an emergent guided reading lesson supports one or more reading skills and standards. The following chart summarizes the procedures and purposes of each component.

Emergent Lesson Procedures and Purposes		
Component	**Procedures**	**Purposes**
Sight Word Review	Students write three sight words you have taught them.	• Increase visual memory • Practice letter formation • Build automaticity with sight words
Introduce a New Book	• Preview and discuss pictures. • Teach new vocabulary. • Rehearse challenging grammatical structures.	• Support oral language • Help students make predictions • Encourage students to ask questions • Build schema • Extend vocabulary
Read and Discuss Books	• Students read independently while teacher confers with each student. • Differentiate prompting based on student needs.	• Teach and prompt for strategic activity • Increase and extend comprehension
Teaching Point	Model a strategic action based on observations during the reading.	• Demonstrate word-solving strategies and other strategic activities
Word Study Activity	• Teach a new sight word. • Students use manipulatives to develop phonemic awareness and learn how words work.	• Teach sight words • Teach phonemic awareness and phonics • Establish visual scanning skills • Hear and record sounds in sequence
Guided Writing	Students write a sentence that is carefully crafted and dictated by the teacher.	• Learn language structures • Improve letter formation • Practice spelling (inventive and traditional) • Teach phonemic awareness • Apply phonics skills • Learn conventions

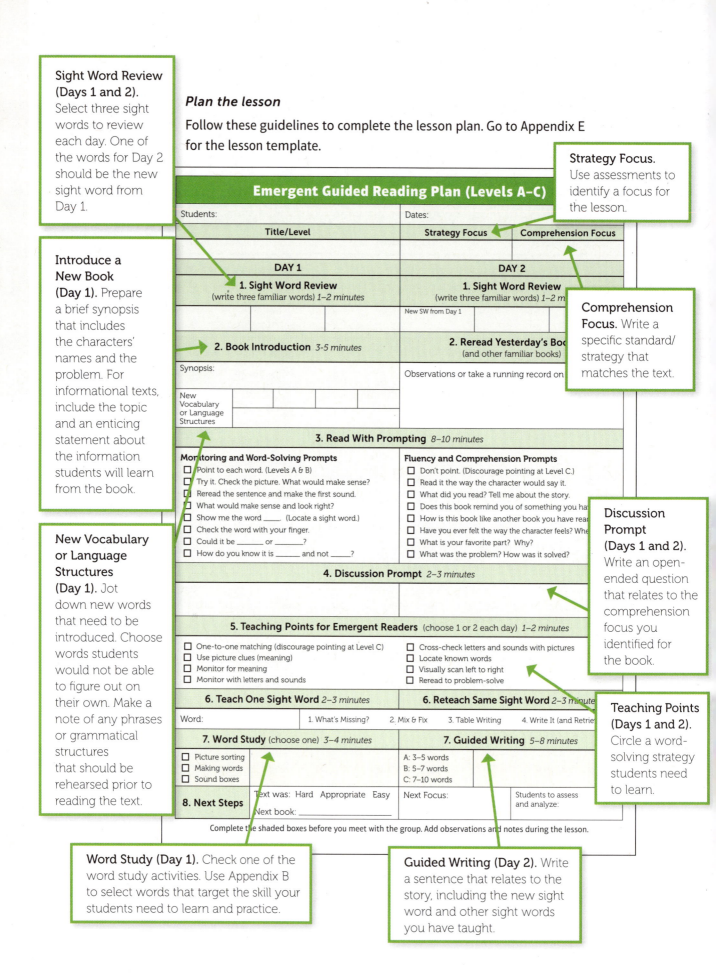

DESCRIPTION OF DAY 1

The Day 1 lesson has six basic components:

- Sight Word Review
- Introduce a New Book
- Read the Book With Prompting
- Discuss and Teach
- Teach a New Sight Word
- Word Study Activity

The lesson takes about 20 minutes. If you have more time, extend the reading or writing components.

Sight Word Review (1–2 minutes)

Distribute materials

Give each student a dry-erase marker and an alphabet chart that has been inserted into a plastic sleeve.

Dictate three words

Choose three sight words for students to write. Always review the most recent word you taught. The other two words should be words students learned in previous lessons. When possible, select familiar words that are in the new book. This gives students "footholds in print" as they read (Clay, 1993). Students can use the alphabet chart if they need support with letter formation. Teach them to cover their writing with their hand so they cannot copy each other. Emergent readers have wandering eyes!

Intervene when necessary

It is common for emergent readers to struggle with the first few words. They might write *on* for *in*, *ot* for *to*, or *cna* for *can*. To solve this problem, have them say the word softly as they write it, without segmenting the sounds. This helps them use sounds to retrieve the word from their memory.

Clay (2013) cautions that two-letter words can be challenging for emergent readers, especially for children with serial order issues. Intervene as soon as you notice the

> **Tip**
>
> *The alphabet chart (Appendix C) is a great scaffold for letter formation. If a child writes a letter backward say, "Check the ABC chart."*
>
>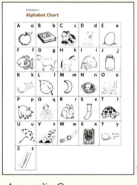
>
> *Appendix C*

student writing the wrong letter. Give a clue or tell him or her the correct letter. It is better to help a student write the word correctly than allow a child to write it incorrectly. The more a child writes a word correctly, the better chance of building visual memory for that word.

Model letter formation

If you notice several children using incorrect letter formation, take a few seconds to model correct formation and have them practice the letter on the bottom of their alphabet chart. Use big movements and simple verbal directions to teach letter formation. Writing letters in the air, shown here, is a way to incorporate gross motor movement. Verbal pathways for each lowercase letter are on pages 43–44.

> **Tip**
>
> *Remind students to use lowercase letters. If they can't recall how to make a lowercase letter, show them the letter on their alphabet chart. You want them to use lowercase letters because that is the way they will see the word in books.*

Record progress

Use the Sight Word Chart to select appropriate words and record progress. Add a check each time a student writes the word without help. This is not a test. If a student misspells a word, intervene quickly and give a clue. For example, if you dictate the word *here*, and a student writes *her*, say, "There's one more letter." If that doesn't help, say, "There's an *e* at the end." If you had to prompt the student, do not put a check on the Sight Word Chart for that student.

Children need to work with a sight word many times until it is firmly known. Don't be surprised if they know the word one day and forget it the next. That is why you should review three words every day. When a child has about six check marks for a word, the word is usually firm.

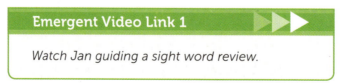

Emergent Video Link 1

Watch Jan guiding a sight word review.

Description of Day 1

Sight Word Chart for Monitoring Progress—Level A

	Student 1	Student 2	Student 3	Student 4	Student 5	Student 6
am						
at						
can						
go						
is						
like						
me						
see						
the						
to						

Sight Word Chart for Monitoring Progress—Level B

	Student 1	Student 2	Student 3	Student 4	Student 5	Student 6
dad						
he						
in						
it						
look						
mom						
my						
on						
up						
we						

Sight Word Chart for Monitoring Progress—Level C

	Student 1	Student 2	Student 3	Student 4	Student 5	Student 6
and						
are						
come						
for						
got						
here						
not						
play						
said						
you						

Emergent

Appendix F

Troubleshooting Sight Word Review

If students . . .	Then . . .
ask for help or write a sight word that begins with a different letter	say, "Make the first sound. Use your ABC chart to find the letter that matches that sound. Think of what the word looks like."
write the word from right to left **m a**	draw a dot on the left side of the box. Tell students to begin writing at the dot. ● **a m**
write left to right but reverse letter order **m a** →	have students say the word slowly, emphasizing the initial sound. This helps them hear the sounds in sequence. **/a/ m**
use all uppercase or a mixture of uppercase and lowercase letters **THE** or **tHe**	point to the lowercase letter form on the alphabet chart and have students rewrite the word using lowercase letters.
write a letter backward **dig** for **big**	have students find the correct letter on the alphabet chart and fix the word.
use sound spelling and misspell one or two letters in a word **sed** for **said**	erase the wrong letter(s) and draw a line for each missing letter. Say, "You almost have it. What's missing? What would make it look right?" If this doesn't help, write the word on the whiteboard and have students copy it. Don't let students segment the sounds. Teach for visual memory. **s _ _ d**

Description of Day 1

Introduce a New Book (3–5 minutes)

Prepare students for a successful reading of the new book by discussing the pictures and teaching challenging words.

Provide a synopsis

State the title and give a brief main idea statement of the book. For example, "This book is called *Camouflage*. It's about different animals that blend into their surroundings so their enemies can't find them. Let's look at the pictures and talk about how the animals are camouflaged."

Watch Jan introducing a new book.

Preview and predict

Invite students to make predictions about the illustrations. This builds schema and supports comprehension. Encourage complete sentences by saying, "What do you see? Tell me more." You do not need to discuss every page, but you should draw students' attention to important information and unfamiliar concepts in the pictures. Make sure every student participates.

Introduce new vocabulary

As students preview the book, discuss unfamiliar concepts and new sight words. For DLLs, use illustrations and gestures to discuss unfamiliar concepts. If there is a new sight word, have students predict the first letter and locate the word in the text. For example, say, "What letter would you expect to see at the beginning of the word *like*? Point to the word *like* in your book."

> **Tip**
>
> *If you have to introduce more than five words, the book is too difficult. Choose an easier book.*

Practice new language structures

Some books contain text structures that may be unfamiliar to students. To set them up for a successful first reading of the book, say the challenging sentence or phrase and ask students to repeat it with you. For example, say, "Turn to page 2. It says, 'Here it comes.' Read that sentence with me."

Encourage cross-checking

An important strategic action for emergent readers is checking one source of information against another. Students usually cross-check meaning and the first letter, but they may also cross-check structure and visual information, making sure it looks right and sounds right. To encourage cross-checking behavior, give students choices for familiar concepts. For example, say, "Look at the picture on page 14. It could be an alligator or a crocodile. You'll have to check the first letter to figure it out."

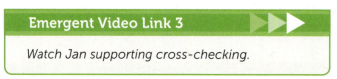

Emergent Video Link 3
Watch Jan supporting cross-checking.

Troubleshooting the Introduction to the Book	
If students . . .	**Then . . .**
need oral language support	have students take turns talking about the pictures. Prompt them to use complete sentences and discuss details that are in the picture.
are dual language learners (DLLs)	model a simple sentence for students to repeat.
need support to cross-check	give students options for some picture concepts. It could be a bunny or a rabbit.
are disengaged	you may be talking too much. Engage students in discussing the pictures.

Description of Day 1

Read the Book With Prompting (8–10 minutes)

Encourage independent reading

Students independently read the book for about five to eight minutes while you confer with individuals. If they finish the book before you call time, have them reread the story.

Prompt students to problem-solve

Listen to individual students and praise them for monitoring, even if they don't fix the error. Once children notice an error, prompt for strategic actions to problem-solve. The goal is not accurate reading but active processing. You want children to encounter challenges and attempt to solve problems. Use the chart on page 76 to differentiate your instruction.

Foster attention to print

The patterned books at Levels A–C help children experience success, but they can be memorized. If children are reading quickly, they probably aren't looking at the words. (One child told me he could read the book with his eyes closed!) Insist that students use their finger or a pointer to point under each word. This will foster attention to print and support one-to-one matching.

> **Tip**
> Do not have students read the book chorally or round-robin. This limits the amount of text they read and impedes independence.

> **Tip**
> If you notice two students reading the same page, have one student go to the previous page and read it to you.

Emergent Video Link 4

Watch Jan prompting students while they read.

Prompts for Emergent Readers		
Behavior	**Goal**	**Prompts**
Stops and appeals, or ignores the picture	Use meaning	You noticed something wasn't right! Now reread the sentence and think what would make sense. Use your picture to help you.
Inserts or omits words	Match one-to-one	Point to each word.
Misreads known words	Use known words	Show me _____. Reread the sentence.
Error doesn't make sense	Monitor for meaning	Are you right? Does that make sense? Try that again and think about the story.
Uses the picture but ignores first letters	Use first letters	That makes sense, but look at the first letter. Sound the first part. What would make sense and look right?
Ignores the end of the word (e.g., *run/runs*)	Visually scan	Check the end of the word. What would look right? Run your finger under the word.
Reads accurately	Confirm strategy	How do you know it is _____ and not _____?

Discuss and Teach *(3–5 minutes)*

Discuss the book

Engage students in a short, meaningful conversation about the story. Ask them to recall what they read. At least one of the discussion prompts should support your comprehension focus for the book. Even though the emergent level books have simple story lines, you can still use the text and pictures to discuss the characters and make connections to personal experiences.

Discussion Starters for Emergent Readers
- *What did we read?*
- *What was your favorite page? Why?*

> **DLL Tip**
>
> *Children learning English will likely need help during the discussion. Provide sentence starters and scaffold their language. Be encouraging and supportive but make sure students do most of the talking.*

Description of Day 1

- *What did this book remind you of?*
- *What picture shows you how the character was feeling?*

Select a teaching point

After you discuss the book, briefly demonstrate a strategic action to the group. Use your interactions with students during the reading of the book to select your teaching point. Refer to the following chart for emergent teaching points. Your teaching should be quick and clear. Teach by demonstration.

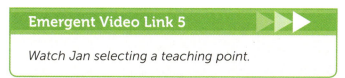

Watch Jan selecting a teaching point.

Teaching Points for Emergent Readers	
Goal	**Demonstration and Teaching**
Apply one-to-one matching	Have students chorally read one page and frame each word with their index fingers. This will demonstrate voice-to-print match.
Use meaning and take risks	Turn to a page and model how to use the picture to figure out a word. Say, "If you don't know a word, always check the picture."
Monitor for meaning	Read a sentence from the book and make an error. Say, "Think about the story and check the picture. Did that make sense? Find my mistake. Let's read that sentence together."
Use letters and sounds	Read a sentence and articulate the first sound of a challenging word. Say, "If you don't know a word, make the first sound to get it started. That will help you figure it out." Point to a few words on the page and ask students to make the first sound.
Cross-check letters and sounds with meaning	Cover the picture and have students read the text. When they come to the challenging word, point to the first letter and say, "Make the first sound." Then reveal the picture. Repeat on another page or two. This action demonstrates the importance of checking one source of information (visual) with another (meaning). It is especially appropriate for children who over-rely on pictures and ignore visual information.
Use known words	Have students turn to a page in the book and ask them to quickly find a sight word. Say, "Show me *go*. Show me *can*. Let's read that sentence together."
Visually scan	Write a word on the dry-erase board. Slide your finger under the word as you say it slowly. Do not segment each sound. Say, "This is the word *can*. Say it slowly as I run my finger under the word. When you read, you need to look all the way to the end of the word."
Reread to problem-solve	Select a page where a student had difficulty. Read up to the tricky word and pretend not to know it. Then model how to reread from the beginning of the sentence. Say, "When you get stuck, reread the sentence and think about the story."

Teach a New Sight Word (2–3 minutes)

Choose a new sight word that was in the book. See the Recommended Sight Words chart (page 58) for a list of appropriate words to teach for each text level. Although there is no specific order for teaching the sight words, phonetic words are easiest for children to learn. Teach them first.

I asked teachers, reading consultants, and Reading Recovery® teachers to explore different procedures for teaching sight words. They affirmed the following steps, which I have found to be efficient, engaging, and effective. These steps will help students develop visual memory, establish left-to-right visual scanning skills, and increase automatic recall. If you follow the procedures with every lesson, most students will develop the process of remembering words by the time they read text Levels E and F.

Start by introducing the word. Write the word on a dry-erase board. Do this in front of students so they can see the left-to-right construction of the word. Tell students the word and ask them to look at each letter as you slide an index card left to right across the word. This prompts students to study the word by scanning left to right. Some students develop a haphazard approach to looking at print, which can lead to visual sequencing problems.

What's Missing?

Turn the board toward you and erase a letter near the end of the word. Show the board to students and ask them to tell you the missing letter. Say, "What's missing?" Students tell you the missing letter and you write it in the word. Repeat the procedure two or three more times by erasing a letter or two at the beginning, middle, or end of the word. Although children may think this is a game, the procedure grabs their attention and teaches them to look closely at the word.

Tip

The sight word is taught after students read the book so they have had an opportunity to read the word several times before you teach them to write it.

Tip

Once you introduce the word, do the activities in order:
- What's Missing?
- Mix & Fix
- Table Writing
- Write It (and Retrieve It)

The activities use a gradual release of responsibility, with you doing more of the work at first and students writing independently by the end.

Tip

Don't teach a new sight word until the old one is firm.

Description of Day 1

Mix & Fix

Give students the magnetic letters to make the new word. Students can use the teacher's model, if necessary. Students read the word using a left-to-right sweep with their finger. Then have them slide each letter to the left or push them up one at a time to make sure they are looking at each letter. Students then mix the letters and remake (fix) the word from left to right. Keep the word on the table.

> **Tip**
>
> *Reteach the same word on Day 2 and review it at the beginning of the next few lessons.*

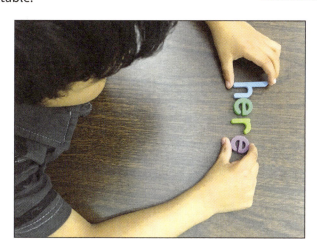

Table Writing

Students use their index finger to "write" the word on the table. Make sure students are looking at their finger while they write. This activity builds a memory trace for the word. Once you observe a child write the word with his or her finger, cover the magnetic letters (from step 2) with an index card and have them do step 4.

Write It (and Retrieve It)

Students write the new word at the bottom of the ABC chart. They should say the word in a natural way as they write it. This mimics what they do when they write stories on their own. Do not encourage students to spell or sound out the word. You want them to learn the word as a complete unit. If they need help, they should lift up the index card and look at the magnetic letters. After they write the word, they should erase it and write it again. Now dictate a *very* familiar word they know how to write. Then dictate the new word again for students to retrieve and write.

> **Emergent Video Link 6** ▶▶▶
>
> *Watch Jan teaching a new sight word.*

Troubleshooting Learning a New Sight Word	
If students . . .	Then . . .
have trouble remembering the missing letter	show them the word again and slide the card across the word. Tell them to look closely.
make the word incorrectly with magnetic letters	intervene immediately and have them check the model on the easel.
are not carefully writing the word on the table	tell them to slow down and look at their finger. Watch them "write" the word.
forget how to write the word	tell them to look under their index card and point to each letter.
write a letter backward	show them the letter on the ABC chart and have them write it correctly.
can't write the familiar word	dictate an easier word.
can't retrieve the new word	tell them to look at their magnetic letters.

Word Study Activity (3–4 minutes)

During the last few minutes of the lesson on Day 1, do a short word study activity to teach phonemic awareness and phonics. The word study is embedded into the small-group lesson so you can show students how to hear sounds and use them to problem-solve unknown words while reading and writing. Choose the target skill and activity that are developmentally appropriate for the students in the group.

> **Tip**
>
> *Organize word study materials on a shelf near your guided reading table.*

Select a target skill for word study

Use children's spelling to identify a focus for word study. Typically, these are the skills most readers need to learn at the following levels:

Level A—initial consonants

Level B—initial and final consonants, short medial vowels

Level C—short medial vowels; initial, medial, and final sounds in CVC words

Description of Day 1

Select the word study activity

I've explored and experimented with dozens of word study activities. The following are engaging, effective, and efficient: picture sorting, making words, and sound boxes. Do only *one* activity. This part of the lesson should be kept short. Most learning about letters, words, and sounds comes from reading and writing text.

Each activity addresses a different aspect of phonemic awareness and phonics. Students learn sounds with picture sorting; they learn how to use the sounds in reading during making words; and they learn how to use the sounds in writing by doing sound boxes. Spend a few lessons (three to four) with picture sorting before moving on to making words and sound boxes. Students need to learn the sounds before they can apply them in reading and writing.

Picture Sorting

Prepare by gathering pictures for initial consonants and medial short vowels. You can find appropriate pictures in *Words Their Way* (Bear, et. al., 2012), or at www.pioneervalleybooks.com. Use the Letter/Sound Checklist to identify two sounds students need to learn. Usually you will firm up all consonant sounds at Level A and teach short vowels at Levels B and C.

Distribute three or four pictures to each student and write the two sounds on a dry-erase board. Each student takes a turn by following these procedures.

Procedures for Sorting Initial Consonants (Level A):

1. Say the word in the picture: *mop*.
2. Say the initial sound: /m/.
3. Say the letter that makes that sound: *m*.
4. Put the picture card under the letter *m*.

> **DLL Tip**
>
> When you have DLLs in the group, give them pictures they know.

> **Tip**
>
> Picture sorts for initial consonants should *not* include digraphs or blends. That would only confuse students.

> **Tip**
>
> When you distribute the picture sorting cards, tell students what the picture is. Don't waste time having them guess what it is.

Procedures for Sorting Medial Vowels (Levels B and C):

Hearing short, medial vowels can be challenging, but the following procedures work. Use one-syllable pictures that have a short vowel in the middle (e.g., *hat, hop, sun*). Teach children how to stretch the word to emphasize the medial sound. This helps them hear the vowel.

> **Tip**
> The short a *and* short o *are the easiest vowels to learn.*

1. Say the word in the picture: *map*.
2. Say the word slowly and stretch the vowel: *maaaap*.
3. Say the letter that makes the vowel sound: *a*.
4. Put the picture card under the letter *a*.

Watch Jan doing a vowel sorting activity.

Making Words

Beginning readers need to match the letters they see to the sounds they hear (Clay, 2005). If the auditory and visual processing systems aren't synchronized, readers may not monitor for visual information while reading and writing (Sousa, 2014). For example, they may read *he* for *here* or write *si* for *is*. The making words activity slows down visual processing to allow auditory processing sufficient time to recognize the sounds. You will see improvement in the left-to-right scanning that is required to build an efficient processing system.

Create a series of words that differ by one letter or use the suggestions in Appendix A. The sequence forces children to attend to the target skill and decide which letter they need to change to make the new word. Each series of words on the chart in Appendix A targets the skill for that text level.

Level A: Change initial consonants.
   can-man-pan-tan-fan

Level B: Change initial and final consonants or change the medial vowel (*a* and *o*). *can-cat-cap-map-mat; cap-cop-mop-map-mat*

Level C: Change initial, medial, and final letters in a CVC word. *can-cap-map-mop-top-tip*

> **Tip**
> *If students have trouble hearing short vowels, do more picture sorts with vowels.*

Description of Day 1

Procedures for Making Words:

1. Give each student the letters he or she will need to make the words.

2. Dictate the first word. "Take three letters and make *cat*. Say *cat* slowly and check it by sliding your finger under the letters. What did you make?"

3. Dictate the next word. "Now change one letter to make the word *bat*. First check the word with your finger so you know which letter you need to change." Have students remove the *c* before they reach for the *b*. "Check the word." At first you will have to tell them which letter to change, but soon they will be able to make the changes without your help.

4. Repeat the process with a few more words. Each time you say a new word, students determine which letter they need to change to make the new word. The process they use to determine the mismatch between sound and letter is the synchrony they will use to self-correct during reading.

> **Tip**
>
> Save preparation time by having a tray of magnetic letters for each student. Before you begin the activity, tell students which letters to select.

Emergent Video Link 8 ▶▶▶
Watch Jan conducting a making words activity.

Sound Boxes

Sound boxes, or Elkonin boxes (Elkonin, 1971), help students hear sounds in words and record sounds in sequence. Use only phonetically regular words with two or three sounds. Do not use sight words unless these words are phonetic (e.g, *can, am, me*). Each phoneme or sound goes in one box. After you teach students how to use sound boxes during word study, you'll be able to use them in guided writing when students need help writing a phonetically regular word.

Two boxes

Three boxes

> **Tip**
> Sound boxes include both the segmenting and blending of sounds.

> **Tip**
> When you first teach this procedure, use a known, phonetically regular word such as *me, go,* or *at*.

> **Tip**
> Some children may need the additional scaffold of segmenting the sounds on their fingers. If so, do this before they write the word in the boxes.

Procedures for sound boxes:

Distribute dry-erase markers and sound box templates that have been inserted into a plastic sheet protector. Tell students you are going to say a word, and that they must write one sound in each box as they say the word slowly. Model each procedure before students do the steps without your support. As soon as possible, transfer the task of slow articulation to the children— otherwise the teacher is doing all the work.

1. Say a word slowly (/m/ - /a/ - /p/).

2. Say the word slowly and touch each box when you say a sound.

   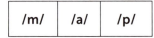

3. Say the word slowly as you write each sound in a box.

   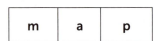

4. Slide your finger under the word to blend the sounds together. Say the word (*map*).

Description of Day 1

Troubleshooting Word Study	
If students . . .	**Then . . .**
can't hear beginning sounds	demonstrate holding the first sound of the word and point to your mouth. Say, "Do what my mouth is doing: *mmmmmm.*"
don't associate the correct letter with the sound	use the picture links on the alphabet chart. Say, "*mmm* is like *moon*. Find the moon on your chart. What letter is that?"
can't hear the medial vowel sound	model how to say the word slowly and give the vowel sound a little punch (*m-a-a-p*).
put a letter in the wrong place when making the new word	show the letters for the previous word (*cat*) and have students slowly run their finger under that word while saying the new word (*can*). Say, "What letter needs to change? What part doesn't look right?" Then have students remove the *t* in *cat* before reaching for the *n* to make *can*. Insist they check the old word and remove the wrong letter before reaching for the new letter they need.
write the sounds out of sequence during sound boxes	use small plastic disks to help students hear sounds in sequence. Say the word very slowly and push a disk into each box, sound by sound. Then have students do the same task.
write the wrong letter in the sound box	have students say the word slowly and hold up a finger for each sound. Then use the ABC chart to link the troublesome sound with a letter. "What sound did you say at the end? What letter makes that sound? Check your ABC chart."

Emergent

Summary of Word Study Activities for Levels A–C

Level	Skill Focus	Picture Sorting	Making Words	Sound Boxes
A	Consonants	Initial consonants	Change initial consonants *cat, fat, mat, bat*	2 or 3 boxes *me, at, we, go, cat, can*
B	Consonants and short vowels (*a, o*)	Initial consonants and short, medial vowels	Change initial and final consonants *pat, pan, pad, mad, man, hat, has, ham, ram, rat*	2 or 3 boxes with short *a* and *o* *am, on, as, mop, mad, hot*
C	Short vowels (*e, i, u*) Hearing sounds in sequence (CVC)	Short, medial vowels (*e, i, u*)	Change initial, medial, and final letters; use all short vowels *pot, hot, hop, hip, lip, lap;* *bad, bed, red, rid, rim*	3 boxes (CVC) *hip, mud, did, get, pet, run*

DESCRIPTION OF DAY 2

The Day 2 lesson takes about 20 minutes and has five components:

- Sight Word Review
- Reread Books With Prompting
- Discuss and Teach
- Reteach the New Sight Word From Day 1
- Guided Writing

Sight Word Review (1–2 minutes)

Review three sight words following the same procedures as Day 1. The new sight word you taught on Day 1 should be one of the review words. This helps you observe how well students are remembering the word. You will likely need to provide some scaffolding when they write yesterday's new word.

Reread Books With Prompting (8–10 minutes)

Students independently read the new book from Day 1 to build automaticity with sight words and increase fluency. Spend a few minutes conferring with each student. Use the Prompts for Emergent Readers chart (page 76) to differentiate your prompting and engage students in short conversations. After students read yesterday's new book, have them reread other books from previous guided reading lessons until time is up.

Discuss and Teach (3–5 minutes)

Have a short discussion of the story and teach one or two strategic actions. Use the Teaching Points for Emergent Readers chart (page 77) for suggestions for teaching points and discussion starters.

> **Tip**
> Prompt students to say the words slowly as they write them. This helps them retrieve the word using the initial letter.

> **Tip**
> If students are receiving an extra guided reading lesson from another teacher, teach the same sight words each week.

> **Tip**
> Students should read for at least five minutes.

> **Tip**
> Reading other familiar books with different sentence patterns guards against memorizing. They need to look at print.

Reteach the New Sight Word From Day 1 *(2–3 minutes)*

Teach the sight word you taught on Day 1. Be sure to follow all procedures:

- Introduce the Word
- What's Missing?
- Mix & Fix
- Table Writing
- Write It (and Retrieve It)

Do not introduce a new sight word until the previous word is firmly known.

Guided Writing *(5–8 minutes)*

Understand the rationale for guided writing

Reading and writing are interwoven in the emergent guided reading lesson framework because they are reciprocal processes. Many of the operations needed in early reading are practiced in another form in early writing (Clay, 2005). Writing letters, sounds, words, and sentences helps children attend to the detail in print (Clay, 2005).

> **Tip**
> Students should write in journals rather than on dry-erase boards so you have a record of their writing.

Guided writing provides an opportunity for you to support students as they write a brief message about the story. It is assisted, not independent, writing. During guided writing students learn the following:

- How print works top to bottom on a page and left to right across a line
- To write known words quickly
- To hear and record sounds in unknown words
- To space between words
- To reread a sentence to monitor for meaning and predict the next word
- To put a period at the end of a sentence
- Simple sentence structures that are common in emergent books

Gather materials

Make a writing journal for each student. Fold about 15 sheets of 8½-x-11-inch blank paper in half and staple at the fold. The bottom half is for students to write their sentence, the top half is for practicing and teaching. Distribute an alphabet chart and pencil to each student.

Description of Day 2

Dictate a sentence and have students repeat it

At Levels A–C, dictate a sentence about the book that includes the new sight word you taught during that lesson, other known sight words, and opportunities for students to hear and record sounds in words they do not already know how to write. Have students repeat the sentence several times until they memorize it. If children have trouble remembering the sentence, it is either too long or too complex. Use a very short sentence at Level A and gradually lengthen the sentence as students progress in levels. This helps students build an auditory memory that will assist them when they write independently.

- **Level A:** sentence should be 3–5 words
- **Level B:** sentence should be 5–7 words
- **Level C:** sentence should be 7–10 words

> **Tip**
>
> Expect accurate spelling on sight words you have taught. Accept approximations on words you have not taught.

Draw a line for each word

As students repeat the sentence, draw a line for each word in their journals. The lines will help children remember to space between words. At first, have children point to the lines as they repeat the sentence so they understand where they should write each word. Once children are able to space without prompting, you do not need to draw the lines.

Confer, scaffold, and teach

Allow students to write at their own pace. Do not dictate the sentence word by word. Work with each student and differentiate your scaffolding based on his or her needs. As students write, use the Prompts for Emergent Writers chart (page 92) to address level-appropriate skills. Use the top part of the writing journal for practicing a sight word, demonstrating correct letter formation, or writing a word in boxes. Prompt students to use an alphabet chart if they need help with letter formation and sound-letter links. If students finish writing the dictated sentence before time is called, tell them to write another sentence. Ask, "What else can you write about the story?"

Focus on spelling

Prompt students to say each word as they write it. This will help them hear sounds in words. You want to encourage them to take risks, but you should expect correct spelling for the sight words you have taught.

Your expectations and teaching points will change as students progress as writers. Children will need many supported writing experiences before skills are internalized.

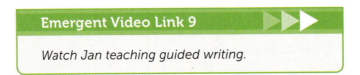
Watch Jan teaching guided writing.

Target Skills and Strategies for Emergent Writers	
Level A	
Draw a line for each word. Use the practice page (the top part of the writing journal) to teach letter formation, write the new sight word, and draw sound boxes.	Dictate a sentence with three to five words. Include the new sight word that was taught that day. Encourage students to stretch unknown words and record dominant consonant sounds. **Target Skills for Level A:** • Segment and record the initial consonant sound in each word • Hear and record long vowel sounds in words (with prompting) • Learn to write about ten sight words • Continue to work on letter formation • Space between words with scaffolding. I like to run.

Description of Day 2

Level B

When you teach a skill during word study, prompt students to apply it in guided writing.

If you sorted short *a* and short *o*, prompt students to write those sounds correctly when they appear in their stories.

Use the practice page for your teaching points. For example, students can write a sight word you have previously taught.

Dictate a sentence with five to seven words. The sentence should include the new sight word that was taught that day, other known sight words, and at least one unknown word for students to problem-solve. When possible, include a word that gives students the opportunity to practice the skill you taught during word study (e.g., words with short *a* and short *o*).

Target Skills for Level B:

- Reread the sentence to predict and monitor (with prompting)
- Hear and record dominant consonant sounds in each word
- Hear and record long vowel sounds in words
- Hear and record short *a* and short *o* sounds in words (with prompting)
- Learn to write about 15–20 high-frequency words
- Write phonetically regular words in sound boxes (with support)
- Place a period at the end of the sentence
- Space between words with the support of teacher-drawn lines

Level C

Stop drawing a line for each word. Students should learn to space with a few verbal prompts.

Connect the sentence to the story.

Continue to use the practice page for your teaching points:
- Letter formation
- Sight words
- Sound boxes

Dictate a sentence that relates to the story and has seven to ten words. Include the new sight word, other known sight words, and CVC words with short vowels. If time permits, dictate a second sentence or guide students to construct their own sentence.

Target Skills for Level C:

- Remember and reread the sentence without prompting
- Say each word slowly while writing
- Learn to write about 30 high-frequency words
- Write phonetically regular words in sound boxes with some support for vowel sounds
- Hear and record CVC sounds in sequence
- Space between words without scaffolding
- Put a period at the end of the sentence without prompting
- Introduce a capital letter at the beginning of the sentence

Emergent

Prompts for Emergent Writers

If the student . . .	Say . . .
forgets the sentence that's being attempted	Reread and point to each word. What comes next? (If this doesn't help, tell him or her the sentence and have the student repeat it.)
forgets to put the period	What goes at the end? (Show the student where to put the period. After writing, have the student circle the periods in his or her story.)
forms a letter incorrectly	Find that letter on your alphabet chart. Practice making it on your practice page. (When necessary, model correct formation.)
needs help hearing sounds in words	Say the word slowly and write the sounds you hear. (If the word has two or three phonemes, draw sound boxes on the practice page and have the student say the word slowly as he or she writes the sounds in the boxes.)
misspells sight words	Does it look right? (Erase the wrong letter(s) and ask, What's missing? If the student can't remember the word, write the sight word on the top part of the journal and have him or her practice writing the word before correcting it in the story.)
forgets to put spaces between words	You need to space between your words. Pick up your pencil and move it over after you write each word. (Teach children to use their finger to make a space between words. If this is too cumbersome for the student, continue drawing a line for each word until the student spaces without prompting.)
doesn't hear inflectional endings	Say the word and listen to the end. What letter(s) do you need at the end of the word? (At Level C, you can expect students to hear and record endings you have taught, such as -s and -ing.)
forgets to use uppercase letters	Go to the first word of your sentence and circle the first letter. This letter should be uppercase. Use your ABC chart to find the uppercase letter if you need help.

Description of Day 2

Reflect on Next Steps

Before you leave the guided reading table, take one to two minutes to reflect on your lesson. In the "Next Steps" box on your lesson plan, write a few notes about your students. Here are some questions to help you determine your next steps:

- Did you choose the right text? Circle the text difficulty. If the text was too easy or too hard, carefully select the next book so that it offers the right amount of challenge.

- Did you pinpoint the right focus? Do students need more lessons with that same focus? Perhaps students are ready for a new focus.

- Is there a specific student you need to assess and analyze? Record his or her name. To help make acceleration decisions, consider doing a running record on the last book he or she read.

☐ Sound boxes			
8. Next Steps	Text was: Hard Appropriate Easy Next book: _____	Next Focus:	Students to assess and analyze:

SAMPLE FILLED-IN LESSON PLAN

Emergent Guided Reading Plan (Levels A–C)

Students: Lilly, Dante, David, Eric, Kaitlyn **Dates:** 12/6-7

Title/Level	Strategy Focus	Comprehension Focus
The Firefighter/C	Monitor	Recall Details

DAY 1

1. Sight Word Review (write three familiar words) *1–2 minutes*

come	said	on

2. Book Introduction *3-5 minutes*

Synopsis: This book tells us the equipment firefighters need to stay safe and to put out fires.

New Vocabulary or Language Structures: going, helmet, climb
Here is my helmet.

DAY 2

1. Sight Word Review (write three familiar words) *1–2 minutes*

New SW from Day 1

here	can	play

2. Reread Yesterday's Book (and other familiar books)

Observations or take a running record on one student. Students used pictures and visual information with little prompting.
Dante read with 100% accuracy. Good comp. Move up.

3. Read With Prompting *8–10 minutes*

Monitoring and Word-Solving Prompts
- ☐ Point to each word. (Levels A & B)
- ☐ Try it. Check the picture. What would make sense?
- ☐ Reread the sentence and make the first sound.
- ☒ What would make sense and look right?
- ☐ Show me the word ____. (Locate a sight word.)
- ☒ Check the word with your finger.
- ☐ Could it be ____ or ____?
- ☐ How do you know it is ____ and not ____?

Fluency and Comprehension Prompts
- ☐ Don't point. (Discourage pointing at Level C.)
- ☐ Read it the way the character would say it.
- ☒ What did you read? Tell me about the story.
- ☐ Does this book remind you of something you have done?
- ☐ How is this book like another book you have read?
- ☐ Have you ever felt the way the character feels? When? Why?
- ☐ What is your favorite part? Why?
- ☐ What was the problem? How was it solved?

4. Discussion Prompt *2–3 minutes*

What special equipment do firefighters need to stay safe?

Turn to the picture on page 15. How do fire hydrants help firefighters put out fires?

5. Teaching Points for Emergent Readers (choose 1 or 2 each day) *1–2 minutes*

- ☐ One-to-one matching (discourage pointing at Level C)
- ☐ Use picture clues (meaning)
- ☒ Monitor for meaning
- ☒ Monitor with letters and sounds
- ☐ Cross-check letters and sounds with pictures
- ☐ Locate known words
- ☐ Visually scan left to right
- ☐ Reread to problem-solve

6. Teach One Sight Word *2–3 minutes*

Word: here

1. What's Missing? 2. Mix & Fix 3. Table Writing 4. Write It (and Retrieve It)

6. Reteach Same Sight Word *2–3 minutes*

7. Word Study (choose one) *3–4 minutes*

- ☒ Picture sorting
- ☐ Making words
- ☐ Sound boxes

ham tap pet man bed

7. Guided Writing *5–8 minutes*

A: 3–5 words
B: 5–7 words
C: 7–10 words

Here is the fireman. He has a hose in his hand.

8. Next Steps

Text was: Hard (Appropriate) Easy
Next book: ____

Next Focus: Work on phrasing. Discourage finger pointing during reading.

Students to assess and analyze: David

Complete the shaded boxes before you meet with the group. Add observations and notes during the lesson.

Analyzing Problem Areas for Emergent Readers

Emergent readers have a lot to learn. They are firming up letter knowledge, learning to hear and use sounds, using pictures and a few known words to read books, and writing short stories. Some children progress quickly through the emergent stage; others may take four to six weeks to move from one level to the next. If you notice a student not making progress, take action. Reflect on your teaching, analyze assessments, and develop a plan for acceleration.

Reflect on your teaching

Have you provided consistent, guided reading lessons? Have you been following the lesson framework to include reading, word study, and writing? Are you using the prompts for emergent readers and writers? Perhaps a child is not accelerating because you've neglected part of the lesson framework.

Observe the student

Take a running record on the last guided reading book, analyze the Sight Word Chart, and administer a dictated sentence. What do you notice? What are the child's strengths? What should be taught next? Ask a colleague to observe the student while you teach a guided reading lesson. He or she might notice behaviors you missed. Use the assessments and your observations to complete the Problem-Solving Chart on the next page. This will help you identify the student's strengths and pinpoint why he or she is struggling.

Mark Strengths and Needs (+ √ -)

Problem-Solving Chart for Levels A–C

Student	Instructional Level	Uses Oral Language Skills	Takes Risks	Monitors for Meaning	Rereads at Difficulty	Cross-checks	Retells Story	Forms Letters	Knows Letter Sounds	Hears and Records Sounds in CVC Words	Writes Sight Words

Directions for completing the Problem-Solving Chart

Columns 1 and 2: Record the student's name and instructional level.

Column 3: Uses oral language skills. Does the student have the language skills to read and retell at this text level? A conversation with the student will usually show if oral language is impeding progress, but you can also check the running record. Is the student making errors on new concepts not in his or her vocabulary? Can the student retell the text? Sometimes dual language learners understand what they read but struggle to retell it because they lack language skills to communicate clearly. Put a plus (+) if language is a strength, a check (√) if the student has adequate language skills, or a minus (-) if language is interfering with progress.

Column 4: Takes risks. Does the student independently try to problem-solve unknown words by using the pictures? Does the student stop reading and wait for your help? Perhaps the child is stopping at a hard word and trying to listen to other students in the group. Are there a lot of "tolds" on the running record? Put a plus (+) if risk taking is a strength, a check (√) if the student has adequate independence, or a minus (-) if lack of risk taking is interfering with progress.

Column 5: Monitors for meaning. Does the student stop when an error doesn't make sense? A reader must notice an error before he or she can fix it. For example, he or she should notice errors such as *horse* for *here* because *horse* wouldn't make sense in the sentence. Of course, self-correction is the goal, but if the student is at least stopping at an error, he or she is monitoring. Put a plus (+) if the student always monitors for meaning, a check (√) if he or she sometimes monitors for meaning, or a minus (-) if monitoring is not observed.

Column 6: Rereads at difficulty. Does the student reread the sentence when he or she encounters an unknown word or notices an error? Put a plus (+) if the student always rereads, a check (√) if he or she sometimes rereads, or a minus (-) if the student does not reread.

Column 7: Cross-checks. Does the student use more than one source of information to problem-solve? Does he or she use both the picture and the first letters to predict unknown words or correct errors? For example, if the child says *frog* for *toad*, does he or she notice *toad* doesn't begin with the letter *f*? Usually cross-checking leads to self-corrections. Put a plus (+) if errors are always meaningful and match first letters, a check (√) if he or she sometimes cross-checks, or a minus (-) if cross-checking is absent.

Column 8: Retells Story. There isn't much to retell in emergent books, but students should be able to recall information they have read. For example, if the book was about playing at the park, they should be able to tell you some of the playground equipment the children used. Put a plus (+) if retelling is a strength, a check (√) if the student recalls some information, or a minus (-) if the student cannot retell a story.

Column 9: Forms letters. Put a plus (+) if letter formation is a strength, a check (√) if the student has adequate letter formation, or a minus (-) if letter formation is a challenge.

Column 10: Knows letter sounds. Put a plus (+) if the student knows at least 20 letters sounds, a check (√) if the student knows 10–20 sounds, or a minus (-) if the student knows fewer than ten sounds.

Column 11: Hears and records sounds in CVC words. Does the student hear sounds in short words and record them in sequence? The best way to analyze this skill is to dictate some simple CVC words, such as *lap, bet, rid, fog, hum*. Does the student spell the words correctly? (If the student is at Level A or B, don't expect vowel sounds to be correct.) It is not unusual to find emergent readers who know letter sounds but do not apply the skill when writing. Put a plus (+) if the student hears and records beginning, medial, and final letters, a check (√) if he or she hears and records beginning and final sounds, or a minus (-) if the student only hears and records a few initial or final sounds.

Column 12: Writes sight words. Record the number of sight words a student can write. Children should be learning about ten words per level. By the time a student is ready for text Level D, he or she should be able to write about 25–30 sight words.

NEXT STEP FOR STRUGGLING EMERGENT READERS

Now that you have analyzed the student, meet with a colleague or reading specialist to create your next steps for acceleration. Discuss ways to build on the student's strengths and plan specific activities that address his or her needs. If another teacher is providing instruction to the student, closely collaborate to ensure you are working toward similar goals. Review the Suggestions for Intervention chart (pages 99–101) and select ideas that might help your student accelerate. Write your ideas on a Next Steps Acceleration Plan (scholastic.com/NSFresources) and share the plan with the parent and other teachers who are working with the student. (See example on the next page.) Give the parent specific activities he or she can do at home to help the student. Each day send home familiar books for the student to read.

Next Steps Acceleration Plan		
Reading	Word Study	Writing
Texts: Write the titles of the next 3–4 books for guided reading. **Focus:** What is your next focus for reading? **Prompts:** What prompts should you use?	**Skills:** What skills does the student need to learn next? **Sight Words:** Write sight words you have taught that need to be practiced. Write 2–3 new words to teach next.	**Language:** What types of language structures can the student remember? **Focus:** What should you focus on in guided writing?

The following chart includes suggestions for each focus area listed on the Problem-Solving Chart. Use these ideas to create the Next Steps Acceleration Plan for your student.

Focus	Suggestions for Intervention
Uses oral language skills	• Select texts that match the student's oral language level. For DLLs choose texts with simple sentences and familiar concepts. Keep it easy to learn. • Encourage conversations during guided reading. Ask the student to discuss the pictures in the book during the introduction. Avoid asking questions that require one-word answers. Instead say, "Talk about this page." Provide sentence starters and praise attempts. After reading, engage the student in a genuine conversation about the book. Use the pictures to prompt the student to include details. Be encouraging and supportive. • Make a special effort to have conversations throughout the day. During interactive read-alouds, have students turn and talk to a partner. Scaffold DLLs with sentence starters such as *My favorite part is . . .* or *The girl is angry because . . .* • During guided writing dictate simple sentences that match the student's language level. Use the structure of the guided reading book when appropriate. Avoid prepositional phrases and complex sentences until the student develops stronger oral language skills. Gradually increase the complexity of the dictated sentence to include adjectives, conjunctions, and varied prepositional phrases. • During whole-group instruction, do shared reading with songs and chants. • Have students listen to simple stories and songs during independent learning time. • Ask an older student to be a reading buddy. Have them read together from the child's box of familiar books.

Focus	Suggestions for Intervention
Takes risks	• Select an easier book. Children will take risks when there are fewer challenges. An easy book will make the child feel successful and confident. • Some children are extremely sensitive to correction and will not attempt a word because they are afraid of being wrong. For a few days, ignore the student's errors. Once confidence is restored and the child begins to try unknown words, be generous with praise and gentle with correction.
Monitors for meaning	• During reading, if the student makes an error that changes the meaning of the sentence, say, "Did that make sense? Think about the story." • Prompt the student to reread and make sense.
Cross-checks	• Most emergent readers quickly learn to use picture clues. The challenging part of the process is using initial letters. Point to the first letter of a word and prompt the student to make the sound and then check the picture. • While you listen to the child read, say, "How did you know it was *flower* and not *daisy*?" The response you want is, "Because it starts with an *f*." This is the first sign the child is cross-checking. • Use the cross-checking teaching point described on page 77. If you teach cross-checking every day, children will quickly apply this strategy as long as they know the letter sounds and the picture concepts.
Retells	• During the discussion after reading, have students take turns retelling one part of the story. If a child can't recall any event, show a picture from the book. • If you want the child to provide more details say, "Tell me more. What else did you read? Think about the pictures you saw in the book." • If the book has a story with a beginning, middle, and end, prompt the student to retell the story in sequence. Scaffold with pictures if necessary.
Forms letters	• If the child has difficulty holding a pencil correctly, experiment with different pencil grips until you find one that works. Usually fat pencils are easier to hold than thin ones. • Ask the occupational therapist to observe the student and make recommendations. • Some handwriting programs, such as Handwriting Without Tears (www.hwtears.com), can help children with weak motor skills. • During guided writing, select a letter the student needs to work on. Have the student form the letter three ways: in the air with big movements, on the table using his or her finger, and on the dry-erase board. Each time the student forms the letter, he or she should say the verbal pathways listed on pages 43–44.

Focus	Suggestions for Intervention
Knows letter sounds	• Assess the student on the letter sounds, and systematically teach the ones he or she doesn't know with picture sorting during word study. Teach the letters with the easiest sounds first (b, d, f, j, k, l, m, n, p, r, s, t, v, z). These letters have the sound in the letter name. • Use picture links and movements to teach the hard-to-learn sounds. Children might learn the /w/ by connecting it to *Walmart*, and the /h/ by breathing on their hand. • Place an alphabet chart next to the student so he or she can refer to it while reading and writing.
Hears and records sounds in CVC words	• If the student knows the sounds but is not using them in writing, use sound boxes during word study. Dictate a word with two or three phonemes. Sometimes three phonemes are easier to hear than two. Follow the procedures for sound boxes on page 84. Support the student with vowels, since they are often hard to hear. Only use phonetically regular words and avoid digraphs, blends, and silent letters. • During guided writing, use sound boxes on the practice page to help the student hear sounds in CVC words. Follow the procedures on page 84. • Always have the student say the words while writing them. • If the student is segmenting the sounds but does not remember the letter that matches that sound, refer him or her to the alphabet chart. Say, "Find the letter in this line that says /m/."
Writes sight words	• Take stock of the words the student can write by dictating the words on the Sight Word Chart. Put a plus (+) next to the words the student wrote quickly and accurately. Now teach one of the words the student doesn't know. Begin with the phonetically regular words so the student can use the letter sounds to learn how to spell them. • Vary sight word instruction by teaching three- and four-letter words along with two-letter words. • When teaching the new sight word in the lesson plan, follow all steps each day: Introduce the Word, What's Missing?, Mix & Fix, Table Writing, Write It (and Retrieve It). Do not skip a step. Do not teach a new sight word until the student has firmly learned this one. • Always include the new sight word and a few familiar sight words in the dictated sentence. • Give magnetic letters to the parents. Each week send home a list of five words you have recently taught and show the parent how to do the steps as homework.

Emergent

ADAPTATIONS FOR DLLs AND STUDENTS WITH IEPs

The emergent lesson is applicable for most kindergartners and students in higher grades who are learning to speak English or have a special learning need. The lesson components teach foundational skills and integrate reading, word study, and writing. Children practice speaking and listening as they participate in conversations about the story. Although the strategies and skills in this chapter are appropriate for any emergent reader, some students may need special technology or adaptations to write the dictated sentence. Others may benefit from more discussion about the story. Regardless of the need, these books are short enough to easily complete the components in the recommended time.

Writing can be especially challenging for DLLs. Begin with simple, short sentences they can remember. Have them repeat the sentence. If they can't repeat it, shorten the sentence. Children need to say each word aloud as they write. Prompt them to reread their sentence to figure out which word to write next.

Don't be too concerned about a DLL's inability to retell the story. These children are still developing language and will need prompting during the discussion. Provide sentence starters, direct them to use the pictures in the books, and model sentences they can repeat. These easy books will help DLLs learn English concepts and sentence structure.

When a student does not fit into a guided reading group (or any time you see a need to provide targeted, individualized instruction), the emergent plan can easily be adapted. Teach the student for ten minutes each day following the plan below.

Ten-Minute Lessons for Individual Instruction		
Day 1	Day 2	Day 3
Sight Word Review	Sight Word Review	Sight Word Review
Introduce and Read New Book	Reread and Discuss Book From Day 1	Guided Writing—Dictate Sentences
Teach One New Sight Word	Reteach Same Sight Word Word Study	

MONITORING PROGRESS

Progress monitoring is a daily part of a guided reading lesson. Take daily anecdotal notes and assess students about every ten lessons to monitor progress and guide your teaching decisions. Because you are working with a small group, you have the opportunity to notice new behaviors and record your observations on the back of the lesson plan or in a separate notebook. Jot down errors and whether the student monitored and self-corrected. These on-the-spot assessments will guide your teaching decisions.

Letters and Sounds

Every two weeks, assess each student on the letters and sounds you have taught. Discontinue this test when the student knows all 52 letters and 26 letter sounds.

Sight Words

Because developing a large bank of sight words is crucial for fluent reading, keep a record of the words you have taught. About every two weeks, take a few minutes at the beginning of the lesson to assess students on the words they have learned over the past two weeks. This will tell you which words are firmly known and which need more review.

Running Record

Use a few minutes at the beginning of the Day 2 lesson to take a running record on one student while the others are reading familiar books. You don't need to listen to the student read the entire book. Just listen to a few pages to assess the text difficulty and the student's problem-solving actions. These assessments will help you decide which students are ready to move up, which students need more time at a level, and which strategies you need to teach next. Students who read with at least 95 percent accuracy and adequate recall are ready to move to the next text level. Reserve formal benchmark testing for the beginning, middle, and end of the year.

MOVING TO THE EARLY LESSON PLAN

Consider moving students to the Early Guided Reading Plan when they can

- Read text Level C with few errors
- Read and write about 25–30 sight words
- Solve new words by using pictures and initial letter sounds
- Monitor for meaning
- Reread to access meaning and structure
- Hear and record CVC sounds in sequence
- Maintain one-to-one matching without pointing

QUESTIONS TEACHERS ASK ABOUT EMERGENT GUIDED READING

My emergent readers are having a hard time remembering sight words. One day they seem to have learned a word and the next day they don't know it. What should I do?

The first sight words can be difficult for some children to learn. Those children might have poor visual memory, weak phonemic awareness skills, or difficulty attending to print. Carefully choose the first words you teach. Don't teach them in alphabetical order. Begin with a few words that are phonetically regular so students can use a sound-to-letter match to build a small bank of known words (e.g., *go, at, can*). Then teach nonphonetic sight words that appear frequently in emergent books (e.g., *my, look, the*). These words have to be remembered as a unit and not sounded out. Shift the emphasis away from phonemic segmentation to visual memory. Vary the length of the word. After you teach a two-letter word, teach a three- or four-letter word. Don't be surprised if children need four or more days to learn one sight word. Avoid introducing a new sight word until students firmly know the first one. Follow all of the steps for teaching a sight word (pages 78–79). After reading and discussing the story, have students find and name the new sight word in the book. Use the new word in the dictated sentence. Once children develop a way of remembering words, they will learn new words at a faster rate.

My students often get "stuck" on Level C. What are some ideas to help them make that leap to Level D?

Review the first column, for Level C, on the Target Skills and Strategies for Emergent Writers chart on page 91 and pinpoint the processing problem. Some children rely too much on a patterned text and don't attend to print. Be sure to select books with a varied pattern. Other children rely solely on the picture at difficult points and ignore first-letter cues. Prompt them to use the first letters at difficult points and carry out the teaching point for cross-checking on page 77. There are children who do not know enough sight words to tackle Level D texts. Use the Sight Word Chart (Appendix F) to assess the A–C words students can write, and teach the ones they can't. Consider how students are doing with the word study and guided writing portion of the lesson. Follow all procedures. The reading, writing, and word study work go hand in hand to build a strong processing system.

What should I do if I am listening to a student and he or she doesn't make any errors?

The first thing I would consider is the text level. Perhaps you need to move the student to a higher one. If the student is reading a patterned book and not making errors, ask him or her to show you a word or two on the page. You could also ask the student, for example, how he or she knows the word is *flower* and not *rose*. You need to know if the student is attending to print or just memorizing the book. Sometimes I'll have a student read a page to me while I place my hand over the picture, which tells me if he or she is using visual information. But most likely, you need to choose a more challenging text for the next lesson.

When should I start teaching for fluency?

Before you teach for fluency, make sure the student is looking at print. I insist students point to the words at Levels A and B until their one-to-one matching is firm. Once students get to Level C, I tell them not to point and begin fluency instruction.

Should I correct spelling errors during guided writing?

Always attend to the misspelling of a sight word you have taught during guided reading. You might write the word on the top page of the student's writing journal and have him or her practice writing it a few times before correcting it in the piece. If the student makes a mistake with only one letter of the word, erase that letter and say, "What's missing? What would make the word look right?" Make a note of misspelled words and review them at the beginning of the next lesson. Do not correct students if they misspell a word that you have not taught them. You want to encourage them to take risks, say unknown words slowly, and write the sounds they hear. If you notice they are not hearing sounds in sequence or misrepresenting short vowel sounds, address those skills during the word study portion of your next guided reading lesson.

> **Professional Study Guide**
>
> *Go to scholastic.com/NSFresources for a downloadable professional study guide written just for this book. In it, you'll find questions and activities about emergent readers to use on your own or with your colleagues in a study group or PLC.*

CHAPTER 4

The Early Reader: Levels D–I

Maryam and her family emigrated to the United States when she was eight years old. Because she didn't know her letters or sounds and didn't speak any English, her third-grade teacher asked me for help. I suggested that the teacher follow the pre-A procedures.

I just happened to be visiting Maryam's school two weeks later and was privileged to teach her very first emergent guided reading lesson. She read a Level A book and learned how to write the word *can*. The classroom teacher continued every day with an individual ten-minute lesson following my framework. By the end of third grade, Maryam was reading and writing at Level J (which corresponds to the beginning of second grade).

Two years later I returned to Maryam's school to shoot videos for *Next Step Guided Reading Assessment: Grades 3–6* (Richardson & Walther, 2013*)*. As I was preparing to film a running record, in walked Maryam! What a delight it was to see her! She was in fifth grade and so proud to be reading on grade level. During that short chance meeting, precious little Maryam posed with me for the cover photo of *Next Step Guided Reading Assessment.*

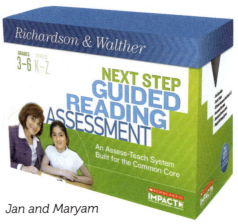

Jan and Maryam

PROFILE OF AN EARLY READER

Early readers read at text Levels D–I. They know their letters and sounds, but they are still learning how to apply these foundational skills to decode challenging words. They are learning to read and write sight words that appear frequently in primary texts. Emergent reading behaviors, such as one-to-one matching, using pictures, and left-to-right directionality, are firm. Early readers become proficient in the following skills and strategic actions as they progress through text levels:

- Monitoring for meaning and structure
- Monitoring for visual information
- Rereading at points of difficulty to access meaning and structure
- Using a variety of strategic actions to solve words
- Reading easy and familiar books with phrasing and expression
- Retelling what they have read
- Reading and writing about 60–80 sight words
- Applying phonetic principles they have learned

ASSESS

As someone who has devoted most of her life to teaching, I'm concerned that we are robbing students of valuable instructional time when we blindly administer assessments that have little or no instructional value. Which assessments are worth sacrificing instructional time? How can we analyze the results of the assessments to inform our instruction? In my opinion, there are two essential assessments for teaching early readers: a reading conference and a spelling assessment.

Assessments for Early Readers		
Assessment	How is it administered?	What does it tell you?
Reading conference	Individual	Instructional text level range Which strategic actions are used and/or neglected
Spelling assessment	Small group	Sight words and phonics skills to teach

Reading Conference

The reading conference includes a running record and an oral retelling. A running record (Clay, 1993, 2005) is the single most valuable tool for teaching early readers. While running records are often taken to assess the text difficulty and to record reading progress, their primary purpose is to guide instruction. Early readers make errors, and the errors tell you how the student is processing text. Running records determine a student's instructional text level and show which strategic actions a student uses and which ones he or she needs to learn. Running records are simple to do. As the student reads aloud, mark his or her miscues on a recording sheet or a blank sheet of paper. After the reading, check for comprehension by asking the student to retell and discuss the passage. For independent reading, students should read texts at easy levels, but for guided reading lessons, choose text levels that students read with 90–95 percent accuracy and some comprehension. Scoring the running record is the easy part. The hard part is analyzing it.

Analyze the strategic actions

The number of errors is not as important as determining why the student made those errors and deciding what strategic actions will accelerate the child. All errors aren't equal. Even though you count every error (to maintain standard assessment procedures), you should look at the kinds of errors the student makes, and what he or she does at the point of difficulty. Ask yourself these questions:

- What kind of action does the child take at difficulty? (I am concerned when I observe a child who always stops and waits for help.)

- Is the student thinking about the story? Were the errors meaningful? (Constructing meaning is the most important factor to consider when analyzing a reader.)

- Did the student monitor using visual information? (A student who notices the visual mismatch between what he or she says and the word on the page is accessing letters and sounds to monitor.)

- Is there a pattern in the child's errors? For instance, did the student repeatedly ignore the middle or the end of a word? (This is often the case with early readers. Understanding the pattern of visual processing will help you prompt the student.)

- Did the student miscue on the same word several times? (Count each miscue, but when you determine the instructional reading range, you should consider the fact that he or she miscued on the same word.)

- Did the student miscue on an unfamiliar word? (If the child has never heard the word before, it is unreasonable to think that an early reader could read it correctly. This is especially important when assessing dual language learners.)

- Did the child notice his or her errors and try to fix them? (Even if the child doesn't correct an error, the process of self-monitoring by stopping, rereading, and making another attempt is important to consider.)

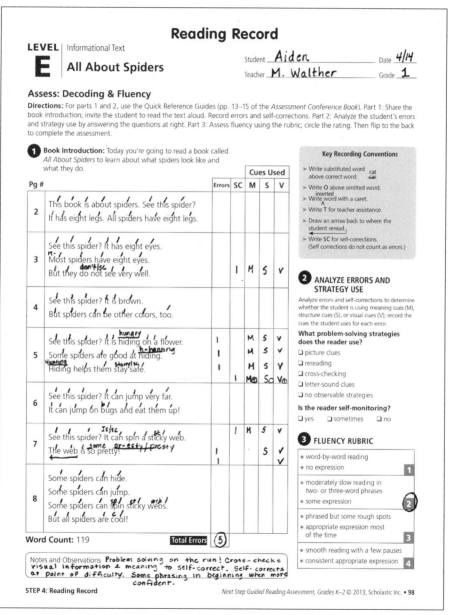

An example of a Level E running record form (from Next Step Guided Reading Assessment: Grades K–2)

Assess fluency and comprehension

Look for phrasing and expression, but don't expect rapid reading at early text levels. And *please* don't time the reader! When a child encounters new words and initiates strategic actions (which is a good thing), it will take time. Early readers should slow down and problem-solve, not mumble through unknown words to beat the clock. Do I expect some phrasing and expression when the student isn't problem solving? Absolutely! I also expect some comprehension, but I don't expect a complete oral retelling that includes every single detail. If the student gets the gist of the story, but doesn't recall every character and event, I can target that in my lessons.

Consider a range of instructional levels

There is a subjective element to scoring running records, one that should always be considered. Background knowledge, interest, genre, topic, and even emotions can contribute to performance. Let's say, for instance, that on Tuesday Sam reads a Level E text about the ocean with 93 percent accuracy and limited comprehension. That would put Sam at Level E. But perhaps Sam has never been to the ocean. Maybe he was upset that day about something that happened on the playground. Maybe he made the same error several times. Should you automatically score Sam at text Level E? It's possible that the next day he could read a Level F text about soccer (a subject he knows) with 96 percent accuracy and good comprehension. I also find that early readers often can read fiction texts at a higher level than nonfiction texts. I'd have Sam read texts at Levels E or F depending on the subject matter, genre, and focus for instruction.

I'm not recommending you give multiple running records on different topics across several days. That would take too much time. I do think you should always look beyond the running record score and consider a range of text levels. You might choose a lower text level to work on fluency but a higher text level to practice decoding strategies. Beware of turning a running record into just a number or letter. There is danger in rigidly scoring a running record without keeping in mind the subjective elements in an assessment.

Determining reading levels is not an exact science. Do your best to get a starting point and form your groups so you can begin teaching as soon as possible. As you begin guided reading lessons and gather more information about each student's processing system, you can plan your next step.

Spelling Assessments

Although a running record is the most useful assessment for teaching early readers, you should also administer a few quick spelling assessments to learn about the child's understanding of letters, sounds, and words. Analyzing the ways children spell words can provide insight into how they decode. Here are a few options for learning more about your students' understanding of letters, sounds, and words.

Use a Sight Word Chart

An early reader who builds automaticity with a bank of known words will read and write more fluently. Administer the Sight Word Chart (Appendix F) to see which words your students can write. The assessment is quick, easy, and useful. Assess students at their instructional level and one level below.

Recommended Sight Words for Levels C–F			
Level C	Level D	Level E	Level F
and	day	all	came
are	down	away	have
come	into	back	help
for	looking	big	next
got	she	her	now
here	they	over	one
not	went	this	some
play	where	want	then
said	will	who	was
you	your	with	what

Use a Word Knowledge Inventory or dictated sentence

You can use a Word Knowledge Inventory (Appendix J) or a dictated sentence (page 112) to provide insight into how children spell words they have not been taught. Administer the assessment like a spelling test and circle the features children miss. Teach those foundational skills during the word study portion of the guided reading lesson.

Dictated Sentences for Early Readers		
Level	Sentence	Skills Assessed
D	I have to sit on the rug to get my chips. I will dig in the sand with my shovel.	Short vowels and digraphs
E–F	I have great friends in my class. I think I will share my snack with them. My teacher is going to read us a story. I will sit on the carpet and be quiet.	Initial blends Endings (-s, -er, -ing)
G–I	I am going to take a bike ride to the park next to the lake. My teacher said we are playing outside today because it might rain tomorrow.	Silent-e rule Complex vowels Endings (-er, -ing) Multisyllabic words

DECIDE

Now that you have assessed and analyzed your early readers, you are ready to summarize the assessments to help you form your groups, pinpoint a focus for instruction, and select a text.

Summarize the Assessments

Summarize the results of the assessments on the Assessment Summary Chart (page 114 and scholastic.com/NSFresources).

Directions for completing the Assessment Summary Chart

Columns 1 and 2: Name and Level Range. Record the student's name and instructional level range. For most children you will write two adjacent levels, such as E/F.

Column 3: Self-monitors. Put an M if the student consistently monitors with meaning. (For example, he or she stops when meaning breaks down and tries to fix the error.) Put a V if the student monitors using visual information (notices visual mismatches at the middle and end of the word). For example, the child reads *skating* for *skates* and notices the miscue.

Column 4: Solves Words. Analyze miscues to determine which parts of words the student is noticing. Put a B if the student consistently matches the beginning letters of the correct word (*place/pool*); put an M if the student attends correctly to the middle of the word (*playing/stayed*); and an E if the student matches the letters at the end of the word (*landed/stayed*). As children move up in levels they will gradually use more visual information to problem-solve.

Column 5: Reads Fluently. Use the following rubric to rate fluency when a student is not in the process of problem solving:

1. Reading is very slow, mostly word by word.
2. Reading is choppy, mostly two-word phrases.
3. Reading is mostly phrased, but lacks some aspect of fluency, such as intonation, expression, or attention to punctuation.
4. Reading is fluent and phrased with appropriate expression and intonation.

Column 6: Retells. Use the following rubric to record a child's basic understanding of the text. Don't penalize a child if you have to prompt him or her for details.

+ Complete and detailed retelling; includes all major ideas and important details

√ Adequate retelling; includes most major ideas and some details

− Limited retelling; misses the main ideas, central characters, and essential details

Column 7: Spells Phonetically. List phonics skills the student uses. Important skills for early readers include short vowels (SV), digraphs (D), blends (B), and complex vowels (CV).

Column 8: Other. Note the factors you need to consider when planning instruction. These include classifications, such as dual language learners (DLL), specific language disorder (SLD), speech therapy (SP), occupational therapy (OT), and other factors such as weak on sight words, lack of risk taking, poor handwriting, etc.

Assessment Summary Chart for Early Readers, Levels D–I

Name	Level Range	Self-monitors M V	Solves Words B M E	Reads Fluently 1 2 3 4	Retells + √ –	Spells Phonetically SV D B CV	Other

Form Groups

Once you've summarized the assessments, group students with similar text ranges. Try to limit the number of guided reading groups to four or five. You can have up to six students in a group, but if students are struggling, limit the group size to no more than four so you can provide targeted instruction. If you have a child who doesn't fit into a group, give him or her a daily ten-minute lesson following the lesson framework until he or she can join one of your groups (see page 154). Another option is to find a colleague who has a guided reading group at that student's level.

Don't get too comfortable with your groups. They are likely to change. Update the Assessment Summary Chart as you notice students making progress in a specific area. Consider regrouping about every two weeks.

Pinpoint Your Focus

Once you decide which students to group together, use the Assessment Summary Chart to pinpoint a strategy focus for each group. Always consider self-monitoring first. This is the most important action to teach any reader. If students are already monitoring for meaning, work on monitoring for visual information, word-solving strategies, and fluency. Once monitoring, word solving, and fluency are strong at that text range, choose retelling as your focus. For early readers, it is wise to delay teaching comprehension strategies until students are independent word solvers (Lipson & Wixson, 2010).

Write the focus on your lesson plan. Identifying a primary focus for the lesson will help you be explicit in your teaching. You will still be able to differentiate your prompting according to individual student needs.

Early Guided Reading Plan (Levels D–I)

Students:		Dates:	
Title/Level		Strategy Focus	Comprehension Focus
DAY 1		DAY 2	

Select a Text

Choose a text at the group's instructional range that offers opportunities to apply the strategy focus. It sounds easy, but it's not. Publishing companies use different criteria to level books. Don't rely on the letter or number on the book; you have to read it to determine if it is a good match for your students. The overarching goal is to select interesting texts that provide enough support to keep students reading independently but enough challenge to provide opportunities for them to problem-solve. Don't be locked into one specific text level. Remember, early readers can read a range of texts.

Selecting Texts That Match Your Focus	
Focus	Text Features
Self-monitoring	Select texts with familiar concepts and strong picture support. Students will be able to access meaning when they have background knowledge about the topic.
Word solving	Select texts that have challenging words students will be able to decode. New words should be in their listening vocabulary and have decodable features, such as known parts and familiar endings. Look for picture support for the challenging vocabulary.
Reading fluently	Use a text at an easier level so students will have few decoding challenges. To work on expression and intonation, select a fiction story with interesting dialogue.
Retelling	Choose stories with strong picture support and a clear beginning, middle, and end. When choosing informational texts, look for mostly familiar concepts, supportive illustrations, and headings that capture the main idea of the section.
Comprehending	At this level, you'll weave your comprehension focus into your discussion questions. Well-written guided reading books will support a variety of comprehension strategies.

Gather Other Materials

Organize the following materials and place them within reach:

- Dry-erase boards, markers, and erasers
- 6–8 sets of magnetic letters on individual trays or sorted in a box
- Sight Word Chart (Appendix F)
- Pictures for sorting sounds
- Sound box and analogy chart templates in plastic sheet protectors (Appendices H & I)
- Guided writing journals
- Leveled books
- Timer

GUIDE

You've assessed your students, analyzed the assessments, formed your groups, and selected the text. Now you are ready to prepare for your guided reading lesson.

The Early Guided Reading Lesson

The early lesson is carried out over two days, about 20 minutes each day. The same book is read and discussed on both days. Each lesson covers one or more strategic actions and skills that are developmentally appropriate for students reading at text Levels D–I.

Overview of the Early Guided Reading Lesson	
Day 1	Day 2
Sight Word Review	Sight Word Review
Introduce a New Book	
Read the Book With Prompting	Reread Books With Prompting
Discuss and Teach	Discuss and Teach
Teach a New Sight Word	Reteach the New Sight Word From Day 1
Word Study Activity	Guided Writing

If you are an intervention teacher and have more than 20 minutes per group, you can extend the part of the lesson that needs more attention. For example, if students need to improve fluency, have students reread books for an extra five minutes; if phonics and phonemic awareness are weak, add a few extra minutes of word study. Use student assessments to make those decisions.

TEACHING COMPREHENSION

The ultimate goal of every guided reading lesson is comprehension, even at the early stage. Read the book to determine an appropriate comprehension focus, write your chosen focus on the lesson plan, and weave that focus into your discussion.

Comprehension instruction should begin with whole-class read-alouds during which you model your thinking and engage students in a conversation about the story. During guided reading, students work on comprehending texts they have read. See Chapter 7 for comprehension modules for whole-group and guided reading lessons. Texts at early levels won't have the depth of comprehension found in most picture books, but you can still engage students in a lively discussion about the story.

Comprehension Strategies for Early Readers	
Narrative/Fiction Strategies	**Informational/Nonfiction Strategies**
• Ask and answer questions about key details • Retell stories • Determine the central message • Analyze a character's feelings • Determine different points of view of characters • Use information from illustrations and the text to understand characters, setting, and plot • Determine the meaning of words and phrases	• Ask and answer questions about key details • Identify the main topic of a section • Determine the meaning of words and phrases • Know and use various text features • Identify the author's purpose • Describe how reasons support key points made by the author • Compare and contrast key points

Understand the purpose and procedures for each lesson component

Each component in an early guided reading lesson supports one or more reading skills and standards. The following chart summarizes the procedures and purposes for each component.

Early Lesson Procedures and Purposes

Component	Procedures	Purposes
Sight Word Review	Students write three sight words you have taught them.	• Automaticity with sight words • Visual memory and scanning • Letter formation
Introduce a New Book	• Preview pictures and text features. • Teach new vocabulary.	• Predict • Ask questions • Build schema • Extend vocabulary
Read and Prompt	• Students read independently while teacher confers with each student. • Differentiate prompting based on student needs.	• Scaffold strategic actions, such as monitoring for meaning and visual information, word solving, fluency, and comprehension • Increase fluency and phrasing
Discuss and Teach	Lead a discussion of the text. Students share ideas and ask questions.	• Retell stories • Ask and answer questions • Deepen understanding of characters, settings, and major events • Make inferences • Identify main idea/key details
Teaching Point	Model a word-solving strategy based on observations during the reading.	Teach students to search for and use visual information by rereading, using known parts, and covering endings
Word Study Activity	• Teach a new sight word. • Students use manipulatives to learn phonics elements and how they work in words.	• Increase automaticity with sight words • Learn phonics skills • Hear and record sounds in sequence
Guided Writing	Students extend comprehension by writing about the text with the teacher's support. Plan > Write > Reread	• Respond to a prompt • Construct sentences • Spell sight words correctly • Apply phonics skills • Learn conventions

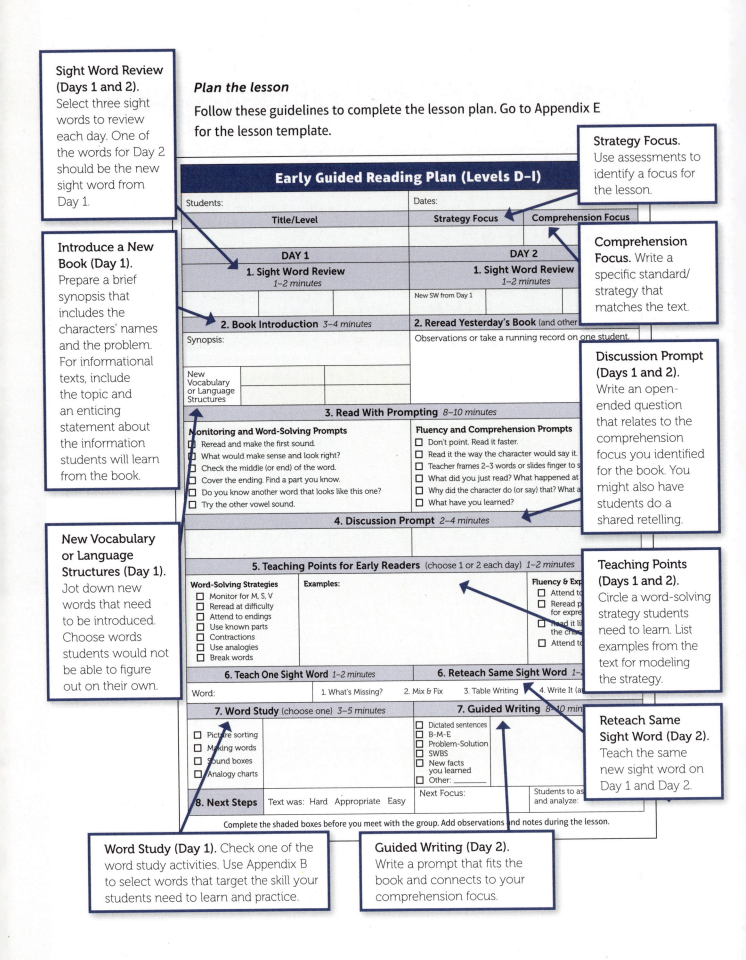

Sight Word Review (Days 1 and 2). Select three sight words to review each day. One of the words for Day 2 should be the new sight word from Day 1.

Introduce a New Book (Day 1). Prepare a brief synopsis that includes the characters' names and the problem. For informational texts, include the topic and an enticing statement about the information students will learn from the book.

New Vocabulary or Language Structures (Day 1). Jot down new words that need to be introduced. Choose words students would not be able to figure out on their own.

Plan the lesson

Follow these guidelines to complete the lesson plan. Go to Appendix E for the lesson template.

Strategy Focus. Use assessments to identify a focus for the lesson.

Comprehension Focus. Write a specific standard/strategy that matches the text.

Discussion Prompt (Days 1 and 2). Write an open-ended question that relates to the comprehension focus you identified for the book. You might also have students do a shared retelling.

Teaching Points (Days 1 and 2). Circle a word-solving strategy students need to learn. List examples from the text for modeling the strategy.

Reteach Same Sight Word (Day 2). Teach the same new sight word on Day 1 and Day 2.

Word Study (Day 1). Check one of the word study activities. Use Appendix B to select words that target the skill your students need to learn and practice.

Guided Writing (Day 2). Write a prompt that fits the book and connects to your comprehension focus.

DESCRIPTION OF DAY 1

The Day 1 lesson has six basic components:

- Sight Word Review
- Introduce a New Book
- Read the Book With Prompting
- Discuss and Teach
- Teach a New Sight Word
- Word Study Activity

Most of the lesson is devoted to reading and discussing the new book with teacher guidance and prompting.

Sight Word Review (1–2 minutes)

Dictate three words

Choose three words you have taught in previous guided reading lessons. Have students write the words on a dry-erase board. Writing the word (as opposed to just reading it) helps imprint the word and reinforces left-to-right sequencing.

This activity is not a test. If students forget how to spell a word, provide a scaffold. For example, if students cannot remember how to write *they*, you might say, "It has *the* in it." If they misspell a letter, erase the wrong letter and prompt them to recall what's missing. If that doesn't help, tell the student the missing letter. Every student should write the words accurately.

Record progress

Use the Sight Word Chart to select appropriate words and record progress. Put a check mark (√) on the chart if the student is able to write the word without help.

Early Video Link 1

Watch Jan guiding a sight word review.

> **Tip**
>
> *Early readers often confuse words that begin with* w *and* wh. *Post a chart with* wh *words and tell students that if the word they want to write is not on the* wh *chart, they should spell it with a* w.

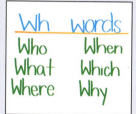

> **Tip**
>
> *Students will likely need multiple experiences with nonphonetic words such as* said, what, *and* they *before they automatically write them. Review these words frequently.*

> **Tip**
>
> *Be sure to teach the words for the lower text levels first, even if students are reading at a higher level.*

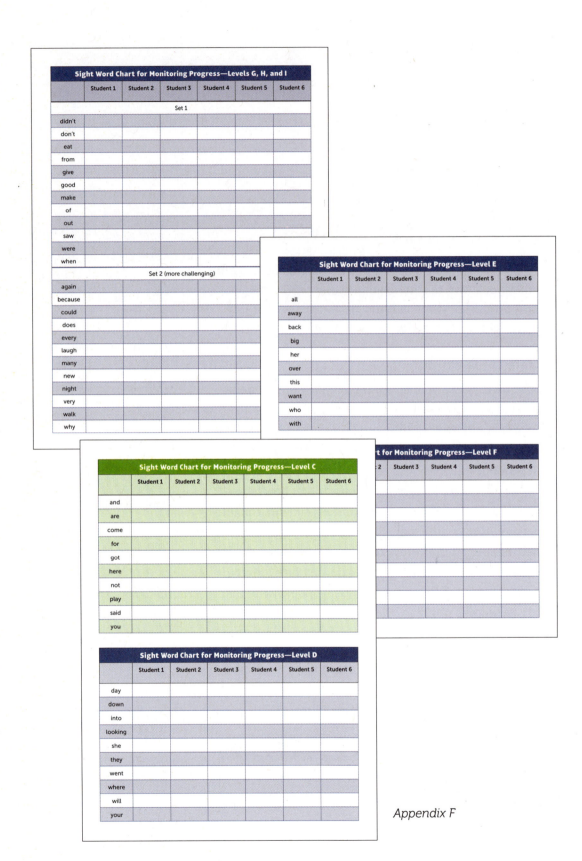

Appendix F

Description of Day 1

Introduce a New Book (3–4 minutes)

Provide a synopsis

State the title and give a brief main idea statement of the book that includes the characters and problem. This gives the reader a foundation for constructing meaning. For example, "In this book, a little puppy is visiting Bella and Rosie's house. He keeps getting into trouble. Let's read to find out how Bella and Rosie feel about the little puppy." For a nonfiction text, you might say, "You will learn all about fireflies: what they look like, why they light up, and how they communicate."

Preview and predict

After you give a brief synopsis of the text, have students quickly preview the illustrations and talk about the story. This activates prior knowledge and builds a foundation for comprehension. Encourage them to ask questions and make predictions from the illustrations or table of contents. You do not need to discuss every page, but you should draw students' attention to important information and unfamiliar concepts in the pictures. When reading nonfiction texts, briefly discuss text features, such as diagrams and the glossary. Maximize time by having children share their questions or predictions with a partner. Support conversations of dual language learners. Do not spend more than two or three minutes with the text preview; otherwise, students won't have enough time to read the book. Gradually release your support so students learn how to preview the text silently.

Introduce new vocabulary

Consider the unique vocabulary needs of your students when choosing words to preteach. Two kinds of words need to be discussed before the reading: words too difficult for them to decode and words not in their listening vocabulary. Write the new words on a dry-erase board and pronounce them. Have students repeat each word. For unfamiliar concepts, discuss the meaning of the word using illustrations and examples from the story. You may want them to read the challenging word in a sentence from the story so they can see the word in context. If possible, make connections to students' personal experiences. Be especially alert to the needs of dual language learners, who will likely need more support and examples.

> **Tip**
>
> *If there are more than four words to introduce, rethink using the book. It might be too difficult.*

Read the Book With Prompting (8–10 minutes)

Encourage independent reading

Have children independently read the book for about five to eight minutes in soft voices while you spend one or two minutes conferring with each student.

If they finish the book before you call time, have them reread the story. If they don't finish on Day 1, have them mark the place where they stopped and let them continue reading from that point on Day 2.

Prompt students to problem-solve

This is where you differentiate your instruction according to their needs. As you listen to a student read a page or two, prompt for strategic, problem-solving actions. Refer to the next page and the lesson plan for some sample prompts. If the student makes no errors, work on phrasing, expression, or comprehension. If you find there is nothing to teach, the book is too easy. Use the chart on the next page to help select appropriate prompts based on student behaviors.

> **Tip**
>
> *Do not have students take turns reading (round-robin style). It will limit the amount of text they can read and impede independent processing.*

Description of Day 1

Prompts for Early Readers

Behavior	Goal	Prompts
Stops and appeals	Take risks	*I'm glad you noticed something wasn't right. Try it. Think about the story and sound the first part.*
Says a word that does not make sense	Monitor for meaning	Wait until the child finishes the sentence and say, *Are you right? Did that make sense? Reread and think about the story.*
Ignores part of the word	Monitor for visual information	*Are you right? Does that look right?* *Check the middle (or end) of the word.* *What would make sense and look right?*
Stops at or miscues on words with inflectional endings	Break words apart	*Cover the ending.* *Find a part you know.* *Sound the first part and think about the story. What would look right?*
Reads accurately but slowly	Read with phrasing and fluency	*Don't point. Read it smoothly. Pretend you are the character.* Slide your finger from left to right to cover the words as the student reads. This pushes the student's eye forward at a faster pace.
Reads accurately and fluently	Check for comprehension	*What happened on this page?* (Retell) *Why did he or she do (or say) that ____? What was the most important event? Tell me about it.* (Infer) *What are you thinking?* (Probe) *What did you learn about ____?* (Key details)

Early Video Link 2 ▶▶▶

Watch Jan prompting students while they read.

Discuss and Teach (3–6 minutes)

Discuss the book

Have a guided conversation about the book. Ask open-ended questions that will facilitate discussion and help students draw inferences. Connect your discussion prompt to the targeted comprehension strategy. For example, if your comprehension strategy is retelling story elements, you could ask different students to describe the characters and setting. You want to engage them in meaningful conversations that will lead them to deeper understanding. The following chart lists examples of discussion starters that correlate to most state reading strategies and standards.

> *See Chapter 7 for more on teaching comprehension strategies, including Somebody-Wanted-But-So, page 281. Video links for specific strategies can be found on pages 4–5.*

Description of Day 1

Discussion Starters for Early Readers

Goal	Discussion Starters
Ask and answer questions about key details	• What questions do you have about _____? • Reread page ____ to find out _____. (Ask a text-dependent question.) • What did you learn (or notice) about (the character, setting, problem, topic, etc.)?
Retell stories, including key details, and demonstrate understanding of the central message or lesson	• Find the most important part of the story. Why is it important? • What important facts did you learn in this book? • What happened at the beginning, the middle, and the end? • Let's retell the story together. • What was the big idea in this story? • What lesson could you learn from this story? • What lesson did the character learn? • Why did the author write this book?
Describe characters, settings, and major events in a story using key details	• Describe the setting. Did the setting change? Find that part in the story. • Describe the character. How did the character change in this story? • Find the page that shows how the character felt at the beginning (or middle or end). Turn and talk. • What was the most important thing the character did? Find that part in the book. Talk to your partner about it. • How were the characters the same (or different)?
Identify words/phrases that suggest feelings or appeal to the senses	• What word on page ____ tells you how the character felt? • What word on page ____ did the author use to help you understand what an ocean sounds like?
Explain major differences between stories and informational books	• How is this book about ____ different from this other book about ____? • How is the fox in this book different from the fox in the other book?

Early

Identify who is telling the story at various points in a text	• Who is telling the story on page _____? • Who is talking on page _____? • Who said _____ on page ___?
Use illustrations and details in a story to describe its characters, setting, or events	• Find the picture that describes the setting in the story. • Find the picture that describes how the puppy feels about dressing up. • How does the picture on page _____ show you more about what happened? • Find the picture that describes the problem. • Find the picture that describes how the problem was solved. • What picture best describes Sam's feelings about the picnic?
Compare and contrast the adventures and experiences of characters in stories	• How do _____ and _____ feel about their adventure? • How do the mom and dad feel about the camping trip? • How is Little Bear's adventure in this story different from (or similar to) Little Bear's adventure in the other story you read?

Do a shared retelling

If students need to improve their retelling skills, give each student a Shared Retelling card (Appendix G) and guide them as they take turns retelling a portion of the book.

> **Early Video Link 3** ▶▶▶
>
> Watch Jan retelling one-on-one with an early reader and doing a shared retelling with a transitional group.

Appendix G

Description of Day 1

Select a teaching point

After you discuss the book, take a few minutes to demonstrate one or two strategic actions to the whole group. Use the notes you took during the individual conferences to select your teaching point. For example, if students struggle with decoding, use a challenging word from the text to teach a word-solving strategy. Be intentional and explicit. Refer to the chart below for the most common teaching points for early readers.

Teaching Points for Early Readers	
Goal	**Demonstration and Teaching**
Monitor for meaning and reread	Ask students to follow along in their books as you read a sentence out loud. Deliberately make an error that does not make sense. Say, "Did that make sense? Find my mistake. Let's reread that sentence together. If it doesn't make sense, always reread and fix it."
Monitor for letters and sounds	Read a sentence from the book and make an error with a word that has visual similarities to the word in the text, such as *laid* for *landed*. Say, "What word doesn't look right? Find my mistake." Write the word from the story (*landed*) on a dry-erase board. Slide an index card left to right across the word (to support visual scanning) and say, "Could this word be *laid*? Why not? When you read, it has to look right and make sense. Be sure you look all the way through the word."
Solve unknown words	Write a challenging word on the dry-erase board or make it with magnetic letters on an easel. Model a word-solving strategy such as • Sound the first part (*after*) • Find a known part (*stand*) • Cover the ending (*plant-ed*) • Use an analogy (link the *ay* in *away* to d*ay*) • Break the word apart (*out-side, bed-room, re-mem-ber*)
Read fluently	Select a page to read with students. Remind them to read with expression, paying attention to punctuation marks. Say, "Let's read this together and pretend we are the characters in the story." If necessary, model reading with expression.

Early Video Link 4

Watch Jan selecting a teaching point.

Teach a New Sight Word (1–2 minutes)

Spend the last few minutes of Day 1 teaching students how words work. Students will learn how to write a new sight word from the story and practice a phonics skill that is appropriate for their reading level.

Early readers need to build rapid recognition of common sight words so they can increase their fluency and free up cognitive space for solving new words. By teaching children how to write these words and not just read them, you help them control visual scanning and improve visual memory, which promotes better spelling skills.

> **Tip**
> *Teach this component after children have read the book so they will have had an opportunity to read the word before you teach them to write it.*

From the story, select a sight word that students don't know how to write. Refer to the Sight Word Chart (Appendix F) for words that frequently appear at each text level. Use the four steps below to help students develop visual memory, establish left-to-right visual scanning skills, and increase automaticity with sight words.

Start by introducing the word. Write the word on a dry-erase board. Tell students the word and ask them to look closely as you slide an index card left to right across the word. This prompts students to study the word by scanning left to right. Some students develop a haphazard approach to looking at print, which can lead to visual sequencing problems.

What's Missing?

Turn the board toward you and erase a letter near the end of the word. Show the board to students and ask them to tell you the missing letter. Say, "What's missing?" Students then tell you the missing letter and you write it in the word. Repeat the procedure two or three more times by erasing a letter or two at the beginning, middle, or end of the word. Beginning readers are easily distracted. Although this game-like activity is quick, it entices group members to attend to the word. You'll notice all eyes on the word when you do What's Missing?

Mix & Fix

Give students the magnetic letters to make the new word. Students can use the teacher's model, if necessary. Students read the word using a left-to-right sweep with their finger. Then have them slide each letter to the left or push them up one at a time. This will ensure that they look at each letter. Students then mix the letters and remake (fix) the word from left to right. Keep the word on the table.

Table Writing

Students use their index finger to "write" the word on the table. Make sure students are looking at their finger while they write. This activity builds a memory trace for the word.

Description of Day 1

Encourage them to say the word as they write it. They shouldn't sound it out. This is a word you want them to remember as a complete unit and to store in their long-term memory. Once you observe them writing the word on the table, use an index card to cover the word they made with magnetic letters and have them do the final step.

Write It (and Retrieve It)

Students write the new word on a dry-erase board. They should say the word in a natural way as they write it. This mimics what they do when they write stories on their own. Do not encourage students to spell or sound out the word. You want them to learn the word as a complete unit. If they need help, they should lift up the index card and look at the magnetic letters. After they write the word, have them erase it and write it again. Now dictate a *very* familiar word they know how to write. Then dictate the new word again for students to retrieve and write.

> **Tip**
> Teach the same sight word for two days, longer if necessary. Don't introduce a new word until students are fluently writing the word you just taught.

If you consistently follow these procedures, most children will have learned to write about 60 sight words by the time they reach Level F. When children have a large bank of sight words they can write, you can omit this component.

Early Video Link ▶▶▶
Watch Jan teaching a new sight word.
(See Emergent Video Link 6, page 79.)

Word Study Activity (3–5 minutes)

Early readers are still learning phonics. Spend the final three or four minutes of the lesson doing picture sorting, making words, sound boxes, or analogy charts. This part of the lesson should be kept short. Most learning about letters, sounds, and words comes from reading and writing text.

Select the target skill

Use the Word Knowledge Inventory or a dictated sentence to select a target skill, or follow the developmental skill sequence in the next chart. Most students reading at text Level D need to learn digraphs because words with digraphs begin to appear in texts (e.g., *they, this, then, shouted*). Children reading at text Levels E and F should learn to hear and use blends. Children reading at text Levels G–I are ready to tackle the silent-*e* feature and complex vowels. If students need more work with short vowels (a target skill for Level C), see the procedures on pages 82–84.

Text Level	Target Skill	Spelling Errors	Word Study Activities
D	Digraphs	*tan* for *than* *muh* for *much*	Picture sorting > Making words > Sound boxes
E/F	Initial and final blends	*pay* for *play* *wet* for *went*	Picture sorting > Making words > Sound boxes
G/H/I	Silent-*e* feature Vowel patterns	*mak* for *make* *fond* for *found* *strt* for *start*	Making words > Analogy charts

Target Skills for Early Readers

Understand the purpose of each activity

Each of the word study activities emphasizes a different aspect of phonics. During picture sorting, children learn to hear the target sound and link it to letters. In the making words activity, they use magnetic letters to make a series of words that differ by one letter. For example, they could make the following: *cap-chap-clap-clop-slop-slot*. This helps them monitor for a visual (letter) and auditory (sound) match. This match, also called synchrony, is critical for the development of reading fluency (Sousa, 2014). When using sound boxes, or Elkonin boxes (Elkonin, 1971), students segment sounds and write the letters that represent those sounds. Analogy charts teach children how to use familiar words to write new words.

Choose one activity to teach digraphs and blends

Use picture sorting, making words, or sound boxes to teach digraphs and blends. The word study activities should be done in sequence because they allow for a gradual release model. For example, when teaching digraphs, do several lessons with picture sorting before you do the making words activity. Children need to learn the sound-letter connection with picture sorting before they can apply the target skill to making words.

> **Tip**
> Only select phonetically regular words (phonetically irregular words will confuse students).

> **Tip**
> Avoid words with silent letters and diphthongs.

Description of Day 1

After a few lessons of making words with digraphs, move to sound boxes. When students are firm with digraphs, repeat the sequence of activities to teach blends. Once they are strong phonetic spellers, it is appropriate to teach them the more challenging spelling features, such as the silent-*e* and vowel teams. The following is a description of each word study activity.

Picture Sorting

Select two examples of the target skill (such as *ch* and *th*). When you sort blends, always choose two consonant clusters that begin with the same letter (such as *cl-cr* or *st-sl*). This helps students attend to the second letter in the blend, which is the most challenging for them to hear. Distribute three or four pictures to each student and write the two digraphs or blends on a dry-erase board. Have students take turns sorting their pictures, following these procedures:

1. Say the word in the picture: *snake*.
2. Say the target sound: /sn/.
3. Say the letters that make that sound: *s-n*.
4. Put the picture card under the digraph *sn*.

Making Words

This activity teaches children how to use sounds to monitor for visual information during reading. It also firms up the left-to-right visual scanning across a word. Each student will need magnetic letters to make a series of words. The minimal changes from one word to the next force students to attend to the specific skill focus. For example, when the focus is digraphs, the series of words the students make differs by the digraph or short vowel (e.g., *mat-math-bath-bash-bush*). When the focus is blends, children make words that differ by their blend or short vowel (e.g., *rim-trim-trip-strip-strap*).

When students have the letters they need, dictate a word for them to make. After they make the word, teach them to check the word by saying it slowly as they run their finger under the letters. Next, dictate a word that differs by one or two letters. Before they make the letter change, have them say the new word as they run their finger under the previous word. This action helps them coordinate the auditory and visual processing speeds. To read successfully, the visual (letters) and the auditory (sounds) have to work together. When children say the new word but look at the letters in the old word, they have to determine which letter needs to change. The process they use to determine the mismatch between sound and letter is the same process they will use to monitor with visual information and self-correct during reading.

After students make each word, have them break apart the word (e.g., *clap*) at the onset (*cl-*) and rime (*-ap*). Then have them point to each part and say it before they remake the word. This reinforces the decoding strategy of reading words in clusters rather than letter by letter. Create your own word sequence or use the suggestions in Appendix A.

Examples of Making Words for Early Readers

Level	Target Skill	Example
C/D	Medial short vowels	*can-man-map-mop-cop-cup*
D	Digraphs	*cat-chat-chap-chop-shop-ship*
E	Initial blends	*cap-clap-clip-grip-grin-spin-span*
F	Final blends	*went-west-pest-past-pant*
G	Initial and final blends	*gasp-grasp-clasp-clamp-stamp*
G/H	Silent *e*	*hat-hate-mate-mat-fat-fate*
I	Vowel patterns	*see-seed-weed-week-cheek-creek-creep*

Early Video Link 5

Watch Jan conducting a making words activity.

Sound Boxes

In this activity children attend to the sounds in a word and record those sounds in sequence. The process used in this activity is well suited to developing

Description of Day 1

phonemic awareness because it helps children blend and segment phonemes.

Each student needs a sound box template inserted into a plastic sheet protector, a dry-erase marker, and an eraser. Dictate a phonetic word that includes the target skill (digraph or blend), and tell students how many boxes they will need. After you say the word, have students say the word slowly. Discourage segmenting the sounds letter by letter (e.g., *mmmaaash* not /m/-/a/-/sh/). Have them touch a box as they say each sound. Students say the word slowly once more as they write the letters in the boxes. The goal is for students to articulate the word slowly, without your support. This will promote independent word solving during writing.

> **Tip**
>
> I don't recommend using sound boxes to teach the silent-e feature or complex vowels. It confuses children since there is no clear sound-to-letter match in the words.

Examples of Sound Boxes for Early Readers

Level	Target Skill	Example
C/D	Medial short vowels	*mop, can, pit, bud, ten*
D	Digraphs	*that, chip, much, shed, hash*
E	Initial blends	*slam, trip, sled, grab*
F	Final blends	*went, fast, tusk, lost*
G	Initial and final blends and digraphs	*grasp, slump, chimp, flask, spent*

Each letter of a consonant blend should be written in a separate box because the blend contains two phonemes. For example, if students write the word *grasp* in sound boxes, they would use five boxes.

g	r	a	s	p

Single sounds represented by two letters, such as *sh, ch, th,* and *ck,* should be placed in the same box. If students are writing the word *chick,* for example, they would use three boxes.

| ch | i | ck |

See Appendix A for examples of sound box activities at each text level.

Early Video Link 6 ▶▶▶
Watch Jan scaffolding a sound box activity.

Analogy Charts

I have found the best way to teach the silent-*e* feature and vowel patterns is to use analogies. Students use the sound patterns in words they know to help them write words they don't know. Wait until students can independently hear and record short vowels, digraphs, and blends before you teach vowel patterns. They need to have a bank of known words that follow the spelling pattern before they'll be able to apply the rule to new words. Follow these procedures for analogy charts.

1. Use a Word Knowledge Inventory or your students' spelling errors to identify two patterns to teach. Choose one that students know fairly well and one new pattern.

2. Distribute an analogy chart template (Appendix I) inserted in a plastic sheet protector, a dry-erase marker, and an eraser to each student.

3. At the top of your chart, write two familiar words for each vowel pattern (e.g., *cow* and *eat*). Students should copy these two words on their own charts and underline the vowel sound in each word. Discuss the sound each vowel pattern makes.

4. Tell students you are going to dictate new words for them to write. They should listen to the vowel pattern in the new word to decide which key word has the same sound. Then they should write the new word under the matching key word and underline the pattern. Randomly dictate three or four words for each pattern. As students grow in proficiency, dictate words with inflectional endings.

> **Tip**
>
> *Using two different patterns requires children to attend to the sounds and make choices based on the patterns. Using only one pattern decreases the need for analysis and problem solving.*

Description of Day 1

5. Before they leave the table, have them read the words in each column. This makes the activity both a reading and writing task. See Appendix A for examples of analogy charts to use at Levels G–I.

map	tape
lap	cape
slap	shape
trap	grape

Silent-*e* analogy chart containing short and long vowel sounds

make	like
take	bike
shake	spike
brake	strike

Silent-*e* analogy chart containing two long vowel patterns

rain	boy
pain	toy
train	enjoy
painful	joyful

Analogy chart with two complex vowel patterns

> **Early Video Link** ▶▶▶
>
> *Watch Jan teaching with an analogy chart. (See Transitional Video Link 6, page 186.)*

DESCRIPTION OF DAY 2

The Day 2 lesson takes about 20 minutes and has five components:

- Sight Word Review
- Reread Books With Prompting
- Discuss and Teach
- Reteach the New Sight Word From Day 1
- Guided Writing

Sight Word Review (1–2 minutes)

Review three sight words following the same procedures as Day 1. The new sight word you taught on Day 1 should be one of the review words. This helps you observe how well students are remembering the word.

Reread Books With Prompting (8–10 minutes)

Students reread yesterday's new book and other familiar books. Rereading books on Day 2 gives students the opportunity to work on fluency while you confer and prompt. Use the Prompts for Early Readers chart (page 125) to differentiate your teaching and engage students in short conversations. If students didn't finish the book on Day 1, they should complete the book on Day 2 and reread it.

Description of Day 2

Discuss and Teach *(3–6 minutes)*

Lead another discussion about the book, just like you did on Day 1. If you notice students were confused when they read a certain part, take them back to that page and help them clarify their understanding. Create your own discussion prompts or use the Discussion Starters for Early Readers (page 127). Thread your state reading standards into your discussions. If you didn't do a shared retelling on Day 1, you might want to do it on Day 2.

Select a teaching point

Use your notes to select another strategic action to teach. Refer to the Teaching Points for Early Readers (page 129).

Reteach the New Sight Word From Day 1 *(1–2 minutes)*

Use the steps described on pages 130–131 to reteach the word you taught on Day 1. If the word is especially challenging and students are not remembering how to write it, teach the same sight word in the next lesson. It is important that you don't introduce a new word until the previous one is firm.

Guided Writing *(8–10 minutes)*

Understand the rationale for guided writing

Guided writing is not writing workshop, nor can it substitute for writing workshop. In writing workshop, students often choose their own topics and write across a range of genres for multiple purposes. They work independently while you circulate among the class and have individual conferences that help students grow as writers. I love writing workshop, but I also love guided writing. Guided writing provides an opportunity to support students as they write about a book they just read. It is assisted writing, not assigned or independent writing. The entire written response is completed at the table. The purpose of guided writing is twofold: it extends comprehension and it can improve your students' writing skills since you are working with them side by side.

Gather materials

Create a guided writing journal for each student so you will have a record of his or her writing. Fold ten sheets of 8½-x-11-inch paper in half and staple at the fold. Position the books so that the stapled fold is on the top. Students reading at text Levels D–E should have about five solid lines on each page to help them form the letters on the lines. After Level E, switch to journals with simple handwriting paper so you can teach letter formation.

There are three steps to early guided writing:

1. Select a response format.
2. Help students plan.
3. Prompt during writing.

Select a response format

Choose a response that connects to the book, matches the comprehension strategy for the lesson, and can be completed in about ten minutes. If you discussed how a character changed in the story, have students write about the character at the beginning, middle, and end. If they did an oral retelling, ask students to write about the major events in the story. For example, after reading a book about horses, students could write facts they learned.

Use a variety of response formats throughout your lessons to give students experience responding in different ways to both narrative and informational texts. On the next page are some writing responses that correlate with comprehension strategies.

Description of Day 2

Response Formats for Early Readers		
Comprehension Focus	**Fiction and Narrative Texts**	**Nonfiction and Informational Texts**
Ask and answer questions about key details	• Pose a question that is answered in the story. • *What was the problem in the story? How was it solved?*	• Ask a question that is answered in the book. • *How do mother squirrels take care of their babies?*
Retell stories or recount important facts	• *Write about the beginning, middle, and end (B-M-E).* • *Summarize using Somebody-Wanted-But-So (SWBS).* • *What was the most important part?*	• *What did you learn about bats?* • *Use key words to summarize the book.* • *Choose an important illustration and write about it.*
Write about the central message or lesson	• *What lesson did the character learn?* • *What did you learn from the characters?*	• *Why did the author write this book?* • *What was the most important thing you learned?*
Describe characters, settings, and major events in a story, using key details	• *Describe the character at the beginning, middle, and end.* • *How do the character's feelings change?* • *How are the characters similar (or different)?* • *Choose an important picture and write about it.* • *Find the picture that describes the most important event. Write about it.*	• *Write key facts about an illustration.* • *Write facts using words from the glossary.* • *Write important facts about the main topic.* • *Use key words from the index to write what you learned about the topic.*
Use illustrations and details in a story to describe its characters, setting, or events	• *Find the picture that shows how the character felt in the middle of the story. Write about it.* • *Use the pictures to describe the setting at the beginning and the end.*	• *Find the page that has a diagram of a butterfly. Write about it.* • *Use the words in the glossary to write about growing carrots.*
Compare and contrast the adventures and experiences of characters in stories	• *How were Luke's feelings about the beach different from Joshua's?*	

Early

Help students plan

Once you explain the writing task, spend a few minutes helping students plan their piece. You might write a few important words on an easel and have students use those words in their sentences. Another idea is to write some key words on sticky notes and distribute the notes to students. Ask them to order the words as they appeared in the story and then use the words to write about the book.

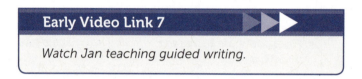

Prompt during writing

As students write, you have an opportunity to differentiate your instruction. Even though your students are reading at about the same text level, they are likely to have different writing needs. Circulate among students and spend a minute or two with each. Observe, analyze, encourage, prompt, and teach. Aim to teach each student something he or she is ready to learn next.

Your prompts and expectations will shift as students progress as writers. Children reading at text Levels D and E may need help constructing sentences. You might even dictate the first sentence to get them started and then prompt them to create the second sentence on their own. You may have to help them spell sight words or prompt them to say words slowly to hear sounds. If students need help with letter formation, show them a model and have them practice writing the letter before they fix the formation in their piece. Students reading at text Levels F, G, and H should write several

Description of Day 2

sentences about the story and have a large bank of known words. You'll still be there to scaffold them, but your prompting will shift to unusual spelling patterns, multisyllabic words, or improving sentence fluency. Students can use the book as a resource for gathering ideas, finding details, and checking the spelling of a character's name. Discourage copying complete sentences.

Writing sample, Level F

Writing sample, Level I

Prompts for Early Writers

If the student . . .	Say . . .
stops writing or forgets the message being attempted	*Tell me what you want to write. Say each word as you write it.* (Repeat the sentence, if necessary.)
misspells sight words you have taught	*That is a word you know how to write. Practice writing it on the top of your journal.* (Write the word for the student to copy.)
leaves out sounds in words such as digraphs and blends	*Say the word slowly and write the sounds you hear.* (Draw sound boxes for the word and have the student write the word in the boxes as you scaffold. If the word has a silent letter, ask the student to think about what letter would make the word look right. This helps him or her balance phonology and orthography.)
uses nonstandard English	*Tell me your sentence.* (Gently correct structure and have the student repeat the sentence.) *Now say each word softly as you write.* (This is an important focus for dual language learners.)
forgets to use capital letters	*What kind of letter should you have at the beginning of your sentence?* *You need a capital letter at the beginning of a name.*
forgets the period	*What should you put at the end? Reread the sentence and listen for the end of your sentence.*
needs help with letter formation	Provide the student with an alphabet strip for lowercase letters.
omits endings on words	*Say the word slowly. What do you hear at the end of the word?*
needs help hearing syllables	*Clap the word. Say each part as you write it.*
omits important details	*Tell me more about that. Find the picture that describes that part and write what you notice.*

Description of Day 2

Reflect on Next Steps

Twenty minutes have passed and the lesson is complete. While students are positioning themselves for the next activity, take one to two minutes to reflect on your lesson. Write a few notes about your students in the "Next Steps" box on the lesson plan. Here are some questions to help you determine your next steps:

- Did you choose the right text? Circle the text difficulty. If the text was too easy or too hard, carefully select the next book so that it offers the right amount of challenge. If students were successful with a fiction text, use an informational text for your next lesson.

- Did you pinpoint the right focus? Did students learn what you were teaching, or do they need more lessons with that same focus? Perhaps you noticed something in the lesson that you want to teach the group. Record your next focus.

- Are some students ready to tackle texts at a higher level? You can regroup students anytime, but make it a habit to consider your guided reading groupings about every two weeks. Write the name of any student who needs a different placement. To help make acceleration decisions, consider doing a running record on the last book he or she read.

- Is there a struggling reader in the group? If you notice a student lagging behind others, there is a good chance the text is too difficult or some part of the child's processing system is breaking down. Write the name of the student and do further analysis. I'll show you in the next section how to analyze your struggling early readers to pinpoint the processing problem and plan a corrective course of action.

		☐ Other: _____	
8. Next Steps	Text was: Hard Appropriate Easy	Next Focus:	Students to assess and analyze:

SAMPLE FILLED-IN LESSON PLAN

Early Guided Reading Plan (Levels D–I)

Students: James, Maria, Lily, Eduardo, Mia **Dates:** 3/30-31

Title/Level	Strategy Focus	Comprehension Focus
The Sledding Adventure	Word-solving	Problem/solution

DAY 1

1. Sight Word Review — 1–2 minutes

they	down	went

2. Book Introduction 3–4 minutes

Synopsis: Little Penguin and Baby Seal went sledding. Something terrible happened when they went too fast down the hill.

New Vocabulary or Language Structures	whee!	again
	shore	uh-oh!

DAY 2

1. Sight Word Review — 1–2 minutes

New SW from Day 1: help

going	out

2. Reread Yesterday's Book (and other familiar books)

Observations or take a running record on one student.

3. Read With Prompting 8–10 minutes

Monitoring and Word-Solving Prompts
- ☐ Reread and make the first sound.
- ☐ What would make sense and look right?
- ☐ Check the middle (or end) of the word.
- ☒ Cover the ending. Find a part you know.
- ☐ Do you know another word that looks like this one?
- ☐ Try the other vowel sound.

Fluency and Comprehension Prompts
- ☐ Don't point. Read it faster.
- ☒ Read it the way the character would say it.
- ☐ Teacher frames 2–3 words or slides finger to support phrasing.
- ☐ What did you just read? What happened at the beginning?
- ☐ Why did the character do (or say) that? What are you thinking?
- ☐ What have you learned?

4. Discussion Prompt 2–4 minutes

Day 1	Day 2
Find the picture that shows the problem. Describe the problem to your partner.	Why did they need Mrs. Polar Bear and Grandpa Walrus to help them? How did they solve the problem?

5. Teaching Points for Early Readers (choose 1 or 2 each day) 1–2 minutes

Word-Solving Strategies
- ☐ Monitor for M, S, V
- ☐ Reread at difficulty
- ☒ Attend to endings
- ☐ Use known parts
- ☐ Contractions
- ☐ Use analogies
- ☐ Break words

Examples:
Magnetic letters: called, pulled, asked
Break off the ending.

Fluency & Expression
- ☐ Attend to bold words
- ☒ Reread page 10 for expression
- ☐ Read it like the character
- ☐ Attend to punctuation

6. Teach One Sight Word 1–2 minutes

Word: help   1. What's Missing?   2. Mix & Fix   3. Table Writing   4. Write It (and Retrieve It)

6. Reteach Same Sight Word 1–2 minutes

7. Word Study (choose one) 3–5 minutes

- ☐ Picture sorting
- ☒ Making words
- ☐ Sound boxes
- ☐ Analogy charts

Magnetic letters:
d, e, g, h, l, p, s, t, u
sled-sped-spud-thud-stud

7. Guided Writing 8–10 minutes

- ☐ Dictated sentences
- ☐ B-M-E
- ☒ Problem-Solution
- ☐ SWBS
- ☐ New facts you learned
- ☐ Other: _____

What was Little Penguin and Baby Seal's problem? How did they solve the problem?

8. Next Steps

Text was: Hard (Appropriate) Easy

Next Focus: Fluency and expression

Students to assess and analyze: Alexis

Complete the shaded boxes before you meet with the group. Add observations and notes during the lesson.

Analyzing Problem Areas for Early Readers

Early readers will progress at varying rates. You might notice a surge in learning followed by a few weeks of staying at the same level. On average, early readers progress one alphabetic level per month. If you notice a student remaining at one level longer than a month, you need to take action. Reflect on your teaching, analyze assessments, and develop a plan for acceleration.

Reflect on your teaching

Have you provided consistent, guided reading lessons? Have you been following the lesson framework to include reading, word study, and writing? Are you using the prompts for early readers and writers? Perhaps a child is not accelerating because you've neglected part of the lesson framework.

Observe the student

Meet with colleagues to share observations and assessments. If another teacher is providing instruction to the student, closely collaborate and discuss your concerns about that student. Use student assessments and observations to pinpoint the problem by completing the Problem-Solving Chart on page 149.

Directions for completing the Problem-Solving Chart

Columns 1 and 2: Record the student's name and instructional level.

Column 3: Uses oral language skills. Does the student have the language skills to read and retell at this text level? A conversation with the student will usually show if oral language is impeding progress, but you can also check the running record. Is the student making errors on new concepts not in his or her vocabulary? Can the student retell the text? Sometimes dual language learners understand what they read but struggle to retell it because they lack language skills to gather their ideas. Put a plus (+) if language is a strength, a check (√) if the student has average language skills, or a minus (-) if language is interfering with progress.

Column 4: Takes risks and works independently. Does the student try unknown words? Is the student working independently or trying to "hitchhike" off other students in the group? Put a plus (+) if risk taking is a strength, a check (√) if the student has adequate independence, or a minus (-) if lack of risk-taking behavior is interfering with progress.

Column 5: Reads for meaning. Do the miscues make sense? Is the student using pictures and the meaning of the story to solve words? Most early readers automatically check the picture at difficulty, but sometimes they still can't make a meaningful attempt on an unknown word. If you notice this, it's possible that the student is thinking at the word level and not at the story level. Early readers should anticipate and predict what might happen in the story. This feed-forward process (Clay, 1994) helps the reader make meaningful predictions on unknown words. Analyze errors to see if the student seems to be thinking about the story at the point of difficulty. Put a plus (+) if reading for meaning is a strength, a check (√) if some errors make sense, or a minus (-) if the student does not read for meaning.

Column 6: Monitors for meaning. Noticing errors is a precursor to applying decoding strategies. If readers aren't aware of their errors, they won't attempt to fix them. The process of monitoring for meaning, also called the "feedback mechanism" (Clay, 1994), is the most important strategic action because it is the basis for all comprehension. Put a plus (+) if you notice the student consistently monitors for meaning, a check (√) if he or she sometimes monitors, or a minus (-) if it is a weakness.

Column 7: Monitors for visual information. Early readers gradually use more visual information as they progress in levels. They begin to notice when their errors don't look right at the middle and end of the word. Put a plus (+) if you notice the student consistently monitors for visual information, a check (√) if he or she sometimes monitors, or a minus (-) if it is a weakness.

Column 8: Takes words apart. Analyze miscues to see if the reader is using parts of words to problem-solve. Actions might include sounding the onset or rime (e.g., *st-and*) or breaking a word at the ending (e.g., *land-ed*). Put a plus (+) if this is a strength, a check (√) if you notice the student attends to a few parts in words, or a minus (-) if the student is not breaking apart unknown words.

Column 9: Uses foundational skills. Check the student's reading miscues and writing sample to see if the student understands and uses short vowels, digraphs, and blends. These foundational skills are essential for problem solving texts at early levels. Put a plus (+) if the student has strong phonetic skills, a check (√) if the student knows and applies most of the short vowels, digraphs, and blends, or a minus (-) if the student lacks these skills.

Column 10: Knows sight words. Does the student have a large bank of function words that he or she can read and write? Check the running record to see if the student frequently misses sight words. Analyze the Sight Word Chart to see if the student has been slow in taking on words. Review the student's writing to see if he or she is misspelling sight words you have taught. Put a plus (+) if sight word knowledge is a strength, a check (√) if the student has an adequate number of known words, or a minus (-) if the student is weak in sight word knowledge.

Column 11: Reads fluently. Does the student read familiar books with phrasing and fluency? Does the student use appropriate intonation and expression when reading dialogue? There should be stretches of fluent, phrased reading when the student is not word solving. Indicate whether fluency is strong (+), adequate (√), or weak (-).

Column 12. Retells. Does the student recall what he or she reads? Does the student engage in discussions after reading? (Use caution here. Some children are just shy.) Rate the student's retelling as complete (+), adequate (√), or weak (-).

Mark Strengths and Needs (+ √ -)

Problem-Solving Chart for Levels D–I

Early

Student	Instructional Level	Uses Oral Language Skills	Takes Risks and Works Independently	Reads for Meaning	Monitors for Meaning	Monitors for Visual Information	Takes Words Apart	Has Foundational Skills	Knows Sight Words	Reads Fluently	Retells

NEXT STEP FOR STRUGGLING EARLY READERS

The first step is to reflect on your teaching. Have you been using appropriate books for guided reading? Sometimes we place struggling readers in texts that are too difficult because we don't want to form another group. Students won't accelerate by reading texts that are too hard. Consider your prompting. Have you been praising the student for monitoring and problem-solving actions even if they don't result in an accurate response?

Meet with a colleague to discuss the student's strengths and needs. Include other teachers who are working with the child, such as the reading interventionist, DLL teacher, or special education teacher. Your goal is to pinpoint an area or two that might be interfering with acceleration. Once you know the problem, discuss ways to solve it.

You or the reading specialist might work with the student individually for an extra ten minutes a day to address specific needs. Plan productive independent activities the student can do when he or she is not in a guided reading lesson. Early readers need lots of independent reading, but if they are just leafing through books and looking at pictures, they are not going to improve. They need eyes-on-text reading, not eyes-on-pictures. Pair students with a buddy or an older student to read familiar books. Meet with the parents and suggest specific activities they can do at home. Find books that match the student's interest and level. Consider dropping the text level for guided reading to see if the student shows more engagement and begins to accelerate. Review the Suggestions for Intervention chart (pages 151–152) and select ideas that may help your student accelerate. The chart lists suggestions for each focus area on the Problem-Solving Chart. Try one of the suggestions for a week or two, and meet with the intervention team again to evaluate progress and determine the effectiveness of the intervention.

Focus	Suggestions for Intervention
Uses oral language skills	• Select guided reading texts with natural language and mostly familiar vocabulary. • Introduce new concepts using illustrations and gestures. Have the student use the words in sentences before reading the book. If the student hesitates on a word not in his or her working vocabulary, explain the word to the student. • Engage the student in conversations before, during, and after reading. Make sure the student does most of the talking. • During guided writing, use dictated sentences to teach sentence structure. Have the student rehearse each sentence before writing it.
Takes risks and works independently	• Select easier texts and provide a supportive introduction. Have the student talk about each picture to become familiar with the story. • When the child stops, say, "Try it," and praise the student for any attempts, even if he or she makes an error. When the student stops at a word, sound the first part of the word for the student. This "jump starts" the processing.
Reads for meaning	• Clarify new vocabulary before reading the book. Have the student describe what is happening in the picture before reading a page. When the student hesitates on a word, say, "Think about the story."
Monitors for meaning	• Temporarily ignore errors that make sense, and focus on those that disrupt meaning. After the student finishes a sentence say, "Are you right? Does that make sense?" Occasionally use this prompt on accurate reading to prompt the student to reflect on meaning. Put your thumb up when the student is making sense and put your thumb down when he or she isn't. To transfer responsibility for monitoring, have the student do it with you.
Monitors for visual information	• If the student only uses pictures and avoids looking at the print, prompt him or her to look at the picture before reading the page. Once he or she starts to read, the eyes should stay on the print. • When the student makes an error, direct attention to the part of the word the student is ignoring and say, "Check here. Say the word slowly. Run your finger under it. Does it look right? It needs to look right and make sense." • Encourage him or her to self-correct at the point of error.
Takes words apart	• During word study, use the making words activity and have the student break the word at the onset and rime (e.g., *sn-ap*). • During reading, prompt the student to cover the ending, find a known part, or break the word at the onset and rime.

Focus	Suggestions for Intervention
Has foundational skills	• Teach one feature at a time and use the word study activities in sequence: picture sorting, making words, and sound boxes. Go slow. For example, spend several days sorting digraphs, then several days doing making words before you spend time with sound boxes. Teach the skills in sequence. • Make sure the student hears and knows the sound before you expect him or her to use it in reading and writing. • During guided writing, encourage the student to say each word slowly as he or she writes. Use sound boxes on the practice page of the journal to help the student hear and record sounds. Target phonetic spelling and provide the silent letters.
Knows sight words	• Take stock of the words the student *can* write. Then systematically teach a new word by following the steps: What's Missing?, Mix & Fix, Table Writing, Write It (and Retrieve It). Teach the same word for two days or until it is known. Coordinate with other support teachers so you are teaching the same words each week. Have the student write three known words at the beginning of every lesson. Hold students accountable for writing known words correctly during guided writing. Select a familiar word from the story and have the student practice writing it on the practice page.
Reads fluently	• Select easier fiction books that have interesting dialogue. • Have the student reread familiar texts with a buddy outside of guided reading. Send familiar books home for the student to read with a parent or sibling. • Record a familiar book so the student can listen to it and read along. • While the student reads with you, frame two to three words with your index fingers and prompt the student to read the words together. Model if necessary. • Slide your finger left to right across the words as the student reads. This pushes the eye ahead of the mouth (a necessary skill for reading fluently). • As a teaching point after reading, select a page for the group to read together. Model intonation and expression, if necessary.
Retells	• Select texts with a clear story line. Before reading, do a supportive picture preview to lay a foundation for comprehension. • Have the student retell a page after reading, prompting him or her to point to the part of the picture he or she is discussing. This will help the student visualize the events when you ask him or her to retell the whole story. After reading, use the Shared Retelling cards (Appendix G) to provide sentence starters. Students will eventually memorize the sentence starters, which will help them retell. Have the student hold up a finger each time he or she retells a part of the story. Tell the student to use all five fingers in the retelling. This will help the student include details. • Create a picture concept map to use during retelling.

ADAPTATIONS FOR DLLs AND STUDENTS WITH IEPs

The "Next Steps" lesson framework is excellent for children with special learning needs and those who are learning English. It includes reading, writing, speaking, and listening—the pillars of literacy development. It integrates phonics and spelling into reading and writing, and teaches skills at developmental levels. You have the opportunity to prompt students to use strategic actions at difficulty. However, you may need to make some adaptations to the lesson to target the specific needs of your students.

Most dual language learners and children with special learning needs do fine with a two-day plan. Some, however, may need additional language development before, during, and after reading. If you find this is necessary, extend the lesson an extra day. The following three-day lesson plan includes all of the components from the two-day plan, but gives more time for teaching vocabulary, discussing the story, and guided writing—all of which are challenging for emerging bilinguals and children with special learning needs. Be sure students do the talking.

Three-Day Early Plan for Children Who Need Extra Time

Day 1	Day 2	Day 3
Sight Word Review (< 1 minute)	**Sight Word Review** (< 1 minute)	**Sight Word Review** (< 1 minute)
Introduce the New Book Talk about the pictures and new vocabulary (5–8 minutes)	**Read and Prompt** Reread the new book and other familiar books with prompting (8–10 minutes)	**Discuss the Writing Response** Encourage oral rehearsal (5 minutes)
Read and Prompt Read new book with prompting (5–8 minutes)	**Discuss and Teach** Discuss the story and teach a word-solving strategy (5 minutes)	**Guided Writing** (15 minutes)
Discuss and Teach Discuss the story and teach a word-solving strategy (5 minutes)	**Reteach Same Sight Word** Use the steps (1 minute)	
Teach a New Sight Word Use the steps (1 minute)	**Word Study** (5 minutes)	

If you have an early reader who does not fit into one of your other groups, teach him or her individually for ten minutes a day, using the following plan.

Ten-Minute Lessons for Individual Instruction		
Day 1	Day 2	Day 3
Sight Word Review	Sight Word Review	Sight Word Review
Introduce and Read New Book	Reread and Discuss Book From Day 1	Guided Writing
Teach One Sight Word	Reteach Same Sight Word Word Study	

MONITORING PROGRESS

Progress monitoring is a daily part of a guided reading lesson. Because you are working with a small group, you have the opportunity to notice new behaviors and record your observations on the back of the lesson plan or in a separate notebook. Jot down errors and whether the student monitored and self-corrected. Comment on fluency and comprehension. These on-the-spot assessments will guide your teaching decisions.

Sight Words

Because developing a large bank of sight words is crucial for fluent reading, keep a record of the words you have taught. About every two weeks, take a few minutes at the beginning of the lesson to assess students on the words they have learned over the past two weeks. This will tell you which words are firmly known and which need more review.

Running Record

Use a few minutes at the beginning of the Day 2 lesson to take a running record on one student while the others are reading familiar books. You don't need to listen to the student read the entire book. Just listen to a few pages to assess the text difficulty and the student's problem-solving actions. These assessments will help you decide which students are ready to move up, which students need more time at a level, and which strategies you need to teach next. Students who read with at least 95 percent accuracy and adequate recall are ready to move to the next text level. Reserve formal benchmark testing for the beginning, middle, and end of the year.

MOVING TO THE TRANSITIONAL LESSON PLAN

Consider moving students to the Transitional Guided Reading Plan when they can

- Independently read text Level I with good fluency and comprehension
- Read and write a large bank of sight words
- Monitor using meaning, structure, and visual information
- Solve new words by integrating a variety of strategic actions
- Reread at point of difficulty to access meaning and structure
- Read familiar texts with fluency, phrasing, and expression
- Remember and retell the main idea and important details
- Apply phonic elements, such as digraphs and blends, to both reading and writing. Begin to understand and use the silent-*e* rule and vowel combinations. You will continue teaching these phonic elements with the transitional lesson plan.

QUESTIONS TEACHERS ASK ABOUT EARLY GUIDED READING

I have some students who can read texts at Levels G and higher but have not mastered the sight words at Levels E and F. Should I continue to teach those words until they know them?

Yes. The words listed for Levels D–F are important to learn because they appear frequently in early books and can be difficult to spell. Words that begin with *th* and *w* are especially confusing. Most students reading at Levels D–I will benefit from the systematic review of known words at the beginning of the lesson and the explicit teaching of sight words after reading. Teach the sight words at the lower levels before tackling the words recommended for Levels G, H, and I. There is no sequence for teaching these words. Choose a word from the book that children don't know how to spell. Once children develop a way of remembering words, they will learn words more quickly.

Should I be teaching during guided writing?

Absolutely! As you work with individual students, select teaching points that match their needs. If students are not recording sounds in sequence, draw sound boxes on the practice page (the top part of the journal) and ask him or her to say the word slowly and write the sound of each letter, blend, or digraph in each box. If a student misspells a sight word you have taught in a previous lesson, write the word on the practice page and have him or her copy it several times before correcting it in his or her story. You can also teach letter formation, periods, capitalization, and spacing, as well as how to use transition words. Always expect children to reread their story to make sure it makes sense.

Why is it a good idea to ask children to talk to a partner at the guided reading table? How can I monitor that?

Having students turn and talk gives everyone the opportunity to participate in discussions. You can lean in, listen to partners, and join in their conversations. After I have students turn and talk, I often ask one or two of them to share something they said (or something their partner said).

How can I help students transfer the skills they are using during guided writing to other parts of the day, such as writing workshop?

You should expect students to transfer what you teach in guided writing to independent writing. Sometimes I'll put a writing goal on a sticky note and tell students to place it in their writing folder so they can remember to practice that skill. During writing conferences, I'll refer to the sticky note and either compliment the student for following through during independent writing or make it a teaching point for the conference.

When do I use B-M-E and when do I use SWBS or Five-Finger Retell? Is there a rule?

I use the B-M-E writing prompt at Levels E and F because I've found it is the easiest to teach. Somebody-Wanted-But-So is a great discussion prompt for any story, but I don't usually include it in guided writing until students are reading texts at Levels F and higher. It is a wonderful scaffold for teaching summarizing, but it requires more cognitive processing than writing a B-M-E. The Five-Finger Retell is even more complex. I begin using it once students move to the transitional lesson plan because they will need a full 20 minutes to write the response.

What is the most important thing to consider when selecting books for guided reading?

The first thing I consider is the strategy focus. For example, if my focus is fluency, I'd select an easier text with interesting dialogue. When my focus is word solving, I want a more challenging text that has new words to solve. Of course, I wouldn't expect fluency on the first reading, when my focus is word solving. It is critically important to choose books that are interesting and engaging.

How do you choose the focus for word study?

Ideally, you should use your students' spelling errors to select your focus. Do they misspell short vowels? Then teach vowel sorts. Use Appendix A to pinpoint your focus. Then choose one of the word study activities to teach the skill. Use picture sorting to teach the sound. Use making words to teach students how to use the sounds in reading, and use sound boxes to teach them how to use the sounds in writing.

What if some students finish sooner than others during guided writing? Should they draw a picture?

I never have students draw a picture during guided writing. I think that is a waste of instructional time. They already have the pictures in the book to help them plan their response. Always prompt them to write more. Say, for example, "What else can you add? Tell me more. How did the character feel at the end? What else did you learn about fireflies?" Students can always turn to a favorite picture and write more about it. Writing for the entire time (about ten minutes) is essential.

How can we help students who try to sound out a word, but are not able to blend the sounds correctly?

I do not prompt students to sound out a word letter by letter. That gets in the way of him or her using meaning at difficult points. Try one of these prompts instead:

- *Sound the first part of the word and think about the story.*
- *What would look right and make sense?*
- *Is there a part of the word you know? Reread and think about the story.*
- *Check the word with your finger and say it slowly.*

> **Professional Study Guide**
>
> Go to scholastic.com/NSFresources for a downloadable professional study guide written just for this book. In it, you'll find questions and activities about early readers to use on your own or with your colleagues in a study group or PLC.

CHAPTER 5

The Transitional Reader: Levels J–P

Kids love to read their first chapter book. It's a rite of passage. Not too long ago, I asked a struggling third grader why reading chapter books is so important. His answer: "Because if you can read chapter books, it means you can really read—and be like everybody else in your class."

PROFILE OF A TRANSITIONAL READER

Although transitional readers typically read at text Levels J–P, they are an extremely diverse group and their specific needs vary. They automatically recognize an increasing number of sight words, but they often struggle with sophisticated vocabulary, especially multisyllabic words with complex vowel patterns and endings. Some at the transitional stage may still need to improve their fluency, while others read so quickly they don't think about what they are reading. I've seen transitional readers who have excellent comprehension and others who can hardly recall the main idea. Most need word study activities that target complex vowels and inflectional endings. All need guided reading lessons that target their needs and teach them strategies for comprehending longer, more complex text.

Most second- and third-grade readers are at this stage, but you will likely find transitional readers at any grade. Advanced readers in kindergarten and first grade, for instance, are transitional readers. So are intermediate students who lag behind their peers. Transitional readers need to work on decoding, fluency, and/or retelling.

Transitional Readers by Grade Level, Text Level, and Instructional Focus		
Grade Level	Text Level	Instructional Focus
K–1	Above Level I	Self-monitoring
2–3	J–M	Word-solving strategies
		Fluency
4–8	J–P	Retelling

Notice that the levels overlap. Second and third graders reading at Levels N–P would likely be fluent readers who need to improve only comprehension and vocabulary. Students in fourth grade or higher who are reading at Levels N–P will probably need to work on decoding, fluency, and/or retelling. Consider both the instructional level and the focus to identify your transitional readers.

Use the Fluent Guided Reading Plan described in Chapter 6 for students who successfully read texts above Level P and do not need to improve decoding, fluency, or retelling. Your instruction with fluent readers should focus on expanding vocabulary strategies and improving deeper understanding beyond basic retelling.

ASSESS

Teachers constantly struggle with finding the balance between teaching and assessing. How can we streamline the assessment process to protect instructional time? Two assessments are essential in identifying a transitional reader's strengths and needs: a Word Knowledge Inventory and a reading conference (Richardson & Walther, 2013).

Assessments for Transitional Readers		
Assessment	**How is it administered?**	**What does it tell you?**
Word Knowledge Inventory	Whole class	Phonics, spelling, and word knowledge

Reading conference
   Running record
   Retelling
   Comprehension conversation
	Individual	Instructional text level range
		Word-solving actions
		Fluency
		Retelling
		Vocabulary
		Comprehension strategies

Word Knowledge Inventory

This assessment is a carefully designed list of words for students to spell. Research has shown that analyzing the ways students spell can provide insight into how they decode and read words (Zutell & Rasinski, 1989). When used at the beginning of the year, a Word Knowledge Inventory will quickly show you which students are struggling and need immediate intervention.

Appendix J

   Transitional readers should be assessed on the following phonics skills:

- Short vowels, digraphs, and consonant blends
- Long-vowel and complex-vowel words (e.g., *drove*, *crawl*)
- Two-syllable words (e.g., *stopping*, *shaking*)

See the Word Knowledge Inventory in Appendix J.

Use the sheet to highlight the spelling features the student missed. Teach these skills during the word study and guided writing components of your lesson.

Reading Conference

The most valuable assessment for transitional readers is a one-on-one reading conference. Consider this time a personal investment in their future. During a reading conference, you meet with each student individually to listen to him or her read a leveled text. The conference should include a running record on at least 100 words, an oral retelling, and a comprehension conversation guided by questions about the passage.

Running record

Teachers primarily use running records (Clay, 2000) to determine a student's instructional level, but there's even greater value in the analysis. The running record will provide insights into the student's word-solving actions and give you an opportunity to observe other reading behaviors such as intonation, phrasing, monitoring for meaning, and self-correcting. This information will help you determine an instructional range of text levels and pinpoint a strategy focus for guided reading.

Have the student read aloud as you record errors, self-corrections, and other reading behaviors. Make a note about the student's phrasing and expression. After you take a running record on about 100 words and determine that the text level is appropriate for the student, have the student finish reading the text silently. You can use this time to analyze errors and note strategic actions the reader used or ignored, such as the following:

Monitoring. Was the student aware of his or her errors? Did the student pause, reread, or attempt to correct a miscue? If so, the student is monitoring.

Rereading. Was the student rereading words, phrases, or sentences to figure out unknown words or to better catch the meaning? Note this on the running record form.

Word solving (decoding). When the student encountered a challenging word, did he or she sound the first part or break the word into smaller units? Record any actions the student used to decode unfamiliar words.

Self-correcting. Did you notice the student correcting errors? Note that.

Reading fluently. Reading speed does not guarantee comprehension, especially after grade 2. It is quite common to find word callers who have high accuracy and reading rates but low comprehension. Research shows that as many as one-third of students who meet the reading rate standard may not have sufficient comprehension (Allington, 2009; Pressley, Hilden, & Shankland, 2005; Schilling, Carlisle, Scott, & Zeng, 2007). Some assessments recommend that you time the reader, but the more important aspects of fluency are phrasing, expression, intonation, and attention to punctuation. Students who stop to monitor or reread may take longer to read the passage, but they are using effective fix-up strategies that should be valued because they improve overall comprehension. Only note the student's fluency when he or she is not problem solving.

Other observable behaviors. Transitional readers may send signals about their thinking through their facial expressions, gestures, or comments. Record and analyze them. What do they tell you about the reader?

Oral retelling

When the student finishes reading, ask him or her to retell the passage by saying, "Tell me what you read." Do your best to make this a casual conversation. You can prompt with phrases such as "Tell me more" or "What else do you remember?" without affecting the rating, but do not allow the student to look back in the story at this point. You want to determine if he or she can demonstrate an overall understanding of the text.

> **Tip**
>
> *Although retelling is widely used to gather information about comprehension (Fountas & Pinnell, 2001; Hoyt, 1999), some students are shy. They may give a general overview of the passage but leave out the details. Dual language learners may give you a meager retelling because they lack confidence and language skills. I've found that many of these students will provide accurate information when prompted. Don't penalize students if you have to prompt them. Your goal is to get a clear picture of their understanding, regardless of prompting.*

Transitional Video Link 1

Watch Jan working with teachers to use assessment data to guide their teaching.

Comprehension conversation

Finally, have a short conversation about the passage to probe deeper into the student's comprehension abilities. Ask questions that require the student to identify the main idea, recall key details, infer, or demonstrate vocabulary strategies.

Individual reading conferences will reveal specific needs for all readers, especially those who struggle. You can address some of those needs through whole-group instruction, but the greatest acceleration will occur through engaging guided reading lessons. Also, confer with a few students each day during independent reading time to talk about the books they are choosing. Invite them to read to you, and then work with them on a specific strategy. Continue to monitor all your readers' book selections to make sure that they are appropriate. In the next section, we will look at how to use the data you've gathered to plan your guided reading lessons. Below and at right are examples of a Level K passage and a running record form (from *Next Step Guided Reading Assessment: Grades 3–6*).

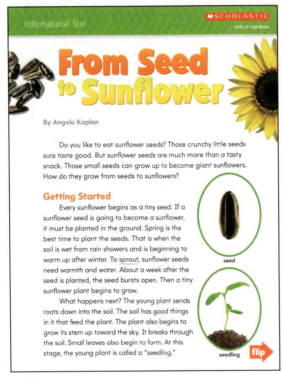

Reading passage

Running record form

The comprehension section of the running record form targets vocabulary, key details, inferring, analyzing relationships, and evaluating.

DECIDE

Now that you have assessed and analyzed your transitional readers, you are ready to summarize the assessments to help you form your groups, pinpoint a focus for instruction, and select a text.

Summarize the Assessments

Summarize the results of the assessments on the Assessment Summary Chart (page 168 and scholastic.com/NSFresources).

Directions for completing the Assessment Summary Chart

Columns 1 and 2: Name and Level Range. Record the student's name and instructional level range. For most students you will write two adjacent levels, such as J/K or L/M. The lower level might be used for informational texts or to work on fluency, whereas the higher level might be more appropriate for teaching word-solving skills and retelling.

Column 3: Self-monitors. Put a plus (+) if the student consistently stops and tries to fix his or her errors when meaning breaks down. Put a check (√) if the student sometimes monitors for meaning. Put a minus (–) if the student consistently ignores errors that distort meaning.

Column 4: Solves Words. Good word-solvers take apart unknown words and attend to all inflectional endings while constructing meaning. Many transitional readers who struggle with word solving have developed a haphazard approach to visual scanning and ignore either the middle or end of the word. Put a plus (+) if the student makes very few errors and attends to all parts of the word. Put a check (√) if the student occasionally ignores the middle or end of a word. Put a minus (-) if the student frequently ignores word parts. Some transitional readers may have strong retelling abilities but struggle with decoding due to inefficient visual scanning skills.

Column 5: Reads Fluently. Use the following rubric to rate fluency when a student is not in the process of problem solving:

1. Word-by-word reading; no expression
2. Moderately slow reading in two- or three-word phrases; some expression
3. Phrased but some rough spots; may read too quickly to notice punctuation
4. Smooth reading with appropriate expression

Column 6: Retells. Use the rubric below to record the student's basic understanding of the text. Take into account a student's language skills, and don't use a lower rating if you have to prompt him or her for details.

- \+ Complete and detailed retelling; includes all major ideas and important details
- √ Adequate retelling; includes most major ideas and some details
- − Limited retelling; misses the main ideas, central characters, and essential details

Column 7: Word Study. Use the results from the Word Knowledge Inventory or other spelling assessments to identify phonics skills the student needs to learn. Write D if the student missed digraphs, B if blends are a problem, V if the reader needs to learn complex vowels, and E if more work is needed on adding inflectional endings.

Column 8: Other. Note other factors you need to consider when planning instruction. You might record specific comprehension needs or language processing issues.

Form Groups

Use the information on the Assessment Summary Chart to form guided reading groups. Locate each student's instructional level range. Begin by placing readers together who are close to the same instructional level (not more than one level apart). Ideally, you want no more than four or five guided reading groups so you can consistently meet with them three to five times a week.

If you have more than six students reading at about the same instructional level, form two groups based on their needs. For example, you might have eight J–K readers. Four may need to work on word solving. Put them in one group. The others might be efficient word-solvers (high accuracy scores), but weak in retelling. Put them in another group. Most likely you will have students in the same reading group who have different instructional needs. That is not an insurmountable problem. You can differentiate your instruction through prompting and coaching. Don't get too comfortable with your groupings anyway. They will likely change about once a month as students progress at different rates.

Assessment Summary Chart for Transitional Readers, Levels J–P

Name	Level Range	Self-monitors + √ −	Solves Words + √ −	Reads Fluently 1 2 3 4	Retells + √ − N	I	Word Study D B V E	Other

Pinpoint Your Focus

Once you decide which students to group together, use the Assessment Summary Chart to pinpoint a strategy focus for each group. Move across the columns to select your focus. Write the focus on your lesson plan. Always teach monitoring for meaning as your first focus. Monitoring for meaning is important to teach any reader, especially transitional ones. If students are already using meaning, work on word-solving strategies. When monitoring and decoding are strong, choose fluency and retelling. Once students are strong in all areas at that text range, it is time to increase the text difficulty.

If you have a group that is strong in all five areas and reading above Level P, change your instructional focus to vocabulary and deeper comprehension and use the Fluent Guided Reading Plan found in Chapter 6.

Select a Text

Choose a text at the group's instructional range, one that offers opportunities to apply the focus. Since publishing companies use different criteria to level books, you should read the book to determine if it is a good match for your students.

\multicolumn{2}{c}{**Selecting Texts That Match Your Focus**}	
Focus	**Text Features**
Self-monitoring	Select fiction or informational texts with familiar concepts and strong picture support. Students will be able to access meaning when they have background knowledge about the topic.
Word solving	Select challenging texts with multisyllabic words so students have multiple opportunities to practice word-solving strategies. These words should be decodable and in their listening vocabulary. Before students read, introduce challenging words that are not decodable.
Reading fluently	Choose a fiction text at the lower text range, one with interesting dialogue. There should be few decoding challenges so students can focus on fluency, phrasing, expression, and intonation.
Retelling	Choose fiction stories with strong picture support and a clear beginning, middle, and end. After students have become proficient with retelling fiction, choose informational texts with supportive illustrations and headings that capture the main idea of the section.
Developing vocabulary	Look for informational texts with unfamiliar concepts. Students should be able to figure out the words using text clues, picture support, and glossaries.
Comprehending	At the transitional level, you may have students write key words, a question, or a sentence to support comprehension. Most transitional texts support a variety of comprehension strategies. See page 173 for suggestions.

The goal in selecting a text for transitional readers is to choose one that provides enough support to keep students reading independently, but enough challenge to provide opportunities for them to problem-solve. Don't be locked into one specific text level. Transitional readers can read a range of texts depending on the genre, background knowledge, and vocabulary.

Gather Other Materials

Organize the following materials and place them within reach:

- Leveled books
- Dry-erase boards, markers, and erasers
- 6–8 sets of lowercase magnetic letters on trays or in a storage box (for word study)

- Analogy Chart templates (Appendix I)

- Guided writing journals
- Personal word walls for guided writing (Appendix K)
- Timer

GUIDE

You've assessed your students, analyzed the assessments, formed your groups, and selected the text. Now you are ready to prepare for your guided reading lesson.

The Transitional Guided Reading Lesson

The transitional lesson is carried out over three days, about 20 minutes each day. On Day 1, students briefly preview the book while you introduce new vocabulary essential to understanding the story. The remainder of the lesson is spent reading the book with prompting, discussing the book, and teaching one or two strategic actions. On Day 2, students usually finish the book and may have time to reread some sections. After you discuss and teach, spend the last three to five minutes on a word study activity that targets phonics skills. Day 3 is spent writing about the book with scaffolding and teaching.

Overview of the Transitional Guided Reading Lesson		
Day 1	**Day 2**	**Day 3**
Introduce a New Book	Read the Book With Prompting	Guided Writing
Read the Book With Prompting	Discuss and Teach	
Discuss and Teach	Word Study Activity	

If you are an intervention teacher and have more than 20 minutes per group, you can extend the part of the lesson that needs more attention. For example, if students need to improve fluency, add more rereading. If they struggle with sight words, spend a few minutes teaching a new word and reviewing the sight words you have already taught. Struggling transitional readers always need more writing support. Use student assessments to make those decisions.

TEACHING COMPREHENSION

Read the book to determine an appropriate comprehension focus. Write your chosen focus on the lesson plan, and weave that focus into your discussion. On Day 2, when students are rereading the book, you might want to insert a few sticky notes for students to write short responses. They can write a key word, a question, or a sentence that fits your comprehension focus. Don't ask for too much writing or there won't be enough time for them to read the book. Two or three short responses is enough. The following chart lists some of my favorite comprehension strategies for transitional readers. See Chapter 7 for more ideas.

Comprehension Strategies for Transitional Readers

Comprehension Strategy	Short Response
Ask Questions	Students write one question about the story.
Beginning-Middle-End (B-M-E)	Students write a sentence about each part of the story.
Retell (STP—Stop, Think, Paraphrase)	After students read each page, they **stop**, **think** about what they read, and **put** it in their own words. They can write their STP for one of the pages.
Determine Key Ideas	Insert a sticky note on three or four pages. Students write one important word on each sticky note.
Who-What	After each page, students think **who** was the important character and **what** did he or she do. Only have them write the **who-what** for one or two pages.
Track the Character's Feelings	Insert a sticky note on a page where the character's feelings change. Students write a feeling word on the note. Provide a list of feeling words students can choose from. See Character Feelings and Traits chart (Appendix M).
Determine Importance (V.I.P.—**V**ery **I**mportant **P**art)	Distribute a few sticky flags. Students use the flags to mark the most important sentence on each page.

Understand the purpose and procedures for each lesson component

Each component in a transitional guided reading lesson supports one or more reading skills and standards. The following chart summarizes the procedures and purposes of each component.

Transitional Lesson Procedures and Purposes		
Component	**Procedures**	**Purposes**
Introduce a New Book	• Preview the book using illustrations and other text features such as the table of contents, diagrams, and glossary. • Introduce new vocabulary.	• Predict • Ask questions • Build schema • Extend vocabulary
Read and Prompt	• Students read independently while teacher confers with each student. • Differentiate prompting based on student needs. • If comprehension is the focus, students may write a short response while reading.	• Scaffold strategic actions such as monitoring for meaning, word solving, fluency, and comprehension • Use text features to extend vocabulary and enhance comprehension
Discuss and Teach	Lead a discussion of the text. Students share ideas and ask questions.	• Ask and answer questions • Retell • Make inferences • Determine importance • Compare/contrast
Teaching Point	Model a word-solving or vocabulary strategy based on observations during reading.	• Take words apart • Use within-word patterns • Use the text and illustrations to extend vocabulary
Word Study Activity	Students use analogy charts and magnetic letters to learn spelling patterns (silent-e feature and diphthongs) and inflectional endings (*e*-drop, doubling, etc.).	• Phonics • Spelling features
Guided Writing	Students extend comprehension by writing about the text with the teacher's support. Plan > Write with prompting > Reread	• Respond to a prompt • Plan with key words • Paragraph organization • Spelling • Reread for meaning and mechanics

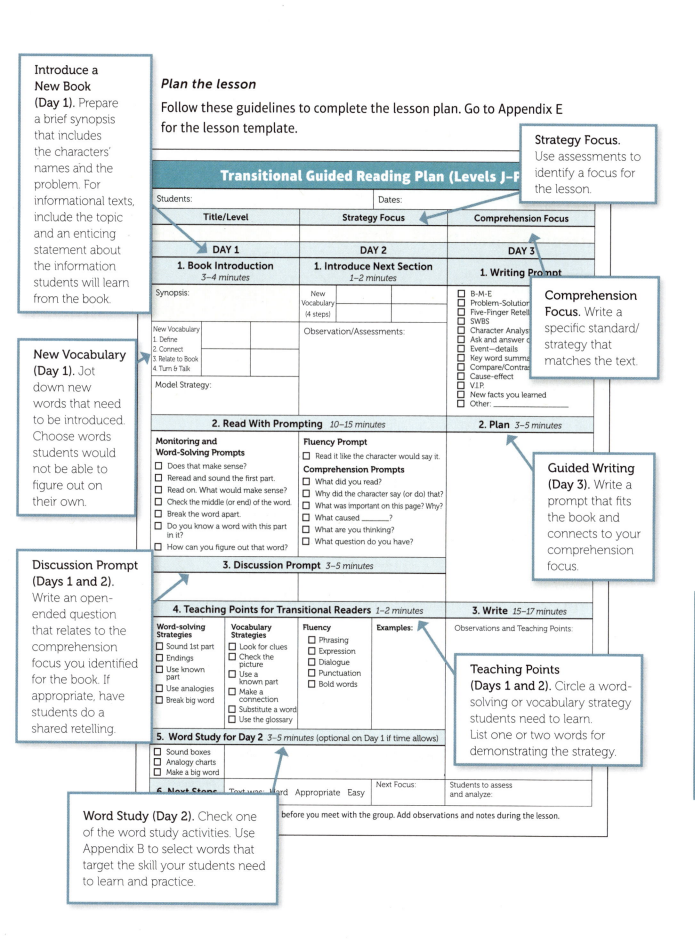

DESCRIPTION OF DAY 1

The Day 1 lesson has three basic components:

- Introduce a New Book
- Read the Book With Prompting
- Discuss and Teach

Introduce a New Book
(3–4 minutes)

Provide a synopsis
State the title and give a brief main idea statement of the book. For example, "This book is called *Life in the Tide Pool*. You are going to learn about plants and animals that live near the seashore."

Preview and predict
Have students briefly preview the illustrations and text features, inviting them to make predictions and ask questions.

Introduce new vocabulary
Discuss new words students are not able to decode or do not know the meaning of. If the word is difficult to *decode*, write it on a dry-erase board and pronounce it for students. Words such as *through, though, enough,* and *precious* can be challenging for transitional readers. When you need to introduce a new word because students do not know what it *means* and the word is not defined in the text, follow these four steps:

1. **Define it.** Prepare a brief, kid-friendly definition. Do not ask students to define the word. That wastes time and causes confusion.

2. **Connect it.** Make a connection between the new word and students' background knowledge and experiences.

3. **Relate it to the book.** Tell students how the word is used in the story and direct them to an illustration if one is provided.

> **Tip**
> Don't spend too much time talking about the book. Expect students to problem-solve as they read.

> **Tip**
> Do not introduce every new word. Prompt students to use strategies and text clues to solve most words.

> **Tip**
> If you have to introduce more than five words, the book is too difficult. Choose another book.

4. **Turn and talk.** Ask students to explain the meaning of the word or give an example to the person sitting next to them.

Model the strategy focus

Remind students of the focus for the lesson. Ideally, you modeled it during a whole-class lesson. If students need a refresher, quickly show them how to do the strategy.

Transitional Video Link 2
Watch Jan introducing vocabulary in four steps.

Read the Book With Prompting
(10–15 minutes)

Read and confer

Have students independently read the book in soft voices while you spend one or two minutes conferring with each student. Use the Prompts for Transitional Readers on the next page to select a focus for your interaction. You'll be targeting these strategies: monitoring, decoding, fluency, vocabulary, and comprehension.

If students finish the book before time is called, have them reread it. If they don't finish the book, have them mark their place with a bookmark and let them continue reading from that point on Day 2. Do not have students take turns reading. It will limit the amount of text they can read and impede independent processing.

Have students write a short response

When comprehension is your primary focus, insert two or three sticky notes in the book and have students write short responses that relate to your specific focus. They could write a key word, a question, or a character trait or feeling. See Chapter 7 for specific procedures and scaffolding steps for teaching comprehension during whole-group and guided reading.

Take notes

On the back of the lesson plan, take notes on students' reading and record the individual teaching points you make. You will use this information to select your teaching points for the entire group later in the lesson.

> **Tip**
> Consider the needs of dual language learners. They may need more support for new vocabulary.

> **Tip**
> Give each student a bookmark to use during guided reading. The bookmark could list strategies for solving words or steps for retelling. Consider the needs of your students.

Prompts for Transitional Readers

Behavior	Goal	Prompts
Stops or miscues on an unknown word	Solve words	You noticed something wasn't right. Reread and sound the first part of the word. What would make sense? Check the middle (or end) of the word. What part do you know? Teach a word-solving action such as • Cover the ending • Take the word apart • Use an analogy with a known word
Does not self-monitor	Monitor for meaning and visual information	Wait until the student finishes the sentence and say, Are you right? Did that make sense? Reread and think what would make sense.
Reads accurately but slowly	Read with phrasing and fluency	Read it as if you are the character. (Slide your finger from left to right to cover the words as the student reads. This pushes the student's eye forward at a faster pace.)
Does not know the meaning of a word	Use vocabulary strategies	Reread and look for clues. How does the picture (or other text feature) help you understand that word? Can you think of another word that would make sense in that sentence? Is the word in the glossary?
Has difficulty retelling	Check for surface comprehension	What happened on this page? Retell the beginning, middle, and end (B-M-E). Tell what you just read. Use the picture to help you.
Has difficulty with comprehension	Check for deeper comprehension	What are you thinking? Why did the character do (or say) that? How is the character feeling now? Why? How is the character changing? What was important on this page? Why? What did you learn about _____ ?

Transitional Video Link 3

Watch Jan prompting students while they read.

Description of Day 1

Transitional Video Link 4
Watch Jan teaching for fluency and phrasing.

Discuss and Teach (3–5 minutes)

Discuss the text
After students read, have a short conversation about what they read. Ask open-ended questions that will facilitate discussion and help them draw inferences. See pages 181–182 for discussion starters.

Do a shared retelling
If students need to improve their retelling skills, give each student a Shared Retelling card (Appendix G) and guide them as they take turns retelling a portion of the book.

Transitional Video Link
Watch Jan doing a shared retelling. (See Early Video Link 3, page 128.)

Do a Five-Finger Retell
Students take turns describing one of the following story elements:

- **Thumb:** The characters are . . .
- **Pointer:** The setting is . . .
- **Tall finger:** The problem is . . .
- **Ring finger:** The events are . . .
- **Little finger:** At the end . . .

Discuss the character's feelings and/or traits
This is a great discussion point for transitional readers. Identify a few words that describe the character's feelings at the beginning, middle, and end. Write the words on sticky notes and distribute to students. Ask, "Who has a word that describes the character at the beginning of the story?" The student with that word uses the word to describe the character's feelings and explains what caused them. Repeat the process with the other words you have written on the sticky notes.

Tip
After you pose a question, invite students to share their ideas with the student sitting next to them. Listen in on conversations and prompt for clarification.

Tip
Be sure every student participates in the discussion.

Tip
Use the dry-erase board or magnetic letters to demonstrate a word-solving strategy.

Tip
Use the Character Feelings and Traits chart to help you think of words to describe the character.

When discussing a character trait, explain that a trait is a word that describes how the character acts most of the time. Many feeling words can be used as a character trait. Distribute the Character Feelings and Traits chart to give students the vocabulary for discussing the characters. Regardless of whether you are discussing feelings or traits, be sure students return to the text to find evidence.

Appendix M

Select a teaching point

After you discuss the book, take a minute or two to demonstrate a strategic action (self-monitoring, decoding, vocabulary, or fluency). Use the notes you took during the individual conferences to select your teaching point. See the following two charts for teaching points and discussion starters.

Teaching Points for Transitional Readers	
Goal	**Demonstration and Teaching**
Monitor for meaning	Read a sentence from the text and make a nonsensical error. Invite students to say, "Stop!" when they hear the word that doesn't make sense.
Monitor for visual information	Read a sentence and intentionally make an error while students follow along in their books. Say, "What word do I need to fix?"
Reread and think	Demonstrate making a miscue, rereading, and using pictures and/or the first part of the word to figure it out.
Cover the ending	Write a word with an ending such as *-s, -ed, -ing, -er,* or *-ly.* Show students how to cover the ending to figure out the word. Then write another word and invite students to show you how they will figure it out.
Chunk big words	Write a multisyllabic word from the book and invite students to break the word into smaller parts. Then put the parts together to decode the big word.
Use analogies	Show students how to use analogies by writing a word part such as *aw* on the dry-erase board and asking, "Do you know a word that has this part in it?" When students respond with *saw,* you say, "Yes, use *saw* to help you figure out other words that have *aw* in them." (Write *crawled* and *awful* on the dry-erase board.)
Reread for clues	Select one or two unfamiliar words that were defined in the text. Guide students to read for context clues and use illustrations to determine the meanings of the words.
Use phrasing	Demonstrate appropriate phrasing, intonation, and/or expression. Then say, "Reread this part with me."
Attend to punctuation	Point out, demonstrate, and discuss the author's use of punctuation.

Description of Day 1

Discussion Starters for Transitional Readers	
Goal	**Discussion Starters**
Ask and answer questions about key details	• What questions do you have about _____? • Reread page ____ to find out _____. (Ask a text-dependent question.) • What did you learn (or notice) about (the character, setting, problem, topic, etc.)?
Retell stories, including key details, and demonstrate understanding of the central message or lesson	• Find the most important part of the story. Why is it important? • What important facts did you learn in this book? • What happened at the beginning, middle, and end? • Let's retell the story together. • What lesson did the character learn? • What was the big idea in this story? • What lesson did you learn from this story? • Why did the author write this book?
Describe and analyze characters, settings, and major events in a story, using key details	• Describe the setting. Did the setting change? Find that part in the story. • Describe the character. How did the character change in this story? • Find the page that shows how the character felt at the beginning (or middle, or end). Turn and talk. • What was the most important event? Find that part in the book. Why was it important? • How were the characters the same (or different)?
Identify words/phrases that suggest feelings or appeal to the senses	• What word on page _____ tells you how the character felt? • What words on page _____ did the author use to describe how the rain forest looks (or sounds)?
Explain major differences between stories and informational books	• How is this informational book about crows different from the fiction book we read called Mia and the Crow? • What facts about crows were in both books?

Transitional

Identify who is telling the story at various points in a text	• Who is telling the story on page _____? • Who is talking on page _____? • Let's reread page _____ together and take turns reading the parts of each character. • Who said _____ on page _____?
Use illustrations and details in a story to describe its characters, setting, or events	• Find the picture that tells you the setting in the story. • Find two pictures that show how the character's feelings change. • What does the diagram on page _____ tell you about sea horses? • Find the picture that describes the problem. • Find the picture that describes how the problem was solved. • What picture best describes Mia's feelings about the injured crow?
Compare and contrast the adventures and experiences of characters in stories	• How do _____ and _____ feel about their adventure? • How are the characters' experiences different (or similar)? • How does each character react to the flood?

Transitional Video Link 5

Watch Jan guiding a discussion of a nonfiction text.

> *See Chapter 7 for more on teaching comprehension strategies, including the Very Important Part (V.I.P.) Nonfiction, page 268, and Turning Headings Into Questions, page 269. Video links for specific strategies can be found on pages 4–5.*

DESCRIPTION OF DAY 2

The Day 2 lesson has three basic components:
- Read the Book With Prompting
- Discuss and Teach
- Word Study Activity

Read the Book With Prompting (10–15 minutes)

Follow the procedures for Read the Book With Prompting on Day 1.

Discuss and Teach (3–5 minutes)

Follow the procedures for Discuss and Teach on Day 1.

Word Study Activity (3–5 minutes)

Transitional readers who struggle with decoding and spelling benefit from systematic word study instruction done in meaningful and interactive ways. By this stage, most students have mastered letters and sounds, but they may have difficulty decoding and spelling multisyllabic words and words with the silent-*e* feature and vowel patterns. If students misrepresent short vowels, digraphs, and blends, use the word study procedures for early readers on pages 131–137.

Target a skill for word study

To determine which phonetic feature to target, use a Word Knowledge Inventory, reading miscues, and spelling errors. If students don't understand the silent-*e* feature, use an analogy chart to help students see the difference between words that have short vowels and long vowels (silent *e*). If they struggle to read and write words with vowel teams such as *oi*, *ou*, and *ai*, use an analogy chart to show them how to use words they know to spell words they don't know. Also use an analogy chart if they need to learn how to add inflectional endings. If long words are difficult for students to decode, Make and Break a Big Word will show them how to take a word apart.

> **Tip**
>
> Insert an analogy chart template into a clear sheet protector. Students can reuse the template for the next word study lesson.

Appendix I

> **Tip**
>
> If some students in the group missed a digraph or blend on the Word Knowledge Inventory, include that skill in the words students write on the analogy chart.

Target Skill	Spelling Errors	Word Study Activity
Silent *e*	*bick* for *bike*	Analogy charts
Vowel patterns	*fond* for *found*	Analogy charts
Endings	*claping* for *clapping*	Analogy charts
Multisyllabic words	*entrng* for *entering*	Make and Break a Big Word

Teach the silent-*e* feature

Distribute an analogy chart template inserted in a plastic sheet protector, a dry-erase marker, and an eraser to each student. Tell students they are going to use the chart to write words that have similar patterns. Begin by writing a CVC word and a CVCe word at the top of your chart. Students copy the key words on their charts. Discuss how the silent *e* makes the vowel say its name.

cap	name

Model. Say a word that matches one of the key-word patterns (*cap* or *name*). Show students how to segment the word at the onset and rime to hear the vowel sound.

For example, "Listen to the word *snap*. Does it have a short vowel like *cap* or a long vowel like *name*? *Sn-ap* has a short *a* like *cap*. I'm going to write *snap* under *cap*. I don't need the silent *e*. Now let's do the word *flame* together."

Dictate more words. Continue to dictate words that match one of the patterns and have students decide in which column they should write the word. Scaffold individual students when necessary. Complete the activity by having students read the words in each column.

> **Tip**
>
> If you have several students who struggle with blends and short vowels, use sound boxes to teach those skills. Follow the procedures on page 135.

> **Tip**
>
> Use only one-syllable words for the silent-*e* lessons. You will teach inflectional endings later (page 187).

Description of Day 2

c**ap**	n**ame**
sn**ap**	fl**ame**
fl**ap**	sh**ame**
sl**ap**	bl**ame**

Increase the challenge. Have students write words that have the same vowel sound (e.g., short *a* and long *a*), but do not have the same rime. This activity forces students to listen to the short or long vowel sound.

c**ap** (short *a*)	n**ame** (long *a*)
chat	snake
mash	grape
brag	spade

See page 137 for more examples of silent-*e* analogy charts.

Teach vowel teams

Always choose two patterns so students have to make a decision about which sound they hear. Since this is a sound sort (not a visual sort), do not choose two patterns that make the same vowel sound such as *new* and *zoo*. The key words students write at the top of their chart should be known words.

s**ee**	c**ow**

Model. Say a word that matches one of the key-word patterns. Show students how to segment a word at the onset and rime to hear the vowel pattern. For example, "Listen to

> **Tip**
>
> *Students often need help learning when to use the -ck at the end of a word. Use -ck words in the first column and silent-e words in the second.*
>
> | si**ck** | l**ike** |
> |---|---|
> | sti**ck** | sp**ike** |
> | sli**ck** | str**ike** |
> | sna**ck** | sn**ake** |

> **Tip**
>
> *If students have trouble deciding where to write the new word, teach them to break the word at the onset and rime (e.g., c-ow). This will help them hear the vowel pattern.*

Transitional

the word *sleep*. Does it have the long-*e* sound you hear in the word *see* or the /ow/ sound you hear in the word *cow*? Listen: *sl-eep/see* or *sl-eep/cow*. Say the words with me. Where should I write *sleep*? I'm going to write *sleep* under *see* because they both have the /ee/ sound."

Dictate more words. Dictate other words (preferably ones students do not know how to spell) that contain the same vowel pattern as one of the key words. Students should repeat the word and listen for the vowel pattern. Then they decide which key word has the same vowel sound and write the new word under the correct key word. If necessary, scaffold individual students. Teach them to underline the pattern in the new word so they can see the analogy.

> **Tip**
>
> *Expect students to overgeneralize when they learn the silent-e rule. A child may put a silent e at the end of any word that has a long vowel sound.*
>
> *You will teach them other combinations for representing long vowels when you teach vowel teams.*

s<u>ee</u>	c<u>ow</u>
sl<u>ee</u>p	n<u>ow</u>
d<u>ee</u>p	h<u>ow</u>
w<u>ee</u>k	pl<u>ow</u>

Increase the challenge. Once students understand how to use the analogy chart to write one-syllable words, dictate compound words and words with inflectional endings. Complete the lesson by having students read the words in each column. This makes the activity both a reading and a writing task.

More challenging analogy chart for vowel teams:

s<u>ee</u>	c<u>ow</u>
sl<u>ee</u>ping	pl<u>ow</u>ed
d<u>ee</u>per	sh<u>ow</u>er
w<u>ee</u>kly	fl<u>ow</u>er

Transitional Video Link 6

Watch Jan teaching vowel patterns with an analogy chart.

Description of Day 2

Teach inflectional endings

Select a feature to teach such as the doubling feature (e.g., *flapping*) or *e*-drop (e.g., *hiking*). Begin with two key words students know. Discuss the feature and dictate words that have the same feature. When you teach the *e*-drop lesson, emphasize that the *e* is dropped when adding an ending that begins with a vowel (*-ing, -er, -ed*), but is not dropped if the ending begins with a consonant (*-ly, -ful*). Gradually increase the challenge as students begin to understand and apply the rule.

Double the final consonant and add -ing:

stop	stopping
hop	hopping
step	stepping
run	running

Drop the e and add -ing:

like	liking
love	loving
hope	hoping
time	timing

> **Tip**
>
> The word study component can be omitted if transitional readers are proficient decoders and no longer struggle with complex vowels or multisyllabic words.

Increase the challenge. Include other inflectional endings (*-ed, -er*) in the analogy chart.

Double the consonant when the rime is two letters (e.g., op, ep, un):

st**op**	st**op**ping
h**op**	h**op**ped
st**ep**	st**ep**ped
r**un**	r**un**ner

Transitional

Drop the silent e if the ending begins with a vowel. Keep the silent e if the ending begins with a consonant:

like	liked	likely
love	loving	lovely
hope	hoped	hopeful
time	timer	timely

Make and Break a Big Word

Select a multisyllabic word with decodable parts, such as *suddenly* or *understand*, from the story. Give each student the magnetic letters to make the word. Have students clap each syllable in the word and use the magnetic letters to construct each part. Once they make the word correctly, have them break it into syllables, say each part, and then remake the word.

Tip

Save time by giving students a letter tray. Tell them which letters to select to make the big word.

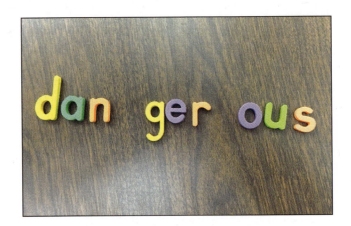

Transitional Video Link 7

Watch Jan scaffolding Make and Break a Big Word.

Description of Day 2

Begin with the easy analogies and gradually increase the difficulty of the task. Remember, these are examples, not a scope and sequence.

Easy Analogy Charts for Teaching Short and Long Vowels
(The rime and vowel sound don't change.)

cap	name	hit	like	hot	hope
clap	same	spit	bike	spot	rope
chap	shame	slit	hike	trot	slope
slap	blame	grit	spike	clot	scope
snap	flame	quit	strike	blot	grope

Easy Analogy Charts for Teaching Short and Long Vowels
(The rime and vowel sound don't change.)

run	cute	pin	dime	sick	line
fun	lute	thin	time	lick	vine
shun	mute	grin	slime	prick	twine
spun	flute	spin	grime	stick	shine
stun	brute	skin	crime	quick	spine

Harder Analogy Charts for Teaching Short and Long Vowels
(The rime changes but the vowel sound stays the same.)

cat	game	him	ride	hop	rode
chat	shake	chip	dike	shop	globe
mash	grape	spit	wife	spot	slope
brag	spade	crib	stripe	smog	spoke
snap	scrape	slim	shine	glob	those

Transitional

\multicolumn{6}{c}{**Harder Analogy Charts for Teaching Short and Long Vowels**}

Harder Analogy Charts for Teaching Short and Long Vowels					
(The rime changes but the vowel sound stays the same.)					
fun	**huge**	**hat**	**same**	**hot**	**note**
stud	fume	chat	brake	spot	spoke
much	mule	champ	quake	drop	stone
brush	crude	last	grave	blog	drove
bump	tube	slam	whale	shock	quote

Hardest Analogy Charts for Teaching Short and Long Vowels					
(Both the rime and vowel sound change.)					
back (short)	**cake** (long)	**did** (short)	**dime** (long)	**pot** (short)	**rope** (long)
duck	trade	spot	broke	drag	drone
clock	pride	crab	spike	skip	frame
stick	chime	flip	smoke	slim	slime
quack	blame	squid	huge	scrap	scrape

Hardest Analogy Charts for Teaching Short and Long Vowels					
(Both the rime and vowel sound change.)					
sun (short)	**name** (long)	**duck** (short)	**made** (long)	**cat** (short)	**ride** (long)
duck	trade	slick	plane	chug	rule
clock	pride	snuck	size	slid	slide
stick	chime	clock	stroke	strip	stripe
quack	blame	check	alone	smog	prune

Description of Day 2

Always choose patterns with two different sounds. Easier patterns are listed on the top rows.

Sample Analogy Charts for Teaching Vowel Patterns

d<u>ay</u>	b<u>all</u>	c<u>ar</u>	<u>and</u>	s<u>ee</u>	f<u>or</u>
m<u>ay</u>	f<u>all</u>	f<u>ar</u>	s<u>and</u>	tr<u>ee</u>	f<u>or</u>t
pr<u>ay</u>	sm<u>all</u>	c<u>ar</u>d	st<u>and</u>	sw<u>ee</u>p	sp<u>or</u>t
st<u>ay</u>ed	sm<u>all</u>er	st<u>ar</u>ted	br<u>and</u>ed	sl<u>ee</u>ping	st<u>or</u>my
spr<u>ay</u>ing	t<u>all</u>est	h<u>ar</u>mful	str<u>and</u>ed	sw<u>ee</u>per	sc<u>or</u>ched

z<u>oo</u>	h<u>er</u>	l<u>oo</u>k	g<u>ir</u>l	<u>ea</u>t	m<u>oo</u>n
sh<u>oo</u>t	g<u>er</u>m	sh<u>oo</u>k	b<u>ir</u>d	tr<u>ea</u>t	p<u>oo</u>l
sm<u>oo</u>th	und<u>er</u>	br<u>oo</u>k	th<u>ir</u>d	dr<u>ea</u>m	sp<u>oo</u>n
gr<u>oo</u>m	ov<u>er</u>	st<u>oo</u>d	sh<u>ir</u>t	ch<u>ea</u>ting	sch<u>oo</u>l
sc<u>oo</u>ter	moth<u>er</u>	cr<u>oo</u>ked	f<u>ir</u>mly	t<u>ea</u>cher	sn<u>oo</u>py

Transitional

sn**ow**	s**aw**	b**oa**t	b**oy**	**out**	n**ight**
bl**ow**	j**aw**	c**oa**t	j**oy**	p**out**	fr**ight**
kn**ow**	cl**aw**	fl**oa**t	t**oy**s	sh**out**ed	m**igh**ty
gr**ow**ing	l**aw**n	c**oa**ch	enj**oy**	sp**out**	f**igh**ter
unkn**ow**n	**aw**ful	t**oa**ster	j**oy**ful	m**out**h	sl**igh**tly

r**ai**n	c**ow**	**oi**l	n**ew**	c**are**	bl**ue**
tr**ai**n	h**ow**	sp**oi**l	f**ew**	sh**are**	gl**ue**
st**ai**n	cl**ow**n	p**oi**nt	gr**ew**	c**are**ful	cl**ue**
r**ai**ned	cr**ow**ded	b**oi**ling	st**ew**	b**are**ly	tr**ue**
p**ai**nful	d**ow**nt**ow**n	av**oi**ded	n**ew**ly	c**are**fully	cl**ue**less

Description of Day 2

eight	found	cause	fur	head	could
weight	round	because	burn	dead	would
eighty	ground	haunt	curl	bread	should
weightless	around	haunted	church	heavy	
neighbor	pounded		hurting	spread	

girl	saw	out	night	eat	rain
squirt	drawn	sprout	bright	sneak	sprain
swirling	squawk	mouthful	rightful	squeak	braid
twirled	thawed	proudly	lightning	squeal	waited
thirsty	crawling	grouchy	frightful	squeaky	faithful

Transitional

DESCRIPTION OF DAY 3

Day 3 is devoted entirely to guided writing.

Guided Writing *(20 minutes)*

Understand the rationale for guided writing

Guided writing doesn't take the place of writing workshop; it supports it. During writing workshop, students independently write at their desks while you circulate and confer with individuals. In guided writing, students complete the response at the table with your support. It is coached, or assisted, not independent or assigned writing. The purpose of guided writing is twofold: it extends comprehension as students write about what they read, and it improves students' writing skills, since you are working with them side by side.

> **Tip**
> Use handwriting paper in the guided writing journal so students have a scaffold for letter formation.

Gather materials

Each student will need a writing journal, a pencil, the guided reading book, and a personal word wall (Appendix K). If students need support for letter formation and handwriting, use lined paper in the journals and provide an individual alphabet strip.

My Word Wall. Have students use their personal word wall as a spelling resource. Although you have taught students how to spell sight words during emergent and early guided reading lessons, they will need to use a spelling resource as their written responses become more sophisticated. The personal word wall includes words elementary students most frequently misspell. You can personalize the word wall by downloading the electronic version and deleting words students already know. Add other words students frequently misspell. The goal is for students to quickly locate a word and copy it correctly in their journal. You may have to show them how to use the alphabetical framework to locate a word. Make additional copies of the personal word wall for students to use during writing workshop.

Appendix K

Have realistic expectations for spelling

Don't expect perfect spelling during guided writing. However, phonetically regular words and words on the word wall should be spelled correctly. Praise students when

Description of Day 3

they use complex vocabulary, and encourage them to use the book as a spelling resource or say the word slowly and write the sounds they hear. There are three steps to transitional guided writing:

1. Select a response format.
2. Help students create a plan or simple concept map.
3. Coach students as they write.

> **Tip**
> *Vary the response format so students experience different ways they can respond to a text.*

Select a response format

Before you meet with students, select a response that fits the structure of the book and supports the comprehension focus for the lesson. During this 20-minute component, you can expect students to write one or two paragraphs. See the following two charts for some suggestions.

Response Formats for Transitional Readers	
Comprehension Focus	**Fiction and Narrative Texts**
Beginning-Middle-End (B-M-E)	Students write about the beginning, middle, and end of the story. Help students plan by generating a few key words for each part. Students then use the key words to summarize the story by sequencing important events. Gradually release your support until students independently create a key-word plan. Give each student the B-M-E card (Appendix N).
Five-Finger Retell	Students use this format after independently writing a B-M-E. Generate a few key words for each element of the Five-Finger Retell: characters, setting, problem, events, and ending. Students write three paragraphs. The first paragraph describes the main characters, setting, and problem. The second paragraph summarizes important events from the beginning and middle of the story. The final paragraph describes how the story ended. Give each student the Five-Finger Retell card (Appendix N).
Somebody-Wanted-But-So	Students use this framework to summarize the gist of the story by describing what the character wanted to achieve (somebody-wanted), what obstacles stood in the way of achieving this goal (but), and how the problem was solved (so) (Macon, Bewell, & Vogt, 1991). For a complex story, students can add "then." For example, *Clare (somebody) wanted to try out for the pirate role in the school play, but she was afraid to do it by herself so she brought the parrot with her. Then the parrot sat on her shoulder and gave her courage.* Give each student the SWBS card (Appendix N).

Problem and Solution	Students describe the character's problem and then explain how the problem was solved. Give each student the Problem-Solution card (Appendix N).
Problem (Feelings) and Solution (Feelings)	Students include the character's feelings as they describe the problem and solution of the story. For example, *Clare's problem was that she felt shy because she didn't want to try out for the play by herself. She solved her problem by bringing her pet parrot to the tryout. That helped her feel more confident.*
Track the Character's Feelings for the B-M-E	Students summarize the major events in the plot by recalling the character's feelings and what caused those feelings. Before students write, record several "feeling" words on sticky notes and distribute them to students. Use the Character Feelings and Traits chart (Appendix M) for descriptive words they might not think of on their own. Students use these words to write about the character's feelings during each part of the story. For example: | B	M	E
---	---	---
excited	terrified	proud	 *In the beginning, Clare felt excited because it was the first time she was going to ride a pony. In the middle, the pony took off running. Clare was terrified she would fall off. At the end of the story, Clare was proud that she had learned how to ride a pony.* (Appendix N)
V.I.P.—Very Important Part	During guided reading, students use sticky notes to mark important parts of the plot. For their guided writing response, students write about the pages they marked to summarize and sequence the most important events in the story (adapted from Hoyt, 1999).
Chapter Summaries	If the book has short chapters, students select a chapter to summarize. Before students write, list some key words on sticky notes and have students select the key words that match the chapter they are summarizing. Students use the key words, chapter titles, and illustrations to write a summary about their assigned chapter.
Use the Discussion Prompt	Students write about the question you discussed on Day 1 or Day 2. For example: *How are the characters similar (or different)?* *Choose three important pictures (B-M-E) and write about them.* *What is the central message or theme?* *How does the character change? Why does the character change?*

Description of Day 3

Response Formats for Transitional Readers	
Comprehension Focus	**Nonfiction and Informational Texts**
Write From the Index or Glossary	Students use words from the index or glossary to write facts about the book.
Chapter Summaries	Students write about one chapter in the book. While students read the book on Day 1 and Day 2, have them write one key word per page on sticky notes that you insert ahead of time in their books. On Day 3, students use the key words to write sentences about their assigned chapter.
Compare/Contrast	Students select two topics from the table of contents or index and write one paragraph describing how the topics are alike and one paragraph telling how they are different. Give each student the Compare/Contrast card (Appendix N).
Write Key Facts About an Illustration or Text Feature	Students describe what they learned from an important illustration, chart, map, diagram, etc.
Write Three Questions About the Topic and Answer Them	Students make a flap book with the questions on the outside of the flap and the answers under the flap.

Transitional Video Link 8

Watch Jan teaching guided writing.

Tip

Use your district or state writing standards to plan the response format.

Tip

If your reading assessments require that students write about the book, use the various question stems on those assessments as writing prompts.

Help students plan with key words

Before students begin to write, take two or three minutes to help them create a key-word plan (concept map). Use sticky notes or an easel to list a few important words they should use. Planning with key words helps students stay focused and organized as they write.

Coach students as they write

As students write their ideas (not dictated sentences), circulate among the group and assist individuals as appropriate. As you read what students have written, you will make on-the-spot decisions based on the strengths and needs of individual students. Think of these interactions as mini writing conferences. The goal of each interaction is not to fix the writing but to teach something that will make the student a better writer. You will attend to some errors and issues and let others go, depending on the individual needs of each student. Use the Prompts and Scaffolds for Transitional Writers on pages 199–200 as you confer with each student. Write the target skill you addressed on a sticky note to remind the student what to do. After the lesson, have students put the sticky note in their writing workshop folder so they can work on that skill during independent writing.

> **Tip**
>
> If students need more scaffolding, have them insert the key-word sticky notes on the appropriate pages in their books. When students write about the beginning, they find the first sticky note and use the picture on that page to get ideas about what to write.

> **Tip**
>
> Encourage students to use their books as a resource, but do not allow them to copy directly from the book.

Prompts and Scaffolds for Transitional Writers

Goal	Sticky Note	Prompts and Scaffolds
Remembering the message being attempted	*Say each word as you write.*	*Tell me what you want to write. Say each word as you write it.*
Word spacing	*Put a space between words.*	*Pick up your pencil and move it over after you write each word.* (If necessary, draw a line for each word in the sentence until students start to space independently.)
Letter formation	*Use an alphabet strip.*	Give students an alphabet guide to support letter formation.
Legible handwriting	*Write slower and use the lines.*	Teach students how to use handwriting paper. Prompt students to use only lowercase letters except at the beginning of a sentence.
Phonetic spelling	*Say words slowly.*	During word study *and* guided writing, use sound boxes to help students segment sounds in one-syllable words (see page 135 for directions). Students need to get in the habit of saying words softly and slowly when they need to write a word they don't know how to spell. This will help them hear and record the sounds. Sound boxes provide an additional scaffold to help students. The goal at this point is phonetic spelling. Do not correct misspelled words if they are spelled phonetically.
Writing sentences that make sense and follow standard structure	*Say each word as you write.*	Orally rehearse each sentence with students and gently correct structure if necessary. Ask students to repeat the sentence, using standard structure. Encourage short sentences students can remember. Students should say each word softly as they write the sentence.
Monitoring for meaning	*Reread with your eraser.*	If students leave out words, remind them to say each word softly as they write it. This slows down the writing process so they are writing what they are thinking. After they write each sentence, remind them to slowly reread each sentence using the pencil eraser to point to each word. This helps them monitor for meaning and find words they left out of the sentence.
Standard spelling	*Use the word wall.*	Teach students how to use My Word Wall (Appendix K) to find frequently misspelled words. Praise them when you see them using the word wall, and draw a star on the top of their paper. Also encourage students to use the guided reading book as a spelling resource.

Complete sentences	Use only one "and" in each sentence.	If you notice students using *and* or *then* to form a series of run-on sentences, tell them they can only have one *and* (or *then*) per sentence. If the sentence lacks a subject or verb, teach students to orally rehearse each sentence using one or two key words from their plan.
Punctuation (periods)	Don't forget the periods.	Prompt students to rehearse the sentence and make a fist after saying the last word. The fist is a physical reminder to use a period.
Capital letters	Use capital letters at the beginning of a sentence.	Prompt students to check the word that follows each period to see if it begins with a capital letter. Always teach periods before you target capital letters. If students mix uppercase and lowercase letters while writing, tell them they can only use capital letters for the first word of the sentence and for a character's name.
Spelling multisyllabic words	Clap big words.	Many transitional writers misspell multisyllabic words. Teach them to clap the parts of big words and stretch out each part as they write it. Use Make and Break a Big Word during word study.
Focus and ideas	Use your plan.	If students lack focus or ideas for writing, the key-word plan is a great scaffold. *Use your plan at the top of the page. Once you write about one of the key words, check it off and write a sentence about the next key word.*
Details	Write more details.	*Tell me more. What else did you learn about that? Turn to the picture that tells you more.*
Sentence variety	Use transition words.	Give students Shared Retelling cards (Appendix G) to provide transitional words.

Reflect on Next Steps

At the end of each three-day lesson sequence, take one to two minutes to reflect on the students in the group and consider your next teaching moves. Write a few notes about your students in the "Next Steps" box on the lesson plan. Here are some questions to help you determine your next steps:

- Did you choose the right text? Circle the text difficulty. If the text was too easy or too hard, carefully select the next book so that it offers the right amount of challenge.

- Should you select a different genre for your next lesson? If students did well with the focus when reading a fiction text, select an informational text for the next lesson.

- If students did not show improvement, evaluate your teaching. Do you need to be more explicit? Would a different focus be more appropriate for this group?

- Did you pinpoint the right focus? Did students learn what you were teaching, or do they need more lessons with that same focus? If students did not show improvement, evaluate your teaching. Do you need to be more explicit? Would a different focus be more appropriate for this group? Perhaps you noticed something in the lesson that you want to teach the group. Record your focus for the next lesson.

- Are some students ready to tackle texts at a higher level? You can regroup your students anytime, but make it a habit to consider your guided reading groupings about every two to four weeks. Write the name of any student who needs a different placement. To help make acceleration decisions, consider doing a running record on the last book he or she read.

- Is there a struggling reader in the group? If you notice a student lagging behind the others, there is a good chance the text is too difficult or some part of the student's processing system is breaking down. Write the name of the student and do further analysis. I'll show you in the next section how to analyze your struggling transitional readers to pinpoint the processing problem and plan a corrective course of action.

☐ Make a big word			
6. Next Steps	Text was: Hard Appropriate Easy	Next Focus:	Students to assess and analyze:

SAMPLE FILLED-IN LESSON PLAN

Transitional Guided Reading Plan (Levels J–P)

Students: Mai, Joey, Nara, Martin, Alison **Dates:** 4/15, 16, 17

Title/Level	Strategy Focus	Comprehension Focus
Life in a Tide Pool	Monitor	Retelling Key Details

DAY 1

1. Book Introduction *3–4 minutes*

Synopsis: A tide pool is a small pool of water you can find at the beach. Many interesting plants and animals live in it.

New Vocabulary
1. Define
2. Connect
3. Relate to Book
4. Turn & Talk

- predators
- camouflage
- tides

Model Strategy: Stop and reread if you don't understand. Use the pictures.

2. Read With Prompting *10–15 minutes*

Monitoring and Word-Solving Prompts
- ☒ Does that make sense?
- ☒ Reread and sound the first part.
- ☒ Read on. What would make sense?
- ☐ Check the middle (or end) of the word.
- ☐ Break the word apart.
- ☐ Do you know a word with this part in it?
- ☐ How can you figure out that word?

3. Discussion Prompt *3–5 minutes*

When is the best time to explore tide pools? Why? Find the evidence on p. 5.

4. Teaching Points for Transitional Readers *1–2 minutes*

Word-solving Strategies	Vocabulary Strategies	Fluency	Examples:
☒ Sound 1st part ☐ Endings ☐ Use known part ☐ Use analogies ☐ Break big word	☐ Look for clues ☐ Check the picture ☐ Use a known part ☐ Make a connection ☐ Substitute a word ☒ Use the glossary	☐ Phrasing ☐ Expression ☐ Dialogue ☐ Punctuation ☐ Bold words	Explore (p. 5) Reread and sound the first part

5. Word Study for Day 2 *3–5 minutes* (optional on Day 1 if time allows)

- ☐ Sound boxes
- ☒ Analogy charts
- ☐ Make a big word

Magnetic letters: a, d, e, g, n, o, r, s, u
dangerous

6. Next Steps — Text was (Hard) Appropriate Easy

DAY 2

1. Introduce Next Section *1–2 minutes*

New Vocabulary (4 steps): abandoned, plankton

Observation/Assessments:

Fluency Prompt
- ☐ Read it like the character would say it.

Comprehension Prompts
- ☐ What did you read?
- ☐ Why did the character say (or do) that?
- ☐ What was important on this page? Why?
- ☒ What caused _____?
- ☐ What are you thinking?
- ☐ What question do you have?

What causes tide pool animals to become camouflaged? What other ways do they protect themselves?

Next Focus: Vocabulary strategies

DAY 3

1. Writing Prompt
- ☐ B-M-E
- ☐ Problem-Solution
- ☐ Five-Finger Retell
- ☐ SWBS
- ☐ Character Analysis
- ☐ Ask and answer questions
- ☐ Event—details
- ☐ Key word summary
- ☐ Compare/Contrast
- ☐ Cause-effect
- ☐ V.I.P.
- ☒ New facts you learned
- ☐ Other: _____

2. Plan *3–5 minutes*

Choose three key words from the glossary and the index. Use the words to write facts you learned about tide pools.

3. Write *15–17 minutes*

Observations and Teaching Points:

Students to assess and analyze: Joshua

Complete the shaded boxes before you meet with the group. Add observations and notes during the lesson.

Analyzing Problem Areas for Transitional Readers

Transitional readers will progress at varying rates. Text Levels J–P have a steeper gradient of difficulty than those at Levels A–I. Although it is not unusual for transitional readers to stay at the same level range for four to six weeks, you should notice progress in their decoding, fluency, and retell. Of course, transitional readers in grades 4–8 will need to make faster progress to reach grade level benchmarks.

If you notice a transitional reader losing ground while others in the group make progress, take one or more of the following steps to discover the problem.

Reflect on your teaching

Have you provided daily guided reading lessons and followed the lesson framework with fidelity? Have you used assessments and your observations to identify a focus for your conferring? Record the prompting and scaffolding portion of the guided reading lesson and script your interactions with the struggling reader. Are you praising the student for partially correct responses? Fragile students need to hear specific praise and encouragement. Let them know when they "almost have it" and help them with the hard part. You might discover that you have overemphasized one part of the reading process and neglected another equally important part. For example, you might have prompted for decoding skills when the student needed to use meaning. Perhaps you have focused on complex comprehension when the student has trouble retelling. Always teach surface-level comprehension before you target deeper comprehension. Examine your prompts to make sure you are supporting a balanced processing system that matches the needs of the student.

Observe the student

Ask a colleague to observe the student during guided reading. The observer may see things you haven't noticed. Is the student taking risks or copying the student sitting beside him or her? The observer can take a running record on the student or script teacher-student interactions. If you can't find an extra pair of eyes, videotape the lesson and review it with your reading specialist or coach. What behaviors (teacher and student) do you notice?

It is also helpful to observe transitional readers during independent reading. Is the student engaged and interested in the book? Do you notice avoidance behaviors such as flipping through the book, gazing around the room, or distracting other students? Have a conference with the student and ask these questions:

- *Tell me about the book you are reading. Do you like it? Why did you choose it?*
- *Do you think this is a good book for you? Read a few paragraphs to me.*

At this point, check on the text difficulty. Many struggling readers choose books that are too difficult, because they want to read the same book as their friends. After the student reads a few paragraphs, have a conversation to check comprehension. If the book is too hard, ask the student if you can help him or her find a different book he or she would like to read. Book choice is the most important factor in reading engagement.

Analyze student assessments and create an intervention plan

Gather recent assessments such as running records, writing samples, Word Knowledge Inventories, and spelling tests. It might be helpful to videotape the student reading so you can watch eye movements and facial expressions. Meet with a colleague to analyze the assessments and share observations. Include other teachers who are working with the student, such as the reading interventionist, bilingual teacher, or special education teacher. The following Problem-Solving Chart lists the most common processing challenges for transitional readers. Pinpoint an area or two that might be interfering with acceleration, and use the suggested activities to create an intervention plan.

Directions for completing the Problem-Solving Chart

Evaluate each student in the following areas. Put a plus (+) if the area is a strength, a check (√) if the student has adequate skills in that area, or a minus (-) if the student is weak in that area.

Columns 1 and 2: Record the student's name and instructional level.

Column 3: Self-monitors. Does the student stop and take action when the reading doesn't make sense?

Column 4: Problem-solves Words. What does the student do to figure out

Mark Strengths and Needs (+ √ -)

Problem-Solving Chart for Levels J–P

Student	Instructional Level	Self-monitors	Problem-solves Words	Applies Phonics Skills	Reads Fluently	Develops Vocabulary	Retells	Writing	Reads Independently

Transitional

unknown words? For transitional readers to become successful decoders, they must initiate a variety of strategic actions to problem-solve words. Actions might include the following:

- Rereading: They repeat a word or phrase to access meaning or to confirm accuracy.

- Using analogies: They use known words or word parts to figure out unknown words (e.g., use *grow* to read *grown-up*).

- Taking apart unknown words: They segment words at the onset and rime (e.g., *ch-at*), find known parts (see *out* in *shout*), and notice endings (cover inflectional endings or break the word at the ending).

If word solving is a weakness, you'll notice the student miscuing on words with endings and multiple syllables. Ask the student to show you the parts in a tricky word to see if he or she knows how to break a word apart.

Column 5: Applies phonics skills. Three assessments will reveal the student's knowledge and application of phonics skills: a running record, a Word Knowledge Inventory, and a writing sample. Is there a pattern of errors? Does the student miscue on and misspell words with short vowels, blends, digraphs, or complex vowels? Are two-syllable words challenging to read or write?

Column 6: Reads fluently. Listen to students read familiar and new texts that are at their independent and instructional ranges. Does the student read dialogue with appropriate phrasing, intonation, and expression? Does the student attend to punctuation? Don't pay too much attention to the reading rate. It is more important that you try to understand why the student is not fluent than to measure how fast he or she can read. Here are some reasons transitional readers struggle with fluency:

- Text is too difficult
- Lack of automaticity with sight words (miscues on short, high-frequency words)
- Poor visual processing skills (doesn't scan left to right across the word)
- Lack of word-solving skills (evidenced by decoding problems)
- Not reading for meaning (using inappropriate phrasing, ignoring punctuation, etc.)

Column 7: Develops vocabulary. Vocabulary is a strength for some struggling readers. They have good oral language and extensive background knowledge. For others, especially dual language learners, vocabulary is still developing. You can discover a great deal about a student's vocabulary just by having a conversation or listening to the student retell a story. Check your anecdotal notes from guided reading to see if the student uses text clues to figure out unfamiliar concepts.

Column 8: Retells. Does the student recall what he or she read? Does the student engage in discussions after reading? (Use caution here. Some students are just shy or still developing English language skills.) If the student provides an adequate retelling that includes important events and ideas, even if he or she needed some prompting, retelling is probably not the problem.

Column 9: Writing. Collect a variety of writing samples from the student. What are the student's strengths? Does he or she have interesting ideas, good penmanship, or strong voice? What does the student need to work on to become a better writer? Use the Target Skills for Transitional Writers (pages 208–209) to identify strengths (+) and needs (-). During guided and independent writing, begin with specific praise: "I like the way you . . . ." Then say, "Today I'd like to help you . . . ."

Column 10: Reads Independently. Striving readers need massive amounts of easy reading in order to increase fluency and word-solving strategies. Unfortunately, the readers who need independent reading the most often read the least. Make it your top priority to increase the amount of time these students read easy, self-selected books for pleasure.

Target Skills for Transitional Writers

Student Name	Writes Legibly	Puts Spaces Between Words	Uses Phonetic Spelling	Makes Sense; Uses Standard Structure	Rereads to Monitor for Meaning	Uses Spelling Resources	Writes With Complete Sentences	Puts a Period at the End of a Sentence	Uses Capital Letters Appropriately	Spells Multisyllabic Words

Target Skills for Transitional Writers (continued)

Student Name	Uses Key Ideas to Plan	Focuses Writing	Includes Interesting Details	Organizes Writing	Uses Transitional Words	Uses a Variety of Sentences	Other

Transitional

NEXT STEP FOR STRUGGLING TRANSITIONAL READERS

Now that you have analyzed the student, meet with a colleague or reading specialist to create your next steps for acceleration. Discuss ways to build on the student's strengths and plan specific activities that address his or her needs. If another teacher is providing instruction to the student, closely collaborate to ensure you are working toward similar goals. Review the Suggestions for Intervention (pages 211–214) and select ideas that might help your student accelerate. Write your ideas on the Next Steps Acceleration Plan (scholastic.com/NSFresources) and share the plan with the parent and other teachers who are working with the student. Give the parent specific activities he or she can do at home to help the student. Each day, send home familiar books for the student to read.

Next Steps Acceleration Plan			
Reading	Word Study	Writing	Home

Try one of the Suggestions for Intervention for a week or two and meet with the intervention team again to evaluate progress. Use student data to assess the effectiveness of the current intervention plan. Brainstorm alternatives. The following chart includes suggestions for each focus listed on the Problem-Solving Chart.

Focus	Suggestions for Intervention
Self-monitors	• During guided reading, have the student whisper-read a page to you. If he or she ignores errors that disrupt meaning, wait until the student finishes the sentence and say, "Are you right? Did that make sense?" Ask the student to reread and find the error. Avoid pointing out the mistake. The student must find the error before he or she can fix it. At this point ignore errors that make sense. • Use nonverbal clues. Place a sticky note or card that says "Make Sense" in front of the student. If the student ignores meaning, don't say anything, just point to the card. When the student stops, rereads, or self-corrects, draw a star on the sticky note. • Specific praise. When the student monitors, smile and say, "I like the way you noticed it didn't make sense." Use praise even if he or she doesn't solve the problem.
Problem-solves words	• Teach word-solving actions described on the Word-Solving Strategies card (Appendix N). • Use the making words activity described on pages 133–134 during word study. This helps improve visual scanning skills and teaches students how to monitor for visual information. • Use Make and Break a Big Word (page 188) during word study. The activity will help students decode multisyllabic words. • During guided reading, give students a sticky flag to mark tricky words. Tell them to use their Word-Solving Strategies card to figure out these words. As you circulate, work with individuals on the words they flagged. • Choose guided reading books that have challenging but decodable words. Students need a great deal of practice using the strategies before they become automatic with solving words.
Applies phonics skills	• Use assessments to target specific skills students need to learn. Use the word study activities in Appendix A to teach those skills. • If students need work with short vowels, digraphs, and blends, use picture sorting (page 133), making words (pages 133–134), and sound boxes (page 135). • Most transitional readers need to learn complex vowels including the silent *e*, *r*-controlled, and vowel combinations. Choose one pattern that is familiar and one that is new and use analogy charts (pages 189–193) during word study. • During guided writing, show students how to use a word they know to spell an unknown word. Write the familiar word in the journal and underline the vowel pattern. Then have the student write the new word using the same vowel pattern. • Some students know skills but fail to apply them when writing. Encourage them to say each word slowly as they write to help them hear and record the sounds in the word. Noisy writing helps students apply phonetic skills.

Focus	Suggestions for Intervention
Reads fluently	• Select easy books for guided reading and prompt for appropriate phrasing and expression. If necessary, model fluent reading of a paragraph before the student reads it with you. • During guided reading, prompt for expression. Some students, especially dual language learners, will need to hear how dialogue should be read. Model and then allow students to practice reading other conversations. • If the student reads accurately but slowly, slide your finger over the words to push the student's eye forward. This Reading Recovery™ procedure (Clay, 2005) is very effective with transitional readers who have developed the habit of reading word by word. By covering the word the student is saying (and possibly even the next word), you are teaching the student to allow his or her eyes to move ahead of his or her mouth. Your goal is to get the student to look one or two words ahead of the one he or she is saying. You will need to listen carefully so you do not push your finger too quickly. If the student stumbles or stops reading, back up and try the procedure at a slower pace. • Have students read familiar books with a partner. Train upper-grade students to coach lower-grade students who need support with fluency. Students read and reread poems, chants, or familiar books. • Include Readers Theater as an independent learning activity. Students practice the script for several days to increase fluency before they perform for their class or another classroom. • If students have trouble tracking print, give them an index card to slide down the page. • Teach a tutor (volunteer or parent) to do neurological impress (Heckelman, 1969) with the student. Procedures for Neurological Impress: 1. Choose a text within the student's reading level. 2. The student and tutor sit side by side. 3. The tutor gently slides the student's finger under the print, making sure the finger and the voice are operating together. 4. The tutor and student read together for 15 minutes without stopping. 5. After 15 minutes (use a timer), have a short, but genuine, conversation about the book.

Focus	Suggestions for Intervention
Develops vocabulary	• Encourage conversations throughout the day. Use the "turn and talk" technique during read-alouds and content instruction. Teach vocabulary in every subject area. Include explicit instruction on prefixes. • During guided reading, introduce unfamiliar vocabulary using the steps on pages 176–177. When appropriate, use gestures and objects to teach new words. • During guided writing, list a few vocabulary words from the story for students to use in their writing. Draw a star on their paper when they include one of the challenging words in their response. • Before reading informational texts, have students preview the words in the glossary and use them in a sentence. • After reading informational texts, invite students to create sentences using the glossary words. • Teach and then prompt students during guided reading to use the vocabulary strategies described on pages 176–177. Select vocabulary as a teaching point after reading. • Choose guided reading books that have text support for new vocabulary.
Retells	• Select texts with a clear story line and picture support. Before reading, do a supportive book preview to lay a foundation for comprehension. • Use the STP strategy (page 259). Have students retell a page or two after reading, prompting them to point to the picture as they discuss the page. This will help them visualize the events when you ask them to retell the story. • Use the who-what strategy (page 263). After students read a page or two, they should say who the most important character was and what the character did. • Insert three sticky notes in the book. On each note, have students write one key word from that page. Have them retell a few pages using the key words they recorded. • After reading, use the Shared Retelling card (Appendix G) to do a shared retelling. Retelling will improve if students memorize the sentence starters. • Have students hold up a finger each time they retell a part of the story. Tell them they have to use all five fingers in their retelling. This will help them include details.
Writing	• Your first goal is to motivate the student to write more. Before writing, ask the student to draw a line down the left side of his or her paper to establish a section for a personal 20-minute writing session. Say, "How many lines do you think you can write in 20 minutes?" During guided writing, encourage the student to keep writing the entire time and praise him or her for meeting or exceeding (or coming close to) the goal. Resist the urge to correct the student's writing. • Once you get the student to write more, select one target skill to work on during guided and independent writing. Choose the easiest thing for the student to learn next. • Use the Prompts and Scaffolds for Transitional Writers on pages 199–200. • Continue to encourage and praise and be gentle with correction. These students are fragile writers who are quickly discouraged.

Focus	Suggestions for Intervention
Reads independently	• Know what interests the student. Most students who say they hate to read have not been successful readers. Our job is to know their interests and reading abilities so we can help them find books they can read and enjoy. Find a book that is appropriate for your reluctant reader. Say, "I found this book I think you will like. Read the first chapter and let me know what you think about it." Most students will not refuse a personal invitation. • Create rich classroom libraries. A well-stocked classroom library is essential for fostering engaged, joyful readers. There should be a wide range of levels and genres to meet every interest and reading ability in your classroom. Organize the books by topic, author, or genre so students can easily find books they want to read. • Initiate book clubs. Form a book club with students who have similar interests and reading levels. Allow them to choose a short novel to read together and then discuss. Striving readers are generally more engaged in independent reading if they know they are going to have an opportunity to discuss the book with a peer or teacher. I've seen some librarians create a monthly book club that anyone can join. Students meet with the librarian before or after school or during lunch to discuss and share. • Plan engaging, independent reading activities students can do when they are not in a guided reading group. These might include buddy reading, Readers Theater, or poetry clubs.

ADAPTATIONS FOR DLLs AND STUDENTS WITH IEPs

Studies show DLLs make progress when they receive small-group instruction in reading, writing, speaking, and word study (Avalos et al., 2007; Nag-Arulmani, Reddy, and Buckley, 2003). Maximize your guided reading instruction for students with special needs and DLLs by

- Selecting culturally responsive texts that match students' interests
- Modeling and supporting comprehension strategies during discussions
- Doing shared retellings
- Using gestures, pictures, and real objects to explain vocabulary
- Scaffolding students during guided writing

Dual language learners and students with special needs are often capable of engaging in higher-level thinking, but it might take them longer to process language. Some DLLs who appear fluent in English may be mentally translating to their first language, especially when reading challenging content. During guided reading, allow extra time for these students to respond to your questions. If a student doesn't respond, model the process or provide a sentence starter. Above all, create a positive and engaging learning experience that ensures student success.

MONITORING PROGRESS

Progress monitoring is a daily part of a guided reading lesson. Because you are working with a small group, you have the opportunity to notice new behaviors and record your observations on the back of the lesson plan or in a separate notebook. Also consider progress monitoring as a tool for evaluating your instruction. Have you selected the right focus? Is your instruction fostering acceleration?

Reading

The average rate of progress for transitional readers is one alphabetic level every eight to nine weeks. Of course, struggling readers need to make accelerated progress to reach grade-level standards. At least once a month, reevaluate your guided reading groups. Update the Assessment Summary Chart (page 168) using anecdotal notes and running records. This will give you a fresh look at your groupings. Move students into higher text levels when you see them repeatedly experiencing success in decoding, fluency, and retelling. If you did not have anything to teach a group, then the text was probably too easy. Match students with the most complex text they can handle with your support and scaffolding.

Writing

About every two weeks, use the Target Skills for Transitional Writers on pages 208–209 to monitor writing progress and select the next focus for instruction. Teach the beginning skills before you tackle the more advanced ones. Use the suggestions on page 213 to help students progress in these areas.

MOVING TO THE FLUENT LESSON PLAN

Consider moving students to the Fluent Guided Reading Plan when they can

- Self-monitor when meaning breaks down
- Decode multisyllabic words with little support
- Read with fluency, phrasing, and expression
- Retell a story by referring to important details and examples in the text

QUESTIONS TEACHERS ASK ABOUT TRANSITIONAL GUIDED READING

Is it okay to model a strategy (such as decoding a multisyllabic word) before students read?

Yes, especially if it is the first time you have targeted the strategy. You might write a challenging word on the dry-erase board and demonstrate how to break it apart. Remind students to always think about what would make sense in the sentence.

What is the purpose of guided writing? Does every transitional reader need it?

Guided writing has two goals: extending and assessing comprehension and improving writing skills. Most transitional readers need both. As they write in front of you, you can prompt, praise, and scaffold them to be more independent and proficient. Guided writing is also an excellent opportunity to extend and assess comprehension because students write about what they have just read.

How much misspelling should I tolerate in guided writing?

Always give transitional readers a personal word wall (Appendix K) during guided writing and expect them to use it. Tell them that if a word is on the word wall, it has to be spelled correctly. If you notice they misspell a word on the wall, put a dot in the margin of that line and say, "There's a word in this line that is on the word wall. Can you find it?" Once students locate the misspelled word, have them use the word wall to correct the spelling. You can download the word wall and personalize it for students by adding words they commonly misspell. If students misspell a word that is not on the word wall, but is on the book's cover, in the table of contents, or in the index, encourage them to use those text features as spelling resources.

What can I do to help my students improve their fluency? Some students are passing the benchmark for accuracy and comprehension, but they aren't reading quickly enough.

The first question to ask yourself is why they didn't pass the fluency test. I've seen some children lose a few seconds because they lost their place and had to reread. Others noticed an error and reread to fix it. I would never penalize a student for those actions. If the student is reading word by word, use the fluency procedures described on page 212. The bottom line, however, is always this: to improve fluency, all students need massive amounts of easy, enjoyable reading.

Should I sometimes use nonfiction text with transitional readers?

I love using nonfiction at every level, but it is especially important for transitional readers. As students advance to text Levels J and higher, it is often difficult for them to retell and comprehend nonfiction. So, when selecting a nonfiction text for guided reading, choose one that is at least one level below the group's current reading level. If there are too many unfamiliar words, students won't have the cognitive capacity they need for comprehension. Teach students to retell nonfiction before you target strategies for deeper comprehension. As you use the strategies described in Chapter 7, prompt students to access all text features to help them understand what they're reading.

> **Professional Study Guide**
>
> *Go to scholastic.com/NSFresources for a downloadable professional study guide written just for this book. In it, you'll find questions and activities about transitional readers to use on your own or with your colleagues in a study group or PLC.*

CHAPTER 6

The Fluent Reader: Level N and Higher

While fluent readers have a sizable core of words they can read easily, some do not want to take time to figure out challenging words. My favorite example of this is when I prompted a student by saying, "You said, 'contributions.' Look at it. Does the word in the book look like 'contributions'?" The student responded, "Doesn't matter. My word is better. Let's go with it!"

PROFILE OF A FLUENT READER

As readers gain automaticity with word recognition and develop efficient and flexible word-solving strategies, they move into the fluent stage. When they make an error (which is rare), they use meaning and parts of words to quickly self-correct. Although fluent readers are proficient decoders, they may need to learn strategies for monitoring comprehension (even when they make no errors) and exploring deeper levels of comprehension as texts become longer and more complex.

The lesson framework in this chapter is designed for students who fluently read texts at Levels N and higher. If you have students who read above Level N but need to improve decoding, retelling, or fluency, you should use the Transitional Guided Reading Plan and strategies described in Chapter 5.

Comprehension instruction is part of every guided reading lesson, but it takes center stage at the fluent levels. As students read a challenging text, they write short responses about their thinking. The teacher uses those responses as well as interactions with students to assess comprehension and plan the next teaching move.

Transitional vs. Fluent Guided Reading		
	Transitional	**Fluent**
Text Level Ranges	J–P	N and Higher
Focus	Monitoring, word solving, fluency, and retelling	Strategies for vocabulary and deeper comprehension
During reading	Students read softly to the teacher. Teacher prompts for monitoring, decoding, fluency, and retelling.	Students read silently and write short responses. Teacher prompts for deeper understanding.
Word study	Silent *e* and vowel patterns Inflectional endings Multisyllabic words	Spelling/meaning Connections Greek/Latin roots New Word List
Guided writing	Occurs on Day 3 of the lesson sequence Target: writing skills	**Optional** May occur after students finish reading the text Target: writing craft

For fluent readers, target higher-level comprehension strategies, including

- Identifying main ideas and important details
- Making inferences
- Summarizing
- Drawing conclusions
- Analyzing relationships between characters and ideas
- Evaluating the author's purpose

Although these strategies can and should be taught K–8 with whole-class instruction (see Chapter 7), the fluent reader is prepared to tackle them during guided reading.

ASSESS

Because instructional time is precious and should be guarded, I recommend streamlining the assessment process for fluent readers. A Word Knowledge Inventory (Appendix J) and an individual reading conference with a comprehension interview will give you enough information to begin guided reading.

Streamlined Assessments for Fluent Readers		
Assessment	How is it administered?	What does it tell you?
Word Knowledge Inventory	Whole class	Phonics, spelling, and word knowledge
Reading conference with comprehension interview	Individual	Instructional text level range Comprehension strategies

Word Knowledge Inventory

Most fluent readers are good spellers and will do well on the Word Knowledge Inventory (Appendix J). Some intermediate students, however, can read and comprehend grade-level text but are poor spellers, mostly because they lack visual memory or phonics skills. A word knowledge assessment will identify the word elements those students need to learn so you can target the needed skills during word study.

Reading Conference With Comprehension Interview

The most useful assessment is an individual reading conference. Select a leveled text or use an assessment kit such as Richardson and Walther's *Next Step Guided Reading Assessment: Grades 3–6*. Since fluent readers make few decoding errors, ask the student to read a few paragraphs aloud to check text difficulty. If the text is too difficult (less than 95 percent accuracy), select an easier passage. If the student makes only a few errors, have him or her read the rest of the passage silently. After the reading, have a conversation about the passage. Ask the questions that accompany the passage or use the questions listed on the appropriate comprehension interview (pages 223–226). You can use prompts such as "Tell me more" or "What else happened?" without affecting the rating. Listen carefully and record your observations. If the discussion indicates that the student has adequate comprehension on that passage, repeat the process on a higher-level text. Your goals are to identify the instructional level range for guided reading and determine which comprehension strategies you need to teach.

Leveling texts is not an exact science. If you've worked with leveled books before, you know that text difficulty is influenced by the reader's background knowledge, interests, oral language proficiency, and vocabulary. Don't be surprised if the student is instructional at several text levels. You'll use this information when you form your guided reading groups and select your texts.

Comprehension interview

Conduct a comprehension interview during a reading conference to assess specific strategies using the appropriate comprehension interview (pages 223–226). You can use a few pages from the student's self-selected reading book or a short, leveled text.

Assess text difficulty. Ask the student to read a few paragraphs to you. During the reading, record miscues. If the text is too difficult, select an easier passage.

Assess comprehension. If the oral reading indicates the passage is at an appropriate level, ask the student to continue reading while you follow along with another copy of the text or read over the student's shoulder. Don't take a running record. Tune in to what's happening in the passage so you can have a discussion with the student. Occasionally stop the reading and assess one or more comprehension strategies by using one of the questions on the interview. Prompt the student to explain his or her thinking or give you more details. Use the rubric to identify which strategies have been internalized (score of 3) and which need to be taught (score of 1 or 2).

Reflect and determine next steps. Once you've completed the reading conference and comprehension interview, reflect on what you learned. Ask yourself, "How can I help this student become a better reader? How will I use this knowledge to guide my instructional next steps?"

Comprehension Interview for Narrative Text

Name	Date	Text

1. **To assess text difficulty,** ask the student to read a few paragraphs (100–200 words) while you listen.
   - Record miscues, self-corrections, and reading behaviors.
   - If the text is too difficult (more than five significant errors), choose an easier text.

Notes on oral reading:

The text was   Easy   Slightly Challenging   Too Difficult
                    (no significant errors)   *(few errors)*   *(excessive errors)*

2. **To assess comprehension,** ask the student to read a few more paragraphs aloud (if you are not familiar with the story) or silently (if you have read the story).

Ask for a retelling.

Notes on retelling:

Retelling Rubric   **1**   **2**   **3**   **4**   **5**
                   (limited)   *(strong)*

Continue the interview if the retelling score is 2 or higher.

Comprehension Strategy	Questions	Rubric
Asks Questions Asks and answers questions to clarify or extend understanding	*What are you wondering?* *What questions do you have?* *What confused you?* Teacher asks a text-dependent question.	1. Limited—incorrect 2. Partial—low-level question 3. Complete—asks **and answers** higher-order questions
Summarizes Main Idea Provides a concise summary that captures the main idea and important details	*Tell me in one or two sentences what you just read.* *What is this part mostly about?* *What are the most important events?*	1. Limited—inaccurate summary 2. Partial—provides some details; misses central idea 3. Complete—provides a clear and concise summary; includes significant details

Comprehension Interview for Narrative Text, *continued*

Analyzes Characters Describes the character, drawing on specific details in the text Identifies specific traits or feelings	*Describe the character.* *Did the character change? How?* *How are ____ and ____ similar? How are they different?* *Why did the character say ___?* *What are you thinking?*	1. Limited—inaccurate description 2. Partial—uses text details to describe character 3. Complete—describes in depth, demonstrating inferential thinking
Understands Vocabulary Determines the meaning of words and phrases as they are used in the text	Select an unknown word that can be solved using text clues. *What do you think this word means?* *What clues help you to figure out the meaning?*	1. Limited—unable to define new words using text clues 2. Partial—demonstrates some understanding of the word but does not articulate strategies 3. Complete—provides correct meaning and articulates strategies for explaining words
Infers Draws inferences from text clues	*What did the author mean by _____?* *What were you thinking when the text said _____?* *What motivated the character to _____?* *What are you thinking about the character?*	1. Limited—no response or makes an illogical inference 2. Partial—states information directly from the text 3. Complete—shows inferential thinking
Evaluates Analyzes and makes judgments about the text Draws conclusions about the author's purpose	*What lesson does this story teach?* *What is the theme/author's message?* *Why do you think the author wrote this piece?* *Is this a good title? Why or why not?* *Why did the author include the part about _____?*	1. Limited—incorrect 2. Partial—refers to the text but does not come to logical conclusions 3. Complete—demonstrates evaluative thinking that goes beyond the story and reveals a depth of understanding related to the author's purpose, message, or theme

Reflection/Next Steps:

Comprehension Interview for Informational Text

Name	Date	Text

1. **To assess text difficulty,** ask the student to read a few paragraphs (100–200 words) while you listen.
    - Record miscues, self-corrections, and reading behaviors.
    - If the text is too difficult (more than five significant errors), choose an easier text.

Notes on oral reading:

The text was   Easy   Slightly Challenging   Too Difficult
                (no significant errors)   *(few errors)*   *(excessive errors)*

2. **To assess comprehension,** ask the student to read a few more paragraphs aloud (if you are not familiar with the story) or silently (if you have read the story).

Ask for a retelling.

Notes on retelling:

Retelling Rubric   **1**   **2**   **3**   **4**   **5**
                   (limited)   *(strong)*

Continue the interview if the retelling score is 2 or higher.

Comprehension Strategy	Questions	Rubric
Asks and Answers Questions Refers to examples in the text to explain what the text says	*What questions did you have?* *What question is answered in this paragraph?* *Teacher asks student to answer a text-dependent question.*	1. Limited—incorrect 2. Partial—low-level question 3. Complete—Asks **and answers** higher-order questions
Identifies Central/ Main Idea Identifies the main idea and important details	*What is this part mostly about?* *Which text features (heading, photo, etc.) help you determine the main idea?*	1. Limited—incorrect 2. Partial—provides some details; misses the main idea 3. Complete—provides a clear main idea; includes significant details

Fluent

Comprehension Interview for Informational Text, *continued*

Summarizes Provides concise summary	Summarize what you read in one or two sentences.	1. Limited—incorrect 2. Partial summary 3. Complete summary
Understands Vocabulary Uses strategies to determine the meaning of unfamiliar words	Were there any words you didn't understand? What could you do to help yourself? Teacher selects a challenging word for the student to define.	1. Limited—incorrect 2. Partial—doesn't fully explain the word 3. Complete—explains the word/ articulates strategies
Analyzes Relationships Identifies cause/effect, compare/contrast relationships	How are __ and __ the same? How are they different? What caused _____? What was the effect of __? What two things does the author compare?	1. Limited—incorrect 2. Partial—mentions details from the text but does not identify relationships 3. Complete—response shows analytical understanding of the text
Infers Captures unstated but implied information	What did the author mean by __? What made you think that? What were you thinking when the text said _____?	1. Limited—incorrect 2. Partial—states information directly from the text 3. Complete—shows inferential thinking
Evaluates Identifies author's purpose, point of view, and reasons Distinguishes between facts and opinions	Why do you think the author wrote this piece? How do you think the author feels about _____? What is the author's opinion about _____? What facts does the author give to support his or her point of view?	1. Limited—incorrect 2. Partial—refers to the text but does not come to logical conclusions 3. Complete—demonstrates evaluative thinking that reveals a depth of understanding
Understands Text Features Interprets and explains visual information	Why did the author include _____ (map, picture, etc.)? What can you learn from this text feature?	1. Limited understanding 2. Partial understanding 3. Complete understanding. Interprets visual information accurately
Describes Text Structure Describes overall text structure	Describe the overall structure of this text. Does the author use sequential, description, comparison, cause/ effect, or problem/solution? Give examples from the text to support your answer.	1. Limited—incorrect 2. Partial—describes correct structure but doesn't give examples from the text 3. Complete—describes correct structure and provides examples from the text

Reflection/Next Steps:

DECIDE

Now that you've analyzed your fluent readers and reflected on their strengths and needs, you are ready to summarize the assessments. This will help you make important decisions about grouping, instructional focus, and text selection.

Summarize the Assessments

Summarize the results of the assessments for narrative and informational text on the Assessment Summary Charts on the next two pages and at scholastic.com/NSFresources. First, record the student's instructional text level range for each genre. Under each strategy, put a plus (+) if the student is proficient and independent in using the strategy, a check (√) if the student is partially proficient but needs some scaffolding, and a minus (-) if the student demonstrates limited understanding of that strategy. The most common standards/strategies are listed, but you may decide to include others based on the standards you are required to teach.

Proficient (+), Partially Proficient (√), Limited Proficiency (−)
R=Retelling, Q=Asks and answers questions, S=Summarizes, V=Applies vocabulary strategies, AC=Analyzes characters, I=Infers, E=Evaluates

Assessment Summary Chart for Fluent Readers, Narrative Text

Name	Level Range	R	Q	S	V	AC	I	E	Other

Proficient (+), Partially Proficient (√), Limited Proficiency (-)

R=Retelling, Q=Asks and answers questions, MI=Main idea/details, S=Summarizes, V=Applies vocabulary strategies, AR=Analyzes relationships (compare/contrast; cause/effect), I=Infers, E=Evaluates, TF=Text Features, TS=Text Structure

Assessment Summary Chart for Fluent Readers, Informational Text

Name	Level Range	R	Q	MI	S	V	AR	I	E	TF	TS

Fluent

Form Groups

Use student data from the Assessment Summary Chart to form temporary, needs-based guided reading groups. Group students who are reading at the same level range and have similar instructional needs. For example, you may have several students reading at text Levels Q–S who need help analyzing relationships when reading informational texts. Perhaps there are others reading at text Levels S–U who need help with summarizing or understanding text features. Or maybe several students have difficulty evaluating the text structure or author's purpose. You may even have two groups with the same focus who are reading at significantly different text levels. Limit your groups to six students so you will have time to conference with each student.

If you notice areas where most of your students struggle, address those strategies in a series of whole-class mini-lessons (see Chapter 7). Target those same strategies in guided reading to give students practice using the strategy with your scaffolding. Some students will quickly apply the strategy while others will need more time. Reflect on your guided reading groups and adjust them as needed. Use anecdotal notes or an individual reading conference to make those decisions.

Pinpoint Your Focus

A powerful guided reading lesson incorporates a focus based on your assessments and observations. Always ask yourself, "What can I teach this group today that will help them be better readers tomorrow?" The Assessment Summary Chart does not list all the focus strategies for fluent readers. It is a useful starting point, but you will need to make decisions based on your students' needs and your state reading standards. Avoid writing "comprehension" as your focus. List a specific strategy (or two) on the lesson plan and communicate the goal to students at the beginning of the lesson. Students should know what they are learning and why they are learning it.

Proficient readers use a combination of strategies in flexible ways to construct meaning. The strategy is not the goal; constructing meaning (comprehension) is the goal. Each strategy you teach in guided reading should be put in the context of comprehending complex texts. As you teach a lesson, always explain to students how the strategy they are learning will help them understand what they read.

Although there is no sequence to teaching comprehension strategies, students need to understand the text at a literal level and be able to ask and answer questions about a text before they can analyze characters or draw conclusions.

Fluent Guided Reading Plan (Levels N and Higher)

Dates	Title/Level	Comprehension Focus	
DAY 1	DAY 2	DAY 3	DAY 4

Select a Text

Selecting an appropriate text for fluent readers can be challenging. You need a short, thought-provoking passage that compels students to read closely. If the text is too easy, students won't have to apply strategies to understand it. Students' body language and facial expressions usually let you know when the text you selected is too difficult. The text also needs to match your focus. Most texts can be used to teach a myriad of comprehension strategies.

In addition to using leveled texts such as *Scholastic's Short Reads for Guided Reading,* look beyond your book room; you can choose any short text (poem, magazine article, short story, or chapter from a novel). Read a few pages and ask yourself, "Does this text contain some challenging vocabulary? Will it give students a chance to practice the focus?" If so, it is a good text for your guided reading lesson.

The *Common Core State Standards for English Language Arts* states, "To build a foundation for college and career readiness, students must read widely and deeply from among a broad range of high-quality increasingly challenging literary and informational texts" (corestandards.org/the-standards, p. 10). Guided reading is the perfect format for meeting that goal.

Example of texts for fluent readers

Domingo's Cat, *a Brazilian Folktale*

Landslide Disaster! *a nonfiction article*

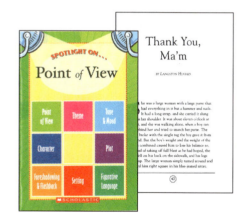

Thank You, Ma'm, *a short story by Langston Hughes*

Selecting Texts That Match Your Focus

Focus	Genre	Text Features
Self-monitoring and decoding*	Short stories Magazine articles	Multisyllabic words with prefixes and suffixes that students can problem-solve because the words are in their listening vocabulary
Retelling	Any text	A straightforward plot with a clear problem and solution Informational texts with short sections students can retell
Asking questions	Any short text	Interesting topics so students have questions to ask and share
Identifying main idea/details	Informational texts	Chapter titles, headings, and picture captions
Summarizing	Any text	Short chapters or sections students can summarize
Applying vocabulary strategies	Short stories Informational books Poetry	Some unfamiliar concepts that are supported with context clues, illustrations, or a glossary Poems with figurative language including similes and metaphors
Analyzing characters	Short stories Fables and myths	Dynamic, multifaceted characters whose actions illustrate character traits
Inferring	Short stories Poems Biographies Fables and myths Informational texts	Characters that have depth and complexity Texts that require the reader to draw inferences from dialogue, character actions, and thoughts Text structure that invites the reader to make inferences and draw conclusions
Evaluating	Persuasive texts Newspaper or magazine articles	An author's bias so students can evaluate the point of view
Using text features	Informational books Magazine articles	Text features such as graphs, charts, diagrams, and maps

* You probably won't have many fluent readers who will need this focus, but I included it just in case. I have had fluent readers who skip tricky words or mumble them instead of using strategies to decode them.

Gather Other Materials

Organize the following materials and place them within reach:

- Dry-erase board and marker (for introducing new vocabulary and demonstrating a strategy)
- Prompts for Fluent Readers (page 239)
- Reading notebooks (one per student) for writing about the text and recording new vocabulary
- Sticky notes and flags
- Comprehension cards (Appendix N)
- Short texts and/or excerpts from longer texts
- Timer

GUIDE

Although the Fluent Guided Reading Plan template has space for four sessions, the actual amount of time you spend with a text depends on the length of the passage. Some short articles, excerpts, and poems may take only one day to read, whereas a short chapter book (fiction or informational) could take several days.

The Fluent Guided Reading Lesson

Each day's lesson takes about 20 minutes. On Day 1, students briefly preview text features to familiarize themselves with

Appendix E

the content. After you introduce a few new vocabulary words, you may need to model the strategy quickly. I recommend that every strategy be taught whole group before you teach it in a small group. This saves time because students will already be familiar with the procedures. Then students spend about ten minutes reading the book while you confer with individuals. The final minutes are spent discussing the passage followed by word study.

On Days 2 and 3, students continue reading and writing. The last five minutes of each day is spent discussing the book and teaching a word study skill they need to learn. If they don't finish reading the passage, extend the lesson an extra day.

Guided writing occurs on the final day of the lesson sequence. This is an optional component for fluent readers who need writing support.

Overview of the Fluent Guided Reading Lesson

Day 1	Days 2 and 3	Day 4
Introduce a New Book	Read and Respond With Prompting	Guided Writing
Read and Respond With Prompting	Discuss and Teach	
Discuss and Teach	Word Study	
Word Study		

TEACHING COMPREHENSION

Write your comprehension focus on the lesson plan. Chapter 7 describes scaffolding steps and procedures for teaching comprehension during whole-group and small-group lessons. There are comprehension cards in Appendix N that match most of the strategies. Give these to students to help them internalize the strategy and respond to the text.

Video links for teaching specific comprehension strategies can be found on pages 4–5 and throughout Chapter 7.

DESCRIPTION OF DAY 1

The Day 1 lesson has four basic components:
- Introduce a New Book
- Read and Respond With Prompting
- Discuss and Teach
- Word Study

Introduce a New Book (3–5 minutes)

Spend a few minutes on Day 1 introducing the text and explaining the focus of the lesson.

Provide a synopsis

For example, "This article is going to teach you about landslides. You are going to learn what causes landslides and what can be done to prevent them."

Preview and predict

Now invite students to preview the text features and share their observations, questions, and predictions. To save time, have them share their ideas with a partner. Do not spend more than one or two minutes on the preview. You want to activate students' background knowledge and get them interested in the book.

Watch the clock! You need about 15 minutes for students to read, write, and discuss the book.

Introduce new vocabulary

Fluent readers should be able to figure out most new words by using vocabulary strategies. However, many scientific and historical texts refer to locations or events that may be unfamiliar to students. Briefly discuss them before students read.

There may be important concepts students would not be able to figure out from the text. Follow these four steps to quickly introduce the word or concept.

1. **Define it.** Prepare a brief, kid-friendly definition. Do not ask students to define the word. That wastes time and causes confusion.

> **Tip**
> Motivate students by choosing interesting books and articles.

> **Tip**
> Be enthusiastic about the text. Say, "You are going to enjoy this book." (If you don't think they will enjoy it, find another book!)

> **Tip**
> Keep a world map at your guided reading table to introduce important cities, countries, and locations. For example, "Today's text is about Mt. Everest, which is located on the border of Nepal and Tibet. Let's find Mt. Everest on the map."

2. **Connect it.** Make a connection between the new word and the students' background knowledge and experiences.

3. **Relate it to the book.** Tell students how the word is used in the story and direct them to an illustration if one is provided.

4. **Turn and talk.** Ask students to explain the meaning of the word or give an example to the person sitting next to them.

> **Tip**
>
> *If you have to introduce more than five words, the text is probably too difficult.*

> **Tip**
>
> *Modeling the strategy during whole-class mini-lessons saves more time for reading and writing.*

> **Tip**
>
> *Expect to scaffold for comprehension on the first day. If you don't have to scaffold, either you chose the wrong strategy or the book was too easy.*

State the comprehension focus

Be clear about the learning expectations. Tell students what they are learning today. Ideally, you modeled the comprehension strategy during a whole-class lesson. Think aloud and demonstrate how the strategy works. For example, say, "I didn't understand what I was reading, so I stopped and reread it a bit slower." Next, decide how you will scaffold students as they practice the strategy. The type of scaffolding will change as students read through the book. As students become more proficient in using the strategy, decrease your support. In Chapter 7 you will find progressive steps for scaffolding students as they practice a particular strategy. Always remember: the goal of a guided reading lesson is to support students as they construct meaning. Tell students how learning to apply the focus will help them become better readers.

Description of Day 1

Read and Respond With Prompting *(10–12 minutes)*

Read, respond, and confer

Students read the text independently and silently while they write short responses that match the comprehension or vocabulary strategy. To improve comprehension, always have students write as they read.

Have students write short responses

I usually have students write a brief response after they read a page or two. Then they read a few more pages and respond. The written response matches the comprehension focus. For example, if students are working on asking questions, they should write a few questions as they read. If inferring is your goal, they can mark the text where they made an inference and jot down their thinking so they can share their inference during the discussion. Writing during reading helps students organize their thoughts and keeps them focused on the task. Students' written responses also help you, as you can monitor their comprehension and know when to scaffold and support.

Occasionally, I'll have students write on a sticky note, but most of the time I have them write in reading notebooks. Sticky notes get lost, but a response in a notebook is a permanent record of a student's thinking.

> **Tip**
> Write a comment about each student. Use these anecdotal notes to plan your teaching point and your next lesson.

> **Tip**
> No round-robin reading!

> **Tip**
> Use informational texts with text features to help students apply vocabulary strategies.

Confer with individuals

While students read and write, circulate among the group and confer with individual students. Keep your conversations personal. You don't want to disturb the other students as they read. You can read a student's written response, ask questions, help clarify confusions, and probe for deeper understanding. Do not have the student read aloud. You already know the student is a fluent reader. This one-on-one time should resemble a mini reading conference. Have a short conversation and provide appropriate scaffolds that lift the level of processing.

Prompt for vocabulary

If you suspect a student is not using text features and clues to extend vocabulary, you might ask one of the following questions:

- *Were there any new words?*

- *Are there clues in the sentence to help you?*
- *Can you think of another word you could substitute for this word?*
- *Can you explain what this word means?*
- *Can you use any text features to tell me more about the word?*

Prompt for comprehension

If there is no new vocabulary to clarify, read the student's response and either clarify any confusions or prompt for deeper understanding. Usually your prompts will match the focus for the lesson, but here are some general prompts you can use to get started. Also use the Prompts for Fluent Readers on page 239.

- *Explain what you just read.*
- *Were there any confusing parts? What can you do to help yourself?*
- *What are you thinking? What makes you say that?*
- *What questions do you have? Ask me a question about this page.*
- *What was the most important thing you read? Why was that important?*
- *Can you summarize what you read in one sentence?*
- *What are you thinking about the character?*
- *What motivated the character to do or say that?*
- *How is the character changing? What's your evidence?*
- *What caused _____? What was the effect of _____?*

> **Tip**
>
> *Don't forget to ask a follow-up question such as, "Why do you think that?" or "What makes you say that?" The second question often helps you explore the depth of their understanding.*

Fluent Video Link 1
Watch Jan prompting students while they read.

Your scaffolding should decrease across a series of guided reading lessons until students independently analyze texts in thoughtful ways. Then it is time to practice a different focus or select a harder text.

Prompts for Fluent Readers

Goal	Prompts
General	*What are you thinking? What are you noticing? Tell me more about that.*
Self-monitor	*Did you understand what you read? What confused you?* *What can you do to help yourself?* (reread, ask a question, summarize, make a connection, use text features, etc.)
Understand vocabulary	*Is there a word you don't understand? What can you do to figure it out?* *Reread and look for clues.* *Does the picture help you understand that word?* *Is there a part you know?* *Do you know a similar word?* *Can you substitute a word that makes sense?* *Is the word in the glossary?*
Identify main/central idea and key details	*What is the most important part you've read so far? Why is it important?* *What is this part mostly about? What is the central idea of this section?* *Use the title, heading, and/or illustrations to describe the central idea.* *What does the author want you to know (learn, notice)?* *What is the theme or message?*
Summarize	**Narrative:** *Summarize this part using Somebody-Wanted-But-So.* *Who was the most important character? What did s/he do?* **Informational:** *Summarize what you read. Use the most important words in the passage. What does the author want you to know (learn, notice)?*
Ask and answer questions	*What questions are you asking yourself? What are you wondering?* Ask the student a literal (green) question about the text: *Who...? What...? Where...? When...? How...?* Ask the student an inferential (red) question: *Why...? What would have happened if...?*
Analyze relationships	*Find two ideas (concepts, etc.) that are similar. How are they similar?* *Find two ideas (concepts, etc.) that are different. How are they different?* *Flag an effect. Write a "what caused" question about it and answer it.*
Analyze characters	*How is the character feeling? What is your evidence?* *Why did the character do (or say) that?* *How is the character changing? What is causing the character to change?* *What is the character thinking? What are **you** thinking?*
Understand text features	*Why did the author include this text feature? How does it help you understand the text?*
Describe text structure	*What is the structure of this section? Why did the author use that structure?*

Discuss and Teach (4–5 minutes)

Discuss the text

After students read for about 10 to 12 minutes, you should set aside time each day for discussion and teaching. Write on the lesson plan a few thought-provoking questions aimed at lifting the processing level of students. They can refer to their notes and the text as they contribute to the discussion. Here are some questions for generating thoughtful discussions:

- *What was the central message/lesson/purpose? Why do you think that?*
- *How is this text similar to (or different from) others we have read on the same topic?*
- *How do the illustrations contribute to the message or mood of the story?*
- *What words would you use to describe the character? What's your evidence?*
- *What was the most important event? What motivated the character to do that?*
- *What facts (or opinions) did the author present?*
- *How did the author use reasons and evidence to support the main idea?*
- *Compare and contrast two ideas (or characters, events, settings, etc.).*

> **Tip**
>
> If one or two students dominate the discussion, use "talking sticks." Each student is given a small stick. After students participate, they put their stick on the table. Repeat the process when everyone has had a chance to share.

Fluent Video Link 2 ▶▶▶
Watch Jan guiding a discussion using shared questions.

Fluent Video Link 3 ▶▶▶
Watch Jan guiding a discussion about important events that support a text's central message.

Teach vocabulary

Select a challenging word from the text and model one or more vocabulary strategies. (See Module 7 on page 264.)

Word Study (1–2 minutes)

Since most fluent readers are advanced spellers, target a word study activity that helps students make connections between words they know and new words in the book. As Donald

Description of Day 1

Bear and his colleagues point out, "The most effective instruction in phonics, spelling, and vocabulary links word study to the texts students are reading" (Bear et al., 2012).

Make spelling/meaning connections

Select a word from the text that can be connected to other words in meaningful ways. For example, you might show students how the word *exhibit* (from the text) is similar to *exhibitor* and *exhibition*.

Explore Greek and Latin word roots

Select a word from the text that has a Greek or Latin root or affix and ask students to think of other words that are similar. For example, *intercontinental* has the Latin prefix *inter,* which means "between." So *intercontinental* means between continents or worldwide. Ask students to think of other words that begin with the prefix *inter* and discuss their connection to *intercontinental* (e.g., *interception, intercom, interchange, intermediate*).

Teach phonics skills

If you have a group of fluent readers who are transitional spellers, use the word study activities described in Chapter 5 to teach vowel patterns and rules for adding inflectional endings. This will improve their spelling skills.

> **Tip**
>
> *Save time by writing the two new words and their definitions on a dry-erase board. Give students the board and have them copy the words in their notebook after they leave the guided reading table.*

Have students add to their New Word List

Most word learning occurs as students read. In fact, Nagy et al. (1987) found that if a fourth grader reads 25 minutes a day, he or she will learn approximately 1,000 words in a year. Research also indicates that direct teaching on the meaning of words will expand students' vocabularies (Anderson & Nagy, 1991). Beck et al. (2002) recommends teachers target words that occur often in literature and are important for reading comprehension. She calls them "Tier 2" words. Close each lesson by having students add two words from the story to their New Word List. They might choose words you defined during the introduction or words you used as a teaching point at the end of the lesson. Encourage students to use the new words in discussions and in their writing. Periodically (every few weeks), test students on the words.

Appendix L

> **Fluent Video Link 4**
> Watch Jan coaching students with a New Word List.

DESCRIPTION OF DAYS 2 AND 3

Students continue to read and respond on Day 2 and Day 3 or until they finish reading the text. The components of Day 2 and Day 3 are the same as Day 1:

- Read and Respond With Prompting
- Discuss and Teach
- Word Study

Read and Respond With Prompting (10–12 minutes)

Follow the procedures for Read and Respond With Prompting on Day 1.

Discuss and Teach (4–5 minutes)

Follow the procedures for Discuss and Teach on Day 1.

Word Study (1–2 minutes)

Follow the procedures for Word Study on Day 1.

DESCRIPTION OF DAY 4

Day 4 is devoted entirely to guided writing. Again, this is an optional component but highly recommended for fluent readers who need writing support.

Guided Writing (20 minutes)

There are basically two types of struggling writers: those who yearn to write but lack the skills, and those who are reluctant to write because they lack the skills. Guided writing is good for both. If you notice students need extra support with writing, or if you want to challenge them to respond in more sophisticated ways, plan a guided writing session.

> **Tip**
> Praise students when you see them addressing the target skill.

> **Tip**
> Struggling writers need more teaching, not just more practice.

Description of Days 2, 3, and 4

Understand the rationale for guided writing

It is not unusual to find fluent readers who are struggling writers. Guided writing helps students improve writing skills and solidify or extend their understanding of the text. The writing is completed during the guided reading lesson with your support. It is not an assignment they complete at their desks. Use this opportunity to prompt and encourage students to apply the principles of good writing you taught them during writing workshop. There are four steps to fluent guided writing:

1. Analyze writing samples and pinpoint a target skill.
2. Select a response format.
3. Plan with students.
4. Scaffold students as they write.

Analyze writing samples and pinpoint a target skill

Analyze samples from students' independent writing to determine strengths and weaknesses. Identify a specific target skill for each student in the group. Some common target skills for struggling intermediate writers include

- Meaningful sentences
- Organization
- Focus
- Sentence fluency
- Spelling
- Details
- Capitalization/punctuation
- Transition words and phrases

> **Tip**
>
> *Choose a response format that is challenging for your group. Guided writing is a perfect opportunity to differentiate your writing instruction based upon students' needs.*

Write the target skill on a sticky note and place it in front of the student. Explain that as they write, they will be working on that one target skill. See the chart on pages 246–247 for suggestions for prompts and scaffolds.

Select a response format

Decide how you want students to respond to the text. When possible, connect the response format to your comprehension focus from the guided reading lesson. See the following chart for some examples of response formats for narrative and informational texts.

Response Formats for Fluent Readers	
Narrative Texts	**Informational Texts**
Describe a character, setting, or event, drawing on specific details in the text. *Summarize the major events (B-M-E).* *Describe how a character responded to the problem.* *Contrast two characters and their points of view.* *Write a poem from the character's point of view. If students need support, provide a few sentence stems such as* • *I feel . . .* • *I laugh . . .* • *I cry . . .* • *I worry . . .* • *I dream . . .* *Write about the author's purpose.* *Respond to a prompt (use your state standards).*	*Explain the topic using examples from the text.* *Describe a point of view and support with reasons from the text.* *Write an opinion, supporting your point of view with reasons from the text.* *Explain how an author uses reasons and evidence to support particular points in a text.* *Describe cause-effect relationships.* *Summarize a chapter using examples/ evidence from the text.* *Compare and contrast ideas.* *Describe the main idea and supporting details.* *Write about the author's purpose.* *Respond to a prompt (use your state standards).*

Plan with students

Before writing, students should always draft a simple plan or concept map using key words and phrases from the text. At first you will need to help them construct a plan, but gradually you'll be able to transfer this responsibility to students. Be sure to check each plan before students begin to write. See the chart on the next page for four simple plans that will help students organize their thoughts before they write. These can be adapted to a variety of response formats.

> **Tip**
>
> *Teach students how to plan. Don't allow them to use complete sentences in their plans. Teach them to use key words and phrases.*

Description of Day 4

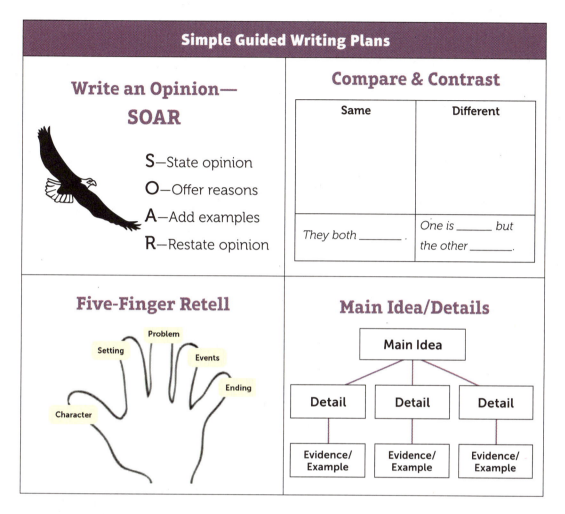

Scaffold students as they write

As students write, assist individuals as appropriate. Just as you differentiate your prompting during reading, differentiate your prompting during writing and teach skills that help students improve as writers. Teach whatever the student is ready to learn next—attend to some issues and let others go.

When you observe students applying the target skill, draw a star next to the target skill you wrote on the sticky note. After the lesson, have students place the sticky note in their writing workshop folder. This will help them make connections between what they are doing in guided writing and what they need to be practicing in writing workshop.

Once students internalize the skill during independent writing, select the next target skill for guided writing. See the chart on the next page for prompts and scaffolds to help teach target skills.

Prompts and Scaffolds for Fluent Writers

Goal	Sticky Note	Prompts and Scaffolds
Spelling	Use the word wall.	Teach students how to use a single-page personal word wall to find frequently misspelled words. Praise them when they use the word wall.
Checking for meaning	Reread for accuracy.	After you write a paragraph, reread it slowly and point to each word with your eraser. Make sure you haven't left out any words.
Writing complete sentences	Use only one and in each sentence.	For run-on sentences, say, You can only have one and (or because or then) per sentence. Start a new sentence.
Punctuating	Don't forget the periods.	Say each sentence before you write it and make a fist at the end. The fist reminds you to put in the period.
Capitalizing	Use capital letters.	After a period, the next word needs a capital letter. Remember to capitalize cities, countries, and people's names.
Spelling multisyllabic words	Clap big words.	If students have trouble spelling multisyllabic words, say, Clap the word and say each part slowly as you write it.
Focusing and organizing ideas	Check off words from your plan.	If students stray off topic or lack organization, help them create a key-word plan before they write. When they use the key word in a sentence, tell them to check it off their plan and write a sentence about the next word.
Adding details	Tell me more. Why? Describe a character's feelings.	Teach students to use a two-column plan. In the first column, they list key words for major events. In the second, they write key words for the supporting details. Students write one sentence about each event and add a sentence for the detail. For fiction pieces, encourage them to add dialogue or describe a character's feelings.
Using vocabulary	Use rich words.	Tell students to avoid common words. Less common words bring more value to the writing, so we call them "rich" words. Praise students for using vocabulary from the text. When they are writing about characters, distribute the Character Feelings and Traits chart (Appendix M).
Creating sentence fluency	Use your transition words.	Write some transition words on index cards and give them to students. Prompt them to use some of the words in their paragraphs. Fiction: *In the beginning, Then, Next, After that, After a while, Finally,* etc. Nonfiction: *First (Second, Third), For example, For instance, On the other hand, In conclusion, Above all, Therefore, Finally,* etc.

Description of Day 4

Target Skill	Sticky Note	Prompts and Scaffolds
Writing the introduction	*Use key words from the prompt in your first sentence.*	*What are the key words in the prompt? Use some of those words in your first sentence. What can you say?*
Creating sentence variety	*Combine two ideas* *While . . .* *Before . . .* *When . . .* *After . . .*	Teach students how to combine two ideas into one sentence by using adverbial clauses or time-passage indicators, such as *While, Before, When, After, At the same time,* etc.
Punctuating dialogue	*Use quotes for dialogue.*	When students begin to add dialogue, teach them how to punctuate a direct quote. • *Put quotation marks around the words that are spoken.* • *Use a capital letter for the first word in the dialogue.* • *Use a comma to separate the words that are spoken and the person who said the words.* (Jack interrupted, "Who took my book bag?")
Indenting paragraphs	*Indent each paragraph.*	Teach this skill once students know how to write a beginning, middle, and end. Give students three sticky dots. Have them write a B, M, and E on each dot. Then tell them to put the B sticker on their paper before they write about the beginning, the M sticker when they start to write about the middle, and the E sticker when they are ready to write about the end. This scaffold reminds them to indent a few spaces as they write each paragraph. You can use the "sticky dot scaffold" for writing any piece. Give students the number of stickers that corresponds to the number of paragraphs they will need. For example, if they are writing about causes and effects, they'll need two stickers—one to help them indent the first paragraph that describes the causes of an event, and the second to remind them to indent the second paragraph when they write about the effects. There are other issues to consider when deciding where to indent a paragraph, but this activity will help struggling writers begin to understand the process.

Reflect on Next Steps

At the end of the three- or four-day lesson sequence, take one to two minutes to consider your next teaching moves. Write a few notes in the "Next Steps" box at the bottom of the Fluent Guided Reading Plan. Reflect on these questions: *How did the lesson go? What did the students learn? Did you choose the right text and strategy? What are your next steps for moving students forward?* Think about the level of support that will be needed at the next guided reading session. Are some students ready to tackle texts at a higher level? Write the name of any student who needs a different placement. You can regroup students anytime, but make it a habit to consider your guided reading groupings about every two weeks.

6. Next Steps	Text was: Hard Appropriate Easy	Next Focus:	Students to assess and analyze:

SAMPLE FILLED-IN LESSON PLAN

Fluent Guided Reading Plan (Levels N and Higher)

Dates	Title/Level	Comprehension Focus	
	When Marian Sang/Level R	Analyzing Character Traits and Motivations	
DAY 1	**DAY 2**	**DAY 3**	**DAY 4**
1. Introduce New Book 2–3 minutes	**1. Before Reading** 1 minute		**1. Writing Prompt**
Synopsis: Marian was a talented singer who had trouble achieving her dreams because of her race.	Review strategy: When you come to a flag, record the motivation.	Review strategy: Flag important actions. Record the motivation.	Connect character traits to major events. What major events in Marian's life shaped her character?

2. New Vocabulary 1-2 minutes

Steps: 1. Define 2. Connect 3. Relate to Book 4. Turn and Talk

p.	Word-Synonym	p.	Word-Synonym	p.	Word-Synonym	**2. Plan** 3-5 minutes
2	velvety smooth	11	opera musical	17	trepidation fear	Flag two or three major events in the book. Write a character trait that is demonstrated by each event.
2	gospel religious	11	passionate emotional	22	momentous important	
6	terminal station	13	opulent rich	23	encore another	
7	tuition money	15	humiliation shame			

Event	Trait

3. Read and Respond 10–12 minutes

Model Strategy (if necessary)	Prompts for Fluent Readers	**3. Write With Prompting** 15–17 minutes
Flag p. 2—What motivated Marian to sing?	Explain what you just read. Were there any confusing parts (words, sentences)? How can you help yourself? What are you thinking? Why do you think that? What questions do you have? What are you wondering? Summarize what you read. What's most important? What motivated the character to do (or say) that? How is the character feeling (changing)? What caused _____? What was the effect of _____? What is the theme/author's message? Why did the author include this text feature? Explain it.	Observations and Teaching Points:

4. Discuss and Teach 4–5 minutes

| What motivated Marian to sing with her eyes closed? Why didn't Marian need encouragement to sing? | What motivated some people to be narrow-minded? (p. 9) Reread p. 13. What trait describes Marian on this page? | multitudes (p. 23)—How did Marian's trip to Europe motivate her? (p. 20)—What event made her dream come true? (p. 26)—Compare Marian to Dr. MLK. | |

5. New Word List 1-2 minutes

Word	Definition	Word	Definition	Word	Definition	
tragedy	sad event	passionate	emotional	multitudes	crowds	
velvety	smooth	humiliation	shame	trepidation	fear	

6. Next Steps	Text was: Hard Appropriate Easy	Next Focus: Make inferences from poetry ("I, Too," by Langston Hughes). Compare & contrast with "When Marian Sang."	Students to assess and analyze:

Complete the shaded boxes before you meet with the group. Add observations and notes during the lesson.

NEXT STEP FOR FLUENT READERS

Although guided reading is essential for struggling readers, all students deserve instruction at their reading level. I'm often asked about guided reading for advanced readers when I conduct staff development, speak at conferences, and visit schools.

Teachers and administrators at a middle school once asked me to model a guided reading lesson for six boys who had scored two to three years above grade level on their last achievement test. I remember how they swaggered into the room and slouched down in their seats at the table. I gave them a highlighter and a copy of "The Mending Wall" by Robert Frost. I told them to read the first stanza and highlight words, phrases, or sentences they didn't understand. All six quickly read the first stanza, then sat back and smiled at me. No one had highlighted anything. Then I said, "Turn to the person next to you and explain what is happening in this stanza." Total silence. "So, it looks like there were some things you didn't understand. Please reread a bit slower and ask yourself, 'Do I understand what I'm reading?' Highlight the part that is confusing you." They sat a bit straighter, leaned over the table, and went to work as I had a conference with each student. It was a wonderful lesson. The boys learned how important it is to monitor their comprehension and reread when meaning breaks down. The teachers learned that many advanced readers push through the text with minimal comprehension. Choosing a challenging text for these young men forced them to gear up their strategies and engage in metacognition. To challenge fluent readers, it's all about the text!

Tips for Planning Effective Guided Reading Lessons for Advanced Readers

Choose challenging texts from print and online sources:
- Newspaper and magazine articles about interesting current events
- Excerpts from longer pieces of literature or informational texts
- Acclaimed short stories
- Poetry. A well-chosen poem will make even your most gifted readers think more deeply.

Compare and contrast ideas, opinions, historical events, and famous people. Have students read two short passages on the same topic and group similar and different ideas on a graphic organizer.

Teach textual analysis. Students examine a text for craft and structure. Sunday Cummins' *Close Reading of Informational Texts* (2013) is a treasure-trove of strategies for helping students read for deep meaning.

Favorite resources for teaching advanced, fluent readers:

- Goodman, B., 1995. *Sudden Twists* (6th grade), *Encounters* (7th grade), and *Conflicts* (8th grade), Jamestown Publishers (a collection of captivating short stories by time-honored authors, such as Poe, O. Henry, and Bradbury).
- Harvey, S., and Goudvis, A., 2007. *Toolkit Texts for Grades 6–7*. Heinemann (a collection of short informational articles specifically selected to teach a comprehension strategy).
- Daniels, H., and Steineke, N., 2011. *Texts and Lessons for Content-Area Reading*. Heinemann (a collection of short informational texts from magazine and newspapers written primarily for middle school students).
- Rasinski, T., 2005. *Primary Source Fluency Activities*. Shell Education Publishing (a collection of primary source articles from American history).
- *Scope* magazine and *Junior Scholastic* magazine. Scholastic Inc.
- *Poetry for Young People*, Sterling (a series of books featuring kid-appropriate poems written by a famous poet).
- *Spotlight on Literary Elements*, Scholastic (anthologies that include engaging stories, poems, or plays that are perfect for teaching specific literary elements).
- *Guided Reading Short Reads*, Scholastic (full-color cards containing high-interest content and attractive illustrations. Texts are leveled using the Fountas and Pinnell alphabetic system).

QUESTIONS TEACHERS ASK ABOUT FLUENT GUIDED READING

Our book room only has sets of novels for fluent readers. Where can I find short fiction and nonfiction materials at the fluent level?

Although novels are wonderful for self-selected reading and literature circles, they are too long for guided reading. That said, some publishers do offer instructional support that targets key portions or excerpts of novels and other longer texts — portions and excerpts that can be used effectively in guided reading. For some of my favorite short-text resources at the fluent levels, see the tips on the previous page.

Should students write while they read or after they read a text?

They can do both. Writing while they read will improve comprehension and provide you with a way to evaluate their understanding. Having students write after they read a text can also be beneficial. Use the comprehension strategy you taught during the lesson or your state writing standards to create a prompt that will extend their comprehension and improve their writing skills.

What should I do while students read silently? Should I ask them to read aloud?

You don't need to listen to students read because you know they are fluent readers. Instead, have a short conversation about what they just read and what they are thinking. You might ask them if there were any words they didn't understand or parts that confused them. Ask them a question or simply say, "What are you thinking?" Listen carefully and respond appropriately. These interactions should resemble a mini reading conference.

How do I assign a reading grade?

Identify categories that measure student performance on independent, instructional, and grade-level texts. Establish expectations for each grading period and create a rubric with your class so students understand how they will be evaluated. See the following chart for some categories and expectations to consider.

Sample Rubric for Evaluating Reading

Category	Expectation for Each Grading Period	Exceeds 10	Meets 9–8	Nearly 7–6	Below 5–0
Independent Reading	Reads seven books from at least two genres				
Reading Responses	Completes seven quality responses				
Home Reading	Reads at home for at least 80 min./week and maintains a home reading log				
Guided Reading	Participates and responds thoughtfully during guided reading lessons				
Reading Strategies	Demonstrates growth in reading levels and strategy use				
Accuracy	Decodes grade-level text with at least 90% accuracy (running record)				
Comprehension	Comprehends grade-level text with at least 75% accuracy				
Vocabulary	Passes weekly (or biweekly) tests on the New Word List with 90% accuracy				
Literature Circles	Prepares for and participates in literature circle discussions				
Whole-Class Lessons	Demonstrates proficiency of the district/state reading standards				
Total	Add the points in each column and total across for final reading grade.				

Fluent

How can I help students improve their comprehension?

Follow the modules in Chapter 7.

> **Professional Study Guide**
>
> *Go to scholastic.com/NSFresources for a downloadable professional study guide written just for this book. In it, you'll find questions and activities about fluent readers to use on your own or with your colleagues in a study group or PLC.*

CHAPTER 7

Moving Forward With Comprehension: Pre-A to Fluent

Teaching comprehension doesn't have to be complicated. Although some teachers have been led to believe that they need to learn hundreds of comprehension strategies to effectively teach reading, that's just not true. In my many years as a classroom teacher and education consultant, I've come to realize that only 12 comprehension strategies are really needed. When you understand these strategies and how readers apply them, you will be able to teach comprehension with any text. They're essential for students to learn and important for teachers to teach, and they produce powerful results.

In the following pages you will find 29 easy-to-follow modules that address at least one of the 12 strategies listed on the previous page. Each module showcases one of my favorite scaffolds for teaching comprehension. After a brief description of the scaffold, you'll find step-by-step guidelines for teaching the strategy across a series of lessons. I use these lessons on a regular basis because they are easy for students to understand and practice.

THE TOP 12 COMPREHENSION STRATEGIES

	Strategy	The reader...	Modules
1	Comprehension Monitoring	is aware when meaning breaks down.	1, 29
2	Retelling	recalls information in nonfiction. retells story elements in fiction.	2, 3, 4, 5, 6
3	Developing Vocabulary	understands the meaning of a phrase or word.	7, 29
4	Asking and Answering Questions	asks and answers questions based on details in the text.	8, 9, 29
5	Identifying Main Idea and Details	is able to identify the main idea/central message and most important details.	10, 11, 12
6	Analyzing Characters	can identify character traits and motives.	13, 14, 15, 16, 17
7	Analyzing Relationships	expresses an understanding of relationships between people, events, or ideas (e.g., cause-effect or compare & contrast).	18, 19
8	Inferring	makes an inference or draws a conclusion from details in the text.	20, 21, 22, 23, 29
9	Summarizing	synthesizes information and prepares a condensed account that covers the main points.	24, 25, 29
10	Evaluating	understands the theme, author's purpose, point of view, and fact vs. opinion, and gathers evidence to support the author's point.	26
11	Using Text Features	uses the table of contents, headings, bold words, sidebars, pictures and captions, and diagrams and maps to clarify and extend his or her understanding of the topic.	27
12	Understanding Text Structure	understands how the author organizes the information within the text: description, problem-solution, cause-effect, compare & contrast, and time order/sequence.	28

How to Use the Modules

Most of the modules can be taught whole group at any grade using an appropriate picture book or a short passage. After you model one of the steps, have students work with a partner to practice it. Thread the strategy into your guided reading lessons during prompting and discussion. For guided reading, the specific steps described in the modules are most appropriate when students are approaching the fluent stage. In addition to the progressive steps for teaching the strategy, there are anchor charts, graphic organizers, comprehension cards (Appendix N), and suggestions for guided writing and independent practice.

Which Module Should You Teach First?

If you've used a comprehension assessment such as the *Next Step Guided Reading Assessment* (Richardson & Walther, 2013), teach the modules that meet the identified needs of your students first. Otherwise, begin with Module 1 and teach the lessons sequentially. I've purposely designed them to be easy to teach. I've also tested them extensively and found them to be effective and powerful. The goal, of course, is for your students to internalize the strategies and use them independently to construct meaning while reading any text.

Module 1

COMPREHENSION MONITORING

Stop and Use Fix-Up Strategies

Genre: Any

Grade Range: K–8

In a Nutshell: When students are confused, they stop and take action to clarify their confusion.

Whole-Class Mini-Lesson

Model: As you read aloud, stop and say, "I'm confused. I need to think about what I just read. If I can't remember, I need to reread (or ask a question, make a connection, etc.) to understand."

Guided Practice: Continue reading and have students hold up their hand when they are confused. Have them discuss their confusion and the strategies they can use to clarify the text.

Video Link

Watch Jan teaching students to monitor and use fix-up strategies.

Tips for Independent Practice

Students can use sticky notes or flags to mark places in their books where they were confused. They can record their thinking in their reading notebooks. During literature circles, students can share the strategies they used to monitor their comprehension.

Progressive Steps for Guided Reading
(Levels K and higher)

1. Distribute sticky flags and tell students to mark places in the text where they were confused. Confer with individuals about their confusions. Model strategies they can use to clarify their understanding.

> **Fix-Up Strategies**
> When you are confused . . .
> - Reread or read on.
> - Ask yourself a question.
> - Use text features.
> - Make a connection.
> - Replace words you don't know with words that make sense.

2. Students mark places where they are confused and write the question they are asking themselves. Students share one of their questions during the discussion.

3. Students mark places where they are confused and record their questions and inferences in their reading notebooks.

4. During guided writing, students write about a confusion they had and what they did to clarify their understanding.

Page	My question	I'm thinking
2	What's wrong with the girl?	She's rude and bossy.

Guided writing by a fifth grader:

When I read that the niece said, "You'll have to deal with me" I was confused. I wondered what was wrong with the girl. I was thinking she was being rude and bossy. After I finished the story, I decided she was tricking the man into believing he was insane. The author used this sentence at the beginning of the story to warn the reader that the niece was going to be important in the story.

Module 2

RETELLING

Stop, Think, Paraphrase (STP)

Genre: Any

Grade Range: K–8

In a Nutshell: After students read each page, they **stop**, cover the text with their hand, **think** about what they just read, and **paraphrase** (softly tell what was read using their own words).

Whole-Class Mini-Lesson

Model: Select a text with pictures. Read a page to students. Cover the text, point to the picture, and retell as many details as you can remember.

Guided Practice: Read a page with students. Students **stop**, **think**, and **paraphrase** with a partner. At first, allow students to use the illustrations. Then remove the picture support and teach them to STP by visualizing what they read.

Video Link
Watch Jan teaching STP.

Progressive Steps for Guided Reading
(Levels F and higher)

STP

Stop—Stop reading; cover the text.

Think—What did I read?

Paraphrase—Put in your own words.

1. **STP one page using the picture.** After each page, students cover the text and STP to themselves. As you confer with individuals, ask them to STP to you. Prompt them to use the picture to add details to their retelling.

2. **STP several pages using the pictures.** After reading two or three pages, students cover the text and STP to themselves. As you confer with individuals, ask them to STP to you. Prompt them to use the pictures to add details.

3. **STP in writing** (Levels K and higher). Insert one or two sticky notes on random pages. After students read a page that has a sticky note, they write their paraphrase on the sticky note.

4. **STP without using the pictures.** Students cover the text and the picture (using both hands) before they retell the page(s).

5. **STP in writing without using the pictures.** After students read a few pages, they close the book and write their STP in their reading notebook (Levels K and higher).

Tip for Independent Practice

During buddy reading, students can take turns using the STP strategy to retell a page. The listening partner can prompt for more details.

Module 3

RETELLING

Beginning-Middle-End (B-M-E)

Genre: Fiction, Biography, Historical Text

Grade Range: K–5

In a Nutshell: Students stop at predetermined places to retell first the beginning, then the middle, and finally, the end of a story.

Whole-Class Mini-Lesson

Model: After reading the first part of the story, retell what happened. Continue reading through the middle of the story. Stop and have students help you retell the middle. Read to the end and have students work with a partner to retell the ending.

Guided Practice: Create a B-M-E chart using symbols or key words for each part of the story. Have students work with a partner to retell the story using the chart.

Tip for Independent Practice

Place the B-M-E chart and the picture book from the whole-class lesson in a learning center for students to practice retelling the story. Older students can write their retelling.

Progressive Steps for Guided Reading
(Levels F–M)

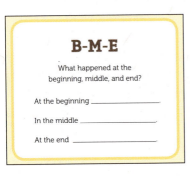

1. **B-M-E with one sticky note.** Insert a sticky note on one page in each book. Some students should have a sticky note at the beginning, some in the middle, and some at the end. When students come to a page with a sticky note, they write a sentence that tells what happened in that part of the story. During discussion, draw a B-M-E chart on an easel and have students match their sticky notes to the correct part of the story.

2. **B-M-E with three sticky notes.** Insert a note near the beginning, one at the middle, and one at the end of each book. On each sticky note have students write one sentence that tells what happened at the beginning, middle, and end. During the discussion, ask students to remove their sticky notes, mix them up, and then place them in the correct sequence.

3. **B-M-E with symbols.** In each book, insert several sticky notes where important events occur. Have students draw a symbol on each sticky note that represents the most important thing that happened on that page. Students sequence their notes during the discussion and use the symbols to retell the story to a partner.

4. **Guided writing.** Students use their sticky notes to write a B-M-E.

Module 4

RETELLING

Five-Finger Retell

Genre: Fiction
Grade Range: K–8
In a Nutshell: After reading, students use their fingers to retell the major elements of a story.

Whole-Class Mini-Lesson

Model: Use your five fingers to retell a familiar story, such as "The Three Little Pigs."

Characters—three pigs and the wolf

Setting—pigs' houses

Problem—The wolf wanted to eat the pigs.

Events—The wolf blew down the house of straw and the house of sticks.

Ending—The pigs found safety in the house of bricks.

Guided Practice: Draw the Five-Finger Retell graphic organizer on a chart and record symbols or key words for each story element. Students retell the story using the graphic organizer.

Tip for Independent Practice

Students can use the Five-Finger Retell card (Appendix N) during buddy reading or independent reading. Younger students can draw a picture for each element; older students can write their retelling.

Progressive Steps for Guided Reading
(Levels I and higher)

1. After reading, students use their fingers to retell the story with your support.

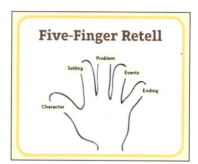

2. Give each student five sticky notes with the following story elements written on each. As students read, they insert the sticky note on the page that matches that story element.

Character	Setting	Problem	Events	Ending

3. Students trace their hand in their reading notebook. As they read, they stop and write about each of the story elements.

4. During guided writing, students use the Five-Finger Retell to write three paragraphs about the story. Paragraph one includes the characters, setting, and problem. Paragraph two describes at least two events that led to solving the problem. Paragraph three includes the solution to the problem and the other events that happened at the end of the story.

> The characters are the worm and Quack. The setting is outside in the rain. Quacks problem is his brother and sister don't want to go outside with Quack. Quack solved his problem by going outside and he found a worm to be his friend. Then the robin wanted to eat the worm. In the end Quack put the worm in his pocket and saved his life. They are BFF.

A Five-Finger Retelling for a Level L fiction text

Module 5

RETELLING

Key Words

Genre: Any

Grade Range: K–8

In a Nutshell: After students read a paragraph or page, they identify a key word that helps them remember the most important event or idea. The key word is often a noun or verb that carries the meaning.

Whole-Class Mini-Lesson

Model: Read a page and think aloud as you choose an important word from the passage. Explain why you chose that word. Write the word on chart paper. Then use the key word to retell the page.

Guided Practice: Read the next page and have students help you choose a key word. Add the key word to the chart and have students use it to retell that page. Continue reading and adding more key words. When you finish the book, students use the key words to retell it to a partner.

Progressive Steps for Guided Reading
(Levels F and higher)

1. Insert a sticky note on one page of each book. When students finish reading that page, they write a key word on the sticky note. Prompt students to use the word on the sticky note to retell what they read.

2. Insert sticky notes on several pages. Students write a key word on each sticky note. Prompt them to use the words on the sticky notes to retell the book.

3. During guided writing, students remove the sticky notes and use the key words to write important facts about the book (primary) or to summarize the text (intermediate).

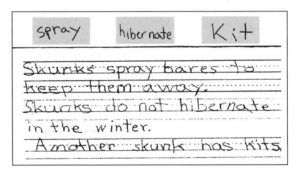

Key words from a Level G nonfiction text are listed at the top of this journal page to guide writing facts about the text below.

Tips for Independent Practice

During independent writing, students can use the chart you created during the mini-lesson to write about the story. (Younger students can add a picture for each key word.) As students read their self-selected books, have them record a key word or two after they read each page. When they finish reading a chapter, they can use the key words they recorded to write a summary of the chapter.

Module 6

RETELLING

Who-What

Genre: Fiction, Biography
Grade Range: K–8
In a Nutshell: After students read a paragraph, page, or chapter, they identify the most important character and retell what he or she did.

Whole-Class Mini-Lesson

Model: Read a page to students and think aloud as you reflect on **who** was the most important character and **what** he or she did.

Guided Practice: Continue reading the book. Students practice the **who-what** strategy with a partner.

Video Link
Watch Jan teaching who-what.

Progressive Steps for Guided Reading
(Levels K and higher)

1. **Who-what for a page (oral).** Students read a page and tell themselves who was the most important character and what he or she did. Confer with individuals and scaffold as needed.

2. **Who-what for a page (written).** Students read a page and write a who-what sentence on a sticky note. For example, *The grasshopper asked the ant if he could come into his home.*

3. **Who-what for a chapter.** Students write a who-what sentence for each chapter.

Tips for Independent Practice

During buddy reading, students can take turns using the who-what strategy to retell a page or short chapter. During independent reading, students can write a who-what statement after they read each chapter.

Module 7

DEVELOPING VOCABULARY

Strategies to Explain New Words

Genre: Any

Grade Range: K–8

In a Nutshell: Students learn to use a variety of strategies to determine the meaning of unfamiliar words.

Whole-Class Mini-Lesson

Model: Before reading a picture book or short informational text to the class, preselect a few vocabulary words that can be defined by using context, illustrations, known parts, or the glossary. Display the words and tell students you are going to show them an important reading strategy. Begin reading and stop when you come to one of the preselected words. Model one of the vocabulary strategies listed on the Vocabulary Strategies card.

Guided Practice: Continue reading. When you come to the next displayed word, have students work with a partner to define the word. Ask them to share the strategy they used.

Video Link

Watch Jan teaching strategies to explain new words.

Progressive Steps for Guided Reading
(Levels K and higher)

> **Vocabulary Strategies**
> 1. Reread (or read on) and look for clues.
> 2. Use the picture to explain the word.
> 3. Use a known part.
> 4. Make a connection.
> 5. Substitute a word that makes sense.
> 6. Use the glossary.

1. Prepare the guided reading texts by inserting sticky notes on pages where students will encounter unfamiliar words that are bolded or can be defined with context clues and illustrations. Write the first letter of the new word on the sticky note. As students read, they write the new word that begins with that letter on the sticky note. Then they use the Vocabulary Strategies card to define it. During discussion, students share new words they learned.

2. Insert sticky notes on pages where students will encounter challenging words. This time don't write the first letter of the word. Students should write a challenging word on the sticky note and use strategies to define it. During discussion, each student shares one new word and the strategy used to define it.

3. Students flag new words and define them in their reading notebooks. Prompt them to use the new words during guided writing.

4. Copy a text and black out some of the challenging words. As students read and come to a word that has been covered, they should think about the sentence and write a word that would make sense.

Tips for Independent Practice

During independent reading or literature circles, have students identify new words, write them in their reading notebooks, and define them. They can share their new words and the strategies they used during discussion time.

Module 8

ASKING AND ANSWERING QUESTIONS

Green Questions

(Adapted from Raphael, 1982)

Genre: Any

Grade Range: K–8

In a Nutshell: Green Questions help students recall information that is explicitly stated in the book. As students read, they take a fact from the text and turn it into a question that is answered in the book. The purpose of this activity is to help children see that asking questions helps them recall information.

Whole-Class Mini-Lesson

1. **Model:** Display a short text and read it to the class. Use a sticky flag to mark one of the sentences and demonstrate how to turn it into a question. Refer to the text to answer the question.

2. **Guided Practice:** Continue reading the text and flag another sentence. Students work together to write a Green Question. Have them answer each other's questions using the text.

Video Link

Watch Jan teaching the questioning strategy with Green and Red Questions.

Tips for Independent Practice

Students can write Green Questions while reading textbooks or doing research for content-area projects.

Progressive Steps for Guided Reading

(Levels K and higher)

Green Questions

I must go to the text and find the answer.

Who...?   When...?
What...?   How...?
Where...? Which...?

1. Students make two columns in their notebooks, one for "Fact" and one for "Question." The *teacher* flags an important sentence on each page. Students write a fact from that sentence in the first column. Then they turn the fact into a question and write it in the second column. During the discussion, students share their questions and call on other students in the group to answer them.

2. While reading their text, *students* flag an important paragraph and write a fact from that paragraph in the first column. They then turn the fact into a question and write it in the second column.

Excerpt from "The History of Gum," *Scholastic Short Reads*: The history of gum begins thousands of years ago, when prehistoric men and women chewed on lumps of tree resin (a sticky brownish substance that oozes from trees). The ancient Greeks chewed on resin and so did Native Americans. Early settlers to New England loved to chew, too.

Fact	Question
Resin oozes from trees.	Where does resin come from?
Prehistoric people chewed resin.	What did prehistoric people chew?

3. Students make two columns in their notebooks, one for "Question" and one for "Answer." This time as students read, they stop and write a Green Question that is answered in the text. Now they close their books and write the answer to their question. Requiring students to close their books prevents them from copying directly from the text. During the discussion, students take turns asking their questions to the group. They should first try to answer the question with their books closed, but they can look back in the text if they want to confirm their answer or if they don't know the answer.

Module 9

ASKING AND ANSWERING QUESTIONS

Red Questions

(Adapted from Raphael, 1982)

Genre: Any

Grade Range: K–8

In a Nutshell: As students read, they take a fact from the text and turn it into a question that is not directly answered in the book. The reader needs to STOP and use text clues and prior knowledge to make inferences about details in the story.

Whole-Class Mini-Lesson

Model: Read a picture book or short text to the class. Stop and model how to ask a Red Question, one not answered in the book. Red Questions often begin with the word *why*.

Guided Practice: Continue reading the text. Stop at an appropriate place where students could ask an inferential question. Have them work with a partner to create a "why" question. Post a few question starters to give students a variety of ways to ask a Red Question. (Repeat this mini-lesson with both narrative and informational text.)

> **Video Link**
>
> *Watch Jan teaching the questioning strategy with Green and Red Questions.*

Progressive Steps for Guided Reading
(Levels K and higher)

1. **Ask a Red Question.** Insert a sticky note on one or two pages in each book. Write the word *why* at the top of the note. When students come to a page that has the sticky note, they write a "why" question about something on that page.

2. **Ask and answer a Red Question.** Students make two columns in their notebooks, one for "Question" and one for "Answer." As students read, they stop and write a Red Question in the first column and answer their question in the second column. During the discussion, students share their questions and call on group members to answer them. Encourage risk by valuing inferential thinking and divergent answers.

Tips for Independent Practice

Students can write Red Questions to prepare for literature circles. You can also use this strategy when students are reading a textbook or doing independent research.

A "why" question for a Level H nonfiction text about hatching chicks

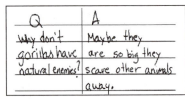

A "why" question for a Level L nonfiction text about gorillas

Module 10

IDENTIFYING MAIN IDEA AND DETAILS

Very Important Part (V.I.P.) Fiction

(Adapted from Hoyt, 1988)

Genre: Fiction

Grade Range: K–8

In a Nutshell: During retelling, readers are asked to recall everything they can remember. As texts get longer, it is impossible to recall every detail. Identifying the Very Important Part (V.I.P.) will help students determine the main idea or central message in texts throughout their schooling—even in college.

Whole-Class Mini-Lesson

First teach students how to determine the important actions. Then repeat the steps to determine the important feelings.

Model: Read a page from a grade-appropriate picture book or short story. Demonstrate how you identified the V.I.P. action from that section. "I think the very important action was . . . because . . . ." Use illustrations if available. Illustrators often depict important actions in their drawings.

Guided Practice: Continue reading and stop to allow students to practice the strategy. If you are displaying the text on an interactive whiteboard, you can highlight the important actions. When you finish the story, use the important actions you identified or highlighted to determine the central message or "Big Idea." The central message is often the lesson the character learned or what the author was trying to teach the reader.

> **Video Link**
>
> *Watch Jan teaching V.I.P. fiction.*

Progressive Steps for Guided Reading
(Levels K and higher)

V.I.P. Fiction

Action—What is the most important thing the character did?

Feeling—What is the most important feeling the character had?

1. **V.I.P. action by page.** After students read a page or two, they use a sticky flag to mark the most important action. During conferring, ask students to tell you why they flagged a specific sentence. If students have trouble determining the important action, direct them to the illustration.

2. **V.I.P. action by chapter.** Students flag the V.I.P. sentence in each chapter and then paraphrase the action in their notebooks. Encourage them to use chapter titles and illustrations to select the most important part. During individual conferences ask for evidence: "Why did you pick that action as the V.I.P.? What were you thinking?"

3. **V.I.P. feeling by page.** Insert a sticky note on alternate pages. Students read and write the important feeling the character had. Give each student a copy of the Character Feelings and Traits chart (Appendix M).

4. **V.I.P. feeling by chapter.** For each chapter, students write a V.I.P. statement that describes the important feeling of the main character.

5. **V.I.P. action and feeling by chapter.** Students identify a V.I.P. action and feeling for each chapter. After reading the book, students use the V.I.P. statements to determine the central idea.

Tip for Independent Practice

Students can identify and share the V.I.P. action and feeling during literature circle discussions.

Module 11

IDENTIFYING MAIN IDEA AND DETAILS

Very Important Part (V.I.P.) Nonfiction

Genre: Nonfiction

Grade Range: K–8

In a Nutshell: Students learn to use text clues such as headings, illustrations, maps, bolded words, and repeated words to determine the most important information. When the text does not have a heading or the main idea is not clearly stated, students must use interpretive and evaluative skills to infer the main idea.

Whole-Class Mini-Lesson

First use texts with supportive text features. Then repeat the mini-lesson using text without headings or illustrations.

Model: Select a grade-appropriate informational picture book or short text. Read a page or paragraph and model how you identified the V.I.P. by using text features. "I think the very important part is gorillas live in central Africa. I noticed the author talked about where they lived and he included a map."

Guided Practice: Continue reading and stop to allow students to practice the strategy of determining importance. If you have a document camera, display the text so students clearly see the text features. When you finish reading the text, show students how to use the V.I.P.s you identified to determine the author's intent or central message.

Progressive Steps for Guided Reading
(Levels K and higher)

1. **V.I.P.** After students read a section that has a heading, they use a sticky flag to mark the most important sentence. Prompt them to use words from the heading, illustrations, repeated words, and possibly words in boldface type. During individual conferences, ask students to clarify their thinking. "Why did you pick that sentence as the V.I.P.? What text features did you use?"

2. **V.I.P.–Key Words.** After students read a page or two, they flag the V.I.P. and write one or two key words. During discussion, help them use the key words to create a main idea statement.

3. **V.I.P.–Key Words–Central Idea.** After students flag the V.I.P. sentence in each section, they write one or two key words in their notebooks. When they finish reading a chapter, they use the key words to write a main idea statement for the chapter.

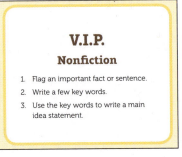

V.I.P.
Nonfiction
1. Flag an important fact or sentence.
2. Write a few key words.
3. Use the key words to write a main idea statement.

Tips for Independent Practice

Gather informational picture books at a variety of levels. Allow students to choose a book for independent practice. Tell them there are two rules: they must be interested in the book, and it must be easy for them to read. During independent reading, students use flags to mark the V.I.P. by section, record key words in their notebooks, and write a main idea statement for each chapter.

Video Link ▶▶
Watch Jan teaching V.I.P. nonfiction.

Module 12

IDENTIFYING MAIN IDEA AND DETAILS

Turning Headings Into Questions

Genre: Nonfiction
Grade Range: 1–8

In a Nutshell: Students learn to turn a heading into a question. As they read the section, they look for information that will answer the question, and they record the information in bullet form. Teaching students how to write their ideas in a bullet format helps them capture the most important details without copying from the text.

Whole-Class Mini-Lesson

Model: Choose a grade-appropriate informational text that has chapter titles or headings. Make a three-column chart and write the heading in the first column. Turn the heading into a question and write it in the middle column. As you read, write key details that answer the main idea question. Then demonstrate how to use the chart to construct a main idea statement.

Guided Practice: Repeat the process using another section of text. Students work with a partner to create a main idea question and identify key details. Students might need to revise the main idea question after they read the section, but that is part of comprehension. Students use the information on the chart to construct a main idea statement.

Video Link

Watch Jan teaching turning headings into questions.

Progressive Steps for Guided Reading
(Levels K and higher)

1. **Flag the heading.** Choose a text with chapter headings in the form of questions. Students flag the heading and write key words for each section, and they bullet key details. During the discussion, students use their notes to answer the question in the heading.

2. **Turn a heading into a question.** Select a text with headings that are not in the form of questions. Students use the headings to create questions and bullet key details as they read. During guided writing, they use their notes to write the main idea of each section.

3. **Use texts without headings (or cover the headings).** As students read, they write their own main idea question and bullet key details. During discussion, students suggest appropriate headings for the passage.

> **Main Idea/Details**
> 1. Turn the heading into a question.
> 2. Bullet key words that answer the question.
> 3. Use the question and key words to identify the main idea of the passage.

Heading	Main Idea Question	Details
Dangers in Tide Pools	Why are Tide Pools dangerous to animals?	• waves • heat • birds

Tip for Independent Practice

Students read nonfiction texts at their level and create a main idea "Question–Details" chart. Then they write a main idea statement for each section.

Module 13

ANALYZING CHARACTERS

Track a Character's Feelings

Genre: Fiction, Biography

Grade Range: K–8

In a Nutshell: Understanding a character and how he or she changes is at the heart of comprehending literary texts. Students track the main character's feelings through the beginning, middle, and end of the story and reflect on what caused those feelings.

Whole-Class Mini-Lesson

Model: Select a short story or picture book that demonstrates a dynamic character, one who changes throughout the story. Begin reading and stop when the author gives a clue as to how the character feels. Think aloud. "In this part of the story, the character felt depressed because other kids were making fun of her." Write B-M-E on chart paper and write a word that describes the character's feelings at the beginning of the book. For primary grades, you can draw the facial expression.

Guided Practice: Continue reading aloud and stop when the character's feeling changes. Students work with a partner to identify a feeling word. Encourage students to think of descriptive words other than *happy*, *sad*, and *mad*. Students in grades 2–8 can use the Character Feelings and Traits chart (Appendix M). List a feeling word for the middle and end of the story. After you finish the story, guide students as they retell the story using the feeling words on the chart.

Video Link

Watch Jan teaching track a character's feelings.

Progressive Steps for Guided Reading
(Levels J and higher)

1. Prepare for the lesson by inserting sticky notes on pages where the character's feelings change. On a dry-erase board, list a few words students should use to describe the character in the book. Use words such as *excited*, *discouraged*, and *determined*. Be sure to discuss the meaning of the words prior to reading. As students come to a sticky note, they write a word from the list that describes how the character is feeling on that page. After reading, have students remove their sticky notes, scramble them and sequence them. Students take turns sharing how the character felt at the beginning, middle, and end of the story.

2. Insert the sticky notes as in step 1, but do not list feeling words. Students use the Character Feelings and Traits chart (Appendix M) to select a word that best describes the character at the beginning, middle, and end. Encourage students to use complete sentences as they retell how the character's feelings changed throughout the story.

3. Provide each student with sticky notes. As students read, they determine where the character's feeling changed, insert a sticky note, and write a feeling word from the Character Feelings and Traits chart.

4. During guided writing, students use the words they wrote on the sticky notes to write a paragraph about the character.

| upset | worried | hopeful | relieved |

Katy was <u>upset</u> because her cat was stuck in a tree. She was <u>worried</u> that the cat wouldn't be able to get down by itself. Then Katy had an idea. She would put some cat food at the bottom of the tree. Katie was <u>hopeful</u> that her plan would work. At the end Katy was <u>relieved</u> because her cat came down the tree and was safe in her arms.

Tips for Independent Practice

After listening to a picture book or after they independently read fiction or biographies, students write about the character's feelings and how and why those feelings change.

Module 14

ANALYZING CHARACTERS

Evidence of Character Traits

Genre: Fiction

Grade Range: K–8

In a Nutshell: Students use evidence from the passage (a character's action or dialogue) to identify a character trait. Students learn to distinguish between a feeling and a trait. A feeling describes the character's emotions in response to a specific event, whereas a character trait is the way a person acts throughout the story. It is part of the character's personality.

Whole-Class Mini-Lesson

Model: Create an anchor chart like the one below. Select a story that has characters who display different traits. *Goggles* by Ezra Jack Keats is one of my favorite examples. As you read, list a character, a trait, and a specific action or dialogue that shows evidence of that trait. Use the Character Feelings and Traits chart (Appendix M) for a list of interesting vocabulary.

Goggles by Ezra Jack Keats

Character	Trait	Evidence
Peter	bold	Didn't back down
Big boys	greedy	Tried to take the goggles
Willie	protective	growled

Guided Practice: Continue reading and have students help you add another character, trait, and evidence.

Progressive Steps for Guided Reading
(Levels K and higher)

1. **Analyze one character.** Prepare the books by inserting sticky notes on a few pages where a character displays a trait. On a dry-erase board, write a few character traits that describe a character. As students read, they stop at the sticky note and write the trait from the list that matches the action. During the discussion, students take turns sharing one of the traits and citing specific evidence (actions) from the story that supports their choice.

2. **Have students flag the evidence.** Continue to provide a list of traits for one of the characters, but let students insert the sticky notes where they find the evidence (action or dialogue). Students write the trait on the sticky note and share during the discussion.

3. **Analyze two or more characters.** Students make the three-column chart in their reading notebooks (Character—Trait—Evidence). Tell students the characters they should analyze and have them write the characters' names in the first column. As students read, they stop and add to the chart when they notice evidence that reveals a character trait.

4. **Guided writing.** Students use their sticky notes or chart to write an opinion paragraph about one of the characters from the story. Use the S.O.A.R. card as a scaffold (Appendix N).

Character—Trait—Evidence

What trait describes the character?
What is your evidence?

Character	Trait	Evidence

The character is _____. In the story she (or he) _____.

I think Pecos Bill was creative. He invented a branding iron that burned a permanent mark into each cow. Now they wouldn't get their cows mixed up with their neighbor's. Another example that he was creative was he made a lasso. This was a rope with a loop at one end. His brothers could throw the loop over the cow's horns and catch a runaway cow. These are reasons why I think Pecos Bill was a creative cowboy.

Tips for Independent Practice

During independent or shared reading, students create a character web that lists character traits and examples (with page numbers) from the story to support each trait.

Module 15

ANALYZING CHARACTERS

Who-What-Why

Genre: Biography

Grade Range: K–8

In a Nutshell: After students read a paragraph, page, or chapter, they identify the most important character, what he or she did, and why the character took that action.

Whole-Class Mini-Lesson

Model: Read a few pages and think aloud as you reflect on **who** the most important character was, **what** he or she did, and **why** he or she did that. "The **who** was King Midas. The **what** was he turned everything to gold. **Why**? Because he was greedy. So my who-what-why is *King Midas turned everything to gold because he was greedy*."

Guided Practice: Continue reading and have students practice the who-what-why strategy with a partner.

Video Link

Watch Jan teaching who-what-why.

Progressive Steps for Guided Reading
(Levels K and higher)

1. **Who-what-why for a page (oral).** Students read a page and tell themselves who was the most important character, what he or she did, and why he or she did that. Confer with individuals and scaffold as needed.

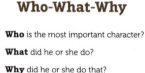

2. **Who-what-why for a page (written).** Students read a page and write a who-what-why sentence on a sticky note. For example, *The grasshopper asked the ant if he could come into his home because he was cold.*

3. **Who-what-why for a chapter.** Students write a who-what-why sentence for each chapter.

    Chapter 2—Dorothy went to Germany to visit a dog school because she wanted to train dogs to help blind people.

    Chapter 3—Buddy was trained to obey commands so he could be Dorothy's very first guide dog.

Tips for Independent Practice

During buddy reading, students can take turns using the who-what-why strategy to retell a page or short chapter. During independent reading, students can write a who-what-why statement after they read each chapter.

Module 16

ANALYZING CHARACTERS

Action-Motivation Chart

Genre: Fiction, Biography, Historical Text

Grade Range: K–8

In a Nutshell: The reader identifies a character's motivation for behaving a certain way by using evidence from the text. Essentially, the reader asks what makes the characters do what they do.

Whole-Class Mini-Lesson

Model: Use a picture book or short biography. Read aloud and stop when the character or person takes action. Share your ideas for why the character did that. You might discuss with primary students the Big Bad Wolf's motivation for attacking the pigs, and with advanced readers you might analyze Jim's motivation for selling his gold watch in O. Henry's "The Gift of the Magi." Create a chart to record the character, action, and motivation.

Guided Practice: Continue reading and stop when a character does something surprising. These are opportune places to examine a character's motivation. Students work with a partner to identify the character's motive.

Progressive Steps for Guided Reading
(Levels M and higher)

1. **Teacher flags the action.** To prepare for the lesson, use sticky flags to mark specific actions of characters in the text. Students make a three-column chart in their notebooks: Character—Action—Motivation. As students read the story and come to the flag, they stop and list the character and the action that occurred. Then they reflect on the character's action and write what motivated the character to act that way. It is not unusual for students to list different motivations for the same action.

2. **Students flag the action.** Give each student a few sticky flags and ask them to mark places where the character does something that surprises them. Then they complete the chart in their notebooks and share their responses during the discussion.

Character	Action	Motivation
Big Bad Wolf	Blew the house down	He was hungry.
Jim	Sold his watch	To buy hair combs.

Character	Action	Motivation
Dr. Martin Luther King	Led a bus boycott	To change the law requiring African Americans to ride in the back of the bus

Tips for Independent Practice

During independent reading or to prepare for a literature circle, students can mark places that surprised them and write about the character's motivation. Use this activity to analyze actions from historical events. For example, what motivated the South to secede? Or what was the motivation behind the Boston Tea Party?

Module 17

ANALYZING RELATIONSHIPS

Sociogram

Genre: Fiction

Grade Range: K–8

In a Nutshell: A sociogram is a visual representation of relationships between characters. It can be used with simple fairy tales or complex novels. Students draw a circle for each character. Then they draw lines between the characters and write a sentence that describes the relationships.

Whole-Class Mini-Lesson

Model: Use a picture book (grades K–3) or an episode from a familiar novel (grades 4–8). Ask students to share the names of the primary characters and write each name in a circle. Then draw a line between two characters and write a sentence that describes their relationship.

Guided Practice: Students work with a partner to describe the relationship between two other characters. As students share their sentences, write them on the sociogram.

Progressive Steps for Guided Reading

(Levels J and higher)

1. Tell students how many circles to draw, one for each character in the story. As they read, students write a character's name in a circle. During individual prompting and discussion, ask questions to help them describe the relationships. "What happened between these characters? How did they feel about each other?"

2. Before reading, list key words or phrases that describe the character relationships. Students draw the sociogram, write the characters' names, and use the key words you provided to describe the relationships. Share and discuss.

3. Students draw the sociogram, insert characters' names, and write a sentence to describe each relationship. Prompt as needed. Have them number the characters in the order they appear in the story. Students use the sociogram as their concept map for guided writing.

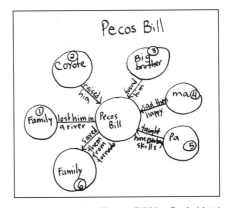

A sociogram for "Pecos Bill" by Ruth Mattison

Tips for Independent Practice

A sociogram is an excellent way for students to understand and remember the relationships between characters. In literature circles, they can create sociograms for different parts of a novel and share them during discussion. After they finish the book, they can use the sociograms to analyze how relationships changed throughout the story.

Module 18

ANALYZING RELATIONSHIPS

Compare and Contrast With Yellow Questions

Genre: Any

Grade Range: K–8

In a Nutshell: Students construct a question that compares and contrasts concepts, ideas, people, or story elements presented in a text. To increase the challenge, students write questions that compare and contrast two different texts on the same topic.

Whole-Class Mini-Lesson

Model: Read a short text to the class, such as "The Tortoise and the Hare." Say, "I need to think of two things I can compare. I can compare the tortoise and the hare. My question is, How are the tortoise and the hare alike? They both want to win the race. How are they different? The hare stops and rests, but the tortoise keeps going."

Guided Practice: Continue reading and identify two other characters, animals, or concepts to compare. Students work with a partner to create a Yellow, or compare and contrast, question. Give student partnerships a Yellow Question card to help them construct their questions. Students can write their question on a dry-erase board, then exchange their board with another partnership and answer each other's questions.

Video Link

Watch Jan teaching compare and contrast with Yellow Questions.

Progressive Steps for Guided Reading

(Levels K and higher)

1. **Find two things to compare.** Distribute several sticky flags to each student. Tell them to read the text and flag two things that are alike or different. During individual conferences, help students construct a question that compares or contrasts the two ideas. This is an oral task. During discussion, students share their questions and answers.

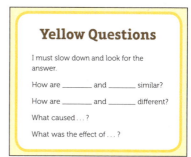

Yellow Questions

I must slow down and look for the answer.

How are _____ and _____ similar?

How are _____ and _____ different?

What caused . . . ?

What was the effect of . . . ?

2. **Write a question.** Insert a sticky note on a page where students can compare or contrast two ideas. When students read that page, they should write a question using one of the question stems on the question card. During the discussion, students take turns asking and answering their questions.

3. **Write a question and answer it.** Students make two columns in their notebooks, one for "Question" and one for "Answer." As students read the text, they write a compare and contrast question and the answer in their notebooks. During the discussion, students share their questions and call on other students in the group to answer them.

Question	Answer
How are moose and elk different?	Moose are larger and have antlers that look like hands. They make a grunting sound. Elk have sharp, pointy antlers and make a bugling sound.

Tips for Independent Practice

Students can write questions that compare and contrast the characters, setting, and problems in two different books they have read. The question card can also be useful in other subject areas.

Module 19

ANALYZING RELATIONSHIPS
Cause-Effect Questions

Genre: Any

Grade Range: K–8

In a Nutshell: Students learn to search for cause-and-effect relationships that are stated or implied in a text.

Whole-Class Mini-Lesson

Model: Read a picture book or short nonfiction text to the class. Say, "I'm going to flag one event. That's the effect. Then I'm going to ask a question about it so I can figure out the cause." (Students might be confused by the interchangeable use of "event" and "effect," but it's the easiest way to introduce the concept.)

- K–2 example: "One event is the Little Red Hen didn't share her bread with the other animals. What caused the Little Red Hen to be so selfish? Let's think about (or reread) the story so we can answer my question."

- 3–5 example: "An effect the author mentioned was people created the Underground Railroad, which helped slaves escape the South. What caused the people to create the Underground Railroad? Let's reread and find the answer to this question."

Guided Practice: Continue reading and stop at another event (effect). Students write a "what caused" question. Give student partnerships a Cause-Effect card so they will have question stems.

Video Link

Watch Jan teaching cause-effect questions.

Progressive Steps for Guided Reading
(Levels N and higher)

1. **Teacher flags the effect.** Before students read the text, insert sticky flags directly on sentences that contain an effect. When they come to a flag, they write a "what caused" question in their notebooks. During discussion, students share their questions and discuss them.

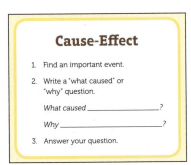

2. **Teacher flags a paragraph that contains an effect.** Before reading, insert sticky flags next to paragraphs that contain a cause-effect relationship. Whenever students come to a flagged paragraph, they place the sticky note on the sentence that contains an effect. Then they write a "what caused" question to share during discussion.

3. **Students flag the effect.** Prepare for the lesson by flagging a different paragraph or page for each student. Tell students they must read the entire selection, but they are responsible for writing a "what caused" question for the paragraph or page that is flagged. Students write a "what caused" question and answer it.

4. **Students write cause-effect statements.** As students read and discover a cause-effect relationship, they write a statement following this pattern: *Because caves maintain the same temperature year round (cause), some people used them as their homes (effect).*

Question	Answer
What caused people to make their homes in caves?	Caves protected them from the heat and the cold.

Cause-effect questions for "Caves" by Michèle Dufrense

Tips for Independent Practice

Students can write cause-effect statements as they read their self-selected books, prepare for literature circles, or read social studies. When reading science texts, an **If-Then** scaffold might be more appropriate. For example, *If you pull down on a rope attached to a pulley (cause), then the load on the other end goes up (effect).*

Module 20

INFERRING

Inferences From Dialogue

Genre: Fiction

Grade Range: K–8

In a Nutshell: Readers examine dialogue and ask themselves, "Why did the character say that? Why did the character say it *that* way? What can I infer about the character?"

Whole-Class Mini-Lesson

Model: Read or display a picture book or short story with dialogue and speaker tags (or write your own story with students' help). Explain that speaker tags tell the reader how a character says something. Be dramatic as you read aloud. Emphasize the speaker tag. "'That porridge is too hot,' *wailed* Goldilocks."

Talk about the inference you made.

Guided Practice: Have students read the rest of the story with you. If you display the text, underline the speaker tags and prompt students to read the dialogue like an actor. Discuss the inferences from the dialogue and speaker tags. Create an anchor chart.

Progressive Steps for Guided Reading
(Levels K and higher)

1. **Understanding speaker tags.** Before reading, discuss vocabulary from the speaker tags, such as *moaned, whined*, etc. (These words can be especially challenging for DLLs.) During reading students should whisper-read so you can listen for appropriate intonation and expression. Use prompts such as, "How would the character say that? Why do you think she *whined*?" If a student is not making an inference from a speaker tag, check to see if the tag includes an unfamiliar word.

2. **Teacher flags the dialogue.** Flag some dialogue in the book. When students come to a flag, they can draw the character's face and write in a thought bubble what the character might be thinking.

3. **Students flag the dialogue.** Students flag important or surprising dialogue and write their inferences using a two-column chart.

Dialogue	Inference
6 (wailed)	She's upset.
7 (giggled)	She's happy.
9 (groaned)	She's hurting.

Tips for Independent Practice

Students can use the speech bubble–thought bubble scaffold or two-column chart to track inferences they are making during self-selected reading. I once did this activity with ninth graders reading Shakespeare's *Macbeth*. It helped the students discover implied meanings.

Module 21

INFERRING

Inferences From Actions

Genre: Fiction

Grade Range: K–8

In a Nutshell: Students attend to a character's actions and consider specific text clues such as adjectives, adverbs, or phrases that describe the character's behavior in order to make inferences about the character.

Whole-Class Mini-Lesson

Model: Read or display a picture book or short story and stop when the character does something. Think aloud as you share your inference. "I'm thinking the character did this because . . . ."

Guided Practice: Continue reading the story and have students help you flag important actions. Students share their inferences. Invite divergent thinking, but students should be able to validate their inference using indicators from the text.

Tips for Independent Practice

Students can use two-column charts in their reading notebooks to track inferences they are making during self-selected reading or to prepare for a literature circle discussion. This works at every grade level.

Progressive Steps for Guided Reading
(Levels K and higher)

1. **Teacher flags actions.** Before reading, scaffold students by inserting sticky flags on a few actions in the book where the reader is expected to draw an inference. Students write what the character might be thinking or what the reader is thinking. Prompt: "What is the character feeling or thinking right now? What are you thinking about the character?"

2. **Students flag actions.** Students mark an action where they made an inference and write about it on a sticky note or in their reading notebooks.

3. **Combine text clues.** Students flag an action or dialogue where they made an inference. They create a two-column chart and in the "In the Book" column, they write the page number and either A for action or D for dialogue. Then they write their inference in the second column, "In My Head."

Make an Inference
Fiction
1. Find an important or surprising dialogue or action.
2. Why did the character say or do that?
3. What is the character thinking?
4. What are you thinking?

I'm thinking _____ because the character _____.

In the Book	In My Head
p. 3 Ricky took his parrot to school. (A)	He wanted to impress his friends.
p. 10 "Come on, Buster, say it." (D)	Ricky is frustrated with Buster.
p. 11 The children laughed. (A)	Ricky is embarrassed.
p. 17 The teacher wasn't smiling. (A)	The teacher is angry with the bird.

Module 22

INFERRING

Inferences From a Character's Inner Thoughts

Genre: Fiction

Grade Range: K–8

In a Nutshell: Students focus on clues about a character's thoughts to make inferences. These words are not spoken in dialogue, but they let the reader know what the character is thinking.

Whole-Class Mini-Lesson

Model: Read or display a picture book or short story that includes a character's thoughts. (*Ready for School, Murphy?* by Brendan Murphy is a great choice for primary grades.) Think aloud as you share your inference. "I am making an inference from the character's thoughts. I'm thinking . . . ."

Guided Practice: Continue reading the story and have students help point out a character's inner thoughts. Make sure they understand how to use quotation marks to distinguish between dialogue and inner thoughts. Invite students to share their inferences. Use the follow-up question "Why do you think that?" to prompt students to validate their inference with text indicators.

Progressive Steps for Guided Reading
(Levels K and higher)

1. **Teacher flags inner thoughts.** Before students read, insert a few sticky flags in their books to draw attention to sentences that include a character's inner thoughts. Students record their inferences on sticky notes or in their reading notebooks.

> **Make an Inference**
> **Fiction**
> 1. Find an important or surprising dialogue or action.
> 2. Why did the character say or do that?
> 3. What is the character thinking?
> 4. What are you thinking?
>
> I'm thinking _____ because the character _____.

2. **Students flag inner thoughts.** Students assume responsibility for flagging a place in the book where they make an inference from a character's inner thoughts. They can use two columns labeled "In the Book" (page number and inner thought) and "In My Head" (inference). Use steps 3 and 4 on the comprehension card above to support students.

3. **Combine text clues.** Students flag a place in the book where they made an inference. They write the page number and either A for action, D for dialogue, or IT for inner thoughts in the "In the Book" column. Then they write their inference in the second column.

Tips for Independent Practice

Students can use two-column charts in their reading notebooks to track inferences they are making during self-selected reading or to prepare for a literature circle discussion. They can identify the text clue as dialogue, action, or inner thoughts.

Module 23

INFERRING

Drawing Conclusions

Genre: Any

Grade Range: K–8

In a Nutshell: Readers use information in the text along with what they already know (schema) to draw a conclusion. The following two scaffolds help simplify this complex process:

What I read + What I know = My conclusion

If-Then.

Whole-Class Mini-Lesson

Model: Choose a picture book or short story that requires the reader to draw conclusions. My favorite authors for teaching this strategy are Mo Willems (primary), Chris Van Allsburg (intermediate), and O. Henry (middle school). Read a page or two and stop to model the process of drawing a conclusion. "I read.... I know.... So I conclude that...."

Guided Practice: Continue reading and stop to involve students in the process.

Use the following anchor chart to track the conclusions students draw as you continue reading the picture book or short story.

I read	I know	I conclude

Progressive Steps for Guided Reading
(Levels N and higher)

Text choice is critical for this strategy. Teach the strategy with fiction first, since children have more schemas for that genre. Then repeat the lessons using nonfiction.

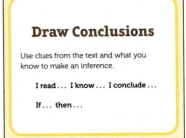

Draw Conclusions

Use clues from the text and what you know to make an inference.

I read... I know... I conclude...

If... then...

1. **Teacher flags the clues.** Prepare for the lesson by flagging a paragraph or illustration where the reader can draw a conclusion. Students write If-Then statements. For example, *If Harriet Tubman plowed fields and moved heavy logs, then she was a strong girl.*

2. **Students flag the clues.** Students flag places in the text where they made a conclusion, and they write an If-Then statement in their notebooks.

3. **Students complete the chart.** Students flag places where they made a conclusion and use the following chart to map the process of drawing a conclusion.

I READ	I KNOW	I CONCLUDE
Harriet didn't go to the doctor when she hurt her head.	It costs money to see a doctor.	If she hadn't been a slave, she would have been able to see a doctor.

Tips for Independent Practice

Divide the class into groups of three or four students. Give each group a short text or picture book with the **If-Then** chart or the **I read–I know–I conclude** chart. Students work together to read the text and complete the chart.

Module 24

SUMMARIZING

Somebody-Wanted-But-So (Then)

Genre: Narrative, Historical Text

Grade Range: K–8

In a Nutshell: The Somebody-Wanted-But-So strategy (Macon, Bewell & Vogt, 1991) can be used during and after reading to help students summarize a story or historical event. Students identify who wanted something (somebody), what they wanted (wanted), what conflict arose (but), and how the problem was solved (so). If there are characters or groups of people with competing points of view, students can do an SWBS paragraph for each character or group. Students can summarize longer texts by connecting a series of SWBS statements with "then."

Whole-Class Mini-Lesson

Model: Use a familiar story (traditional tale, movie, or real-life event) to model the SWBS strategy. Add "then" when it is appropriate.

Guided Practice: Retell another traditional tale or read a short picture book and have students help you do the SWBS(T).

Video Link ▶▶

Watch Jan teaching SWBS.

Progressive Steps for Guided Reading
(Levels F and higher)

1. **SWBS oral.** After reading, guide students to summarize a fiction text using the SWBS strategy.

2. **SWBS written.** Students write an SWBS response for guided writing.

3. **SWBST.** As texts become longer and more complex, students extend their summary by adding "then" and writing a second Somebody-Wanted-But-So statement.

Somebody-Wanted-But-So

little Dinasewre wanted to eat bedos and draginfis and eggs but he got Kot so he ranback in to his hole.

SWBS—Early guided writing

Brandon wanted to beat the Bayfront kids. But he couldent make a free throw. So the ball bounced down the street and it helped him find some friends that had talent. Then he finaly made a shot in the basket and Springton won.

SWBS—Transitional guided writing

Tips for Independent Practice

Students can write an SWBS for each chapter they read during independent reading.

Module 25

SUMMARIZING

Key Word Summary

Genre: Nonfiction

Grade Range: 2–8

In a Nutshell: As students read a text, they identify key words and use them to compose a summary.

Whole-Class Mini-Lesson

Model: Read the first paragraph from a nonfiction text. As you read, underline or list key words. Consider headings, bold words, illustrations, and repeated words when selecting key words. Then use the words to summarize the paragraph.

Guided Practice: Read the next paragraph. Have students help you identify key words. Students work with a partner to orally summarize the text using the key words.

Key Word Summary

Native Americans
ceremonies
messenger
gods

Bald eagles were important to Native Americans. They thought the eagle was a messenger from the gods and used the feathers in ceremonies.

Progressive Steps for Guided Reading
(Levels M and higher)

1. **Students write the key words with initial letters provided.** Give students the initial letters of the key words. Tell them to read the text and write the key words that begin with those letters. During the discussion, they create an oral summary using the key words.

2. **Students write the key words without initial-letter support.** Students read a paragraph or page and record key words. During the discussion, they take turns sharing one of the key words they selected and tell why they chose it. They do not have to agree on the key words, but they should be able to support their choices. They compose a summary with your support.

3. **Students write the key words and a summary.** Students read the text, write three to five key words, and use the key words to compose their own summaries. Remind them to use all the key words in their summaries. After students write their summaries, have them underline the key words. You will probably spend several days at this step. It is imperative that students write their summaries in their own words.

4. **Students revise their summaries.** Students continue to identify key words and write their summaries, but now they focus on revising their first draft and eliminating unnecessary words. Aim for fewer than 20 words per summary. At this step you're helping students write summaries that are clear, concise, and complete.

Tips for Independent Practice

Use this strategy during content-area instruction. Divide the class into four or five groups and give each group a section of text to read and summarize. Students work together to identify key words and write a summary to share with the rest of the class.

Module 26

EVALUATING
Thesis-Proof

Genre: Persuasive Nonfiction

Grade Range: 4–8

In a Nutshell: The thesis-proof scaffold helps students gather and sort information when reading a persuasive text. It can be used to support a single thesis or evaluate and compare two texts on the same topic. *Scholastic News* (sni.scholastic.com/) has opinion articles in almost every weekly edition. You can use them for whole-class and guided reading lessons.

Whole-Class Mini-Lesson

Model: Choose an interesting text that has the thesis stated in the title. For example, "Kids Are Playing Too Many Video Games" or "Is Homework Good for Kids?" Create a thesis-proof chart and use the article's title to write the thesis statement. Then read a paragraph and record bullet ideas that either support or oppose the thesis statement.

Guided Practice: As you continue reading, students identify key ideas that support or oppose the thesis. Use the anchor chart during writing workshop to model how to write an opinion essay.

Tips for Independent Practice

The Thesis-Proof chart is an excellent tool for conducting research. Students choose a thesis statement that interests them and gather evidence that supports or opposes the thesis. They use their chart to write an opinion essay.

Progressive Steps for Guided Reading
(Levels N and higher)

See scholastic.com/teachers/top-teaching/2015/03/graphic-organizers-opinion-writing for short opinion articles to use in guided reading.

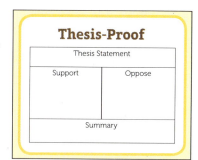

1. **Evaluate one side of an argument.** Select a persuasive text that presents one side. Explain that a thesis statement declares what a writer believes or intends to prove. Give students the thesis statement to write on their thesis-proof chart. As they read, they bullet ideas that support the thesis. During discussion, help them summarize their information using their chart. Teach the language for citing evidence: *According to the text . . . . On page ___ the author stated . . . . An example is . . . .*

2. **Evaluate two sides of an argument.** Select a text that presents both sides of an argument, or choose two texts that have opposing views on the same topic. Students identify the thesis statement and bullet key ideas that support or oppose the thesis. Below is an example using an article from *Scholastic News* titled, "Should Students Have a TV in Their Bedroom?" (sni.scholastic.com/Debates/02_02_15)

Thesis: Students Should Have a TV in Their Bedroom	
Support	Oppose
Fewer arguments over what to watch.	Kids will watch more TV.
Parents can control what their kids watch.	Too much TV can lead to obesity.
Parents can control how much TV time.	Kids don't spend time with friends or family.

3. **Guided writing.** Provide support as students write an opinion paper. Paragraph 1: Briefly state the two viewpoints. Paragraph 2: Explain the *supporting* view with evidence. Paragraph 3: Explain the *opposing* view with reasons. Paragraph 4: State your opinion.

Module 27

USING TEXT FEATURES

Strategies to Enhance Comprehension

Genre: Nonfiction

Grade Range: 1–8

In a Nutshell: This module teaches students how to use text features to locate and understand important information. You will find a variety of text features in Scholastic magazine articles.

Whole-Class Mini-Lesson

Model: Text features include all the components of an article or book that are not in the main body. Although attending to text features greatly enhances comprehension, students often ignore them (Kelley & Clausen-Grace, 2010). So teach one or two text features each day as you complete the anchor chart to the right. Display an example, explain its purpose, and ask Green Questions (page 265).

Guided Practice: Distribute nonfiction magazines to pairs of students and have them create a Green Question that is answered in a text feature.

Tips for Independent Practice

As students read a nonfiction text or news magazine, they write Green and Yellow Questions on sticky notes. Place the books and student questions in a learning center. Students choose a book and answer the questions using text features.

Progressive Steps for Guided Reading
(Levels K and higher)

1. **What's the big idea?** As students read a nonfiction book, they place a small sticky note on a text feature and write why the author included it. *This diagram shows the details of a butterfly's wing.*

Text Feature	Purpose
Contents	Gives chapters and page numbers
Headings	Tell main idea of a section
Photos and illustrations	Show how something looks
Diagrams	Illustrate key ideas with labeled parts
Graphs	Organize and explain data
Maps	Show locations
Captions	Explain the picture
Close-ups	Magnify a picture
Bold words	Identify important words May be in glossary
Glossary	Defines important words
Index	Gives page numbers for key ideas

2. **Just the facts.** Students record facts they learn from a visual text feature. During discussion, students share one of their facts. The other members of the group find the text feature that confirms the fact.

3. **Ask Green Questions.** Students write Green Questions (page 265) that can be answered from a text feature. After reading, students take turns asking and answering each other's questions.

4. **Ask Yellow Questions.** Students write Yellow Questions—questions that compare and contrast information in a map, graph, diagram, chart, etc.

| How are the mouth and hood similar? | What are the differences between the arms and the tentacles? |

Module 28

UNDERSTANDING TEXT STRUCTURE
Graphic Organizers

Genre: Nonfiction

Grade Range: 3–8

In a Nutshell: Text structures are organizational patterns found within informational texts. In this module students learn to recognize five text structures and select appropriate graphic organizers for taking notes and summarizing the article. Scholastic magazines are great resources for teaching text structure.

Whole-Class Mini-Lesson

Model: Select a text that follows one of the main text structures. Use the title and text features to explain why the author chose that structure. Display the graphic organizer from the chart at the right that matches the text structure. Read the first paragraph to students and use bullets to record important information in the graphic organizer.

Guided Practice: Read the next paragraph and have students help you add more bullets to the graphic organizer. Students work in pairs to summarize the passage using the graphic organizer you created together.

Repeat the lesson with the other text structures, then select a text that incorporates more than one structure. Students read a section, determine the structure, record important information in the graphic organizer, and summarize it.

Progressive Steps for Guided Reading
(Levels Q and higher)

1. **Single text structure.** Select a text with a single text structure. Help students determine the text structure using titles and headings. Students draw the appropriate graphic organizer in their reading notebooks and use it to record key details as they read. Support those who need help. During discussion, students take turns summarizing a paragraph or section using the graphic organizer.

2. **Multiple text structures.** Choose a text that has several text structures. As students read the passage, they draw the graphic organizer for that section and record their notes. During discussion, students take turns summarizing a section using the graphic organizer.

Sequential	Description	Compare/Contrast
steps or time sequence	main idea/details	similarities and differences
1. 2. 3. 4.	Main Idea — Detail, Detail	(Venn diagram)

Cause/Effect	Problem/Solution
A causes B	problem is solved
C → E	Problem, Event, Event, Solution

Graphic organizers for common text structures

Tips for Independent Practice

Students work in pairs to make a poster that explains one text structure. They select an article from a news magazine, mount it on an 11-x-14-inch piece of construction paper, draw the graphic organizer that matches the structure, and record their notes. Then they write a summary of the article.

Module 29

COMBINING STRATEGIES

Reciprocal Teaching

Genre: Any

Grade Range: 2–8

In a Nutshell: Reciprocal teaching is an interactive method for improving comprehension (Palinscar & Brown, 1984). Students employ four strategies to lead a discussion:

Predict: Preview text features to anticipate what you will learn next.

Clarify: When you don't understand, stop and use fix-up strategies. See Module 1.

Question: Ask questions about the text.

Summarize: Recall the most important ideas.

Give students a Reciprocal Teaching card to use (Appendix N).

Whole-Class Mini-Lesson

Model: Introduce one of the four strategies listed above and model how to do it with any grade-appropriate text.

Guided Practice: Students work in pairs to practice the strategy.

Follow-up Lessons: Repeat the lesson with the other three strategies. Then teach a series of lessons using all four strategies at the same time.

Progressive Steps for Guided Reading
(Levels M and higher)

1. **Predict.** Insert several sticky notes where students should stop reading and write a prediction. Prompt them to use chapter titles, headings, illustrations, and other text features. During discussion, students take turns sharing one of their predictions.

> **Reciprocal Teaching**
> **Predict:** What will you read next?
>   *I predict I will learn . . . because . . . .*
> **Clarify:** What confused you?
>   *At first, I didn't understand . . . so I . . . .*
> **Question:** What were you wondering?
>   *I wonder . . . . How . . . ? What would happen if . . . ?*
> **Summarize:** Summarize what you read.
>   *This passage is about . . . .*

2. **Clarify.** Provide copies of a text and give each student a Fix-Up Strategies card (Appendix N). As students read, they make an *X* where they stop understanding, and they underline words or phrases they need to clarify. Then they use one of the fix-up strategies to clarify their confusion. After reading, students share the strategies they used to help them clarify their confusions.

3. **Question.** Distribute sticky flags. As they read, students flag a sentence where they ask themselves a question, and they write the question in their notebooks. Prompt them to write questions about important details or places where they made an inference. During the last few minutes of the lesson, students take turns asking and answering each other's questions.

4. **Summarize.** Prepare for the lesson by inserting a sticky flag where students should stop reading and write a summary. If students struggle with summarizing, use Module 25.

5. **Combine strategies.** Assign one reciprocal teaching strategy to each student. As they read, they write a response for their assigned strategy. Prompt as needed. During the discussion, students take the lead and teach the strategy to the group. Your role is to facilitate the discussion and provide feedback.

Tips for Independent Practice

Use reciprocal teaching for literature circles. Students write a short response for each strategy during independent reading and share their responses during the circle discussion. One student takes the teacher's role.

References

Allington, R. (2009). *What really matters in fluency: Research-based practices across the curriculum.* Boston: Pearson.

Allington, R. (2011). What at-risk readers need. *Educational Leadership, 68*(6), 40–45.

Anderson, R., & Nagy, W. (1991). Word meanings. In R. Barr, M. Kamil, P. Mosenthal, & P. D. Pearson (Eds.), *Handbook of Reading Research, Vol. 2,* (pp. 690–724). New York: Longman.

Avalos, M. A., Plasencia, A., Chavez, C., & Rascon, J. (2007). Modified guided reading: Gateway to English as a second language and literacy learning. *The Reading Teacher, 61*(4), 318–329.

Bear, D. R., Invernizzi, M., Templeton, S., & Johnston, F. (2012). *Words their way: Word study for phonics, vocabulary, and spelling instruction* (5th ed.). Boston: Pearson.

Beck, I. L., McKeown, M. G., & Kucan, L. (2002). *Bringing words to life.* New York: Guilford.

Both-de Vries, A., & Bus, A. G. (2008). Name writing: A first step to phonetic writing? Does the name have a special role in understanding the symbolic function of writing? *Literacy Teaching and Learning, 12,* 37–55.

Boushey, G., & Moser, J. (2014). *The daily 5: Fostering literacy independence in the elementary grades.* Portland, ME: Stenhouse.

Clay, M. (1975). *What did I write?* Portsmouth, NH: Heinemann.

Clay, M. (1993). *Reading recovery: A guidebook for teachers in training.* Portsmouth, NH: Heinemann.

Clay, M. (1994). *Reading recovery: A guidebook for teachers in training.* Portsmouth, NH: Heinemann.

Clay, M. (2000). *Concepts about print: What have children learned about the way we print language?* Portsmouth, NH: Heinemann.

Clay, M. (2005). *Literacy lessons designed for individuals: Part two, teaching procedures.* Portsmouth, NH: Heinemann.

Clay, M. (2006). *An observation survey of early literacy achievement* (2nd ed.). (Rev. ed.). Portsmouth, NH: Heinemann.

Clay, M. (2013). *An observation survey of early literacy achievement* (3rd ed.). (Rev. ed.). Portsmouth, NH: Heinemann.

Elkonin, D. (1971). Development of speech. In A. V. Zaporozhets & D. B. Elkonin (Eds.), *The Psychology of Preschool Children.* Cambridge, MA: M. I. T. Press.

Fawson, P., & Reutzel, R. (2000). But I only have a basal: Implementing guided reading in the early grades. *The Reading Teacher, 54*(1), 84–97.

Fernald, G. M. (1943). *Remedial techniques in basic school subjects.* New York: McGraw-Hill.

Fountas, I., & Pinnell, G. S. (1996). *Guided reading: Good first teaching for all children.* Portsmouth, NH: Heinemann.

Fountas, I., & Pinnell, G. S. (2001). *Guiding readers and writers: Teaching comprehension, genre, and content literacy.* Portsmouth, NH: Heinemann.

Fountas, I., & Pinnell, G. S. (2008). *Teaching for comprehending and fluency: Thinking, talking, and writing about reading, K–8.* Portsmouth, NH: Heinemann.

Fountas, I., & Pinnell, G. S. (2016). *Guided reading: Responsive teaching across the grades.* Portsmouth, NH: Heinemann. Manuscript submitted for publication.

Heckelman, R. G. (1969). The neurological impress remedial reading technique. *Academic Therapy, 4,* (pp. 277–282). San Rafael, CA: DeWitt Reading Clinic.

Hoyt, L. (1988). *Revisit, reflect, retell.* Portsmouth, NH: Heinemann.

Hoyt, L. (1999). *Revisit, reflect, retell: Strategies for improving reading comprehension.* Portsmouth, NH: Heinemann.

Hoyt, L. (2007). *Interactive read-alouds: Linking standards, fluency, and comprehension.* Portsmouth, NH: Heinemann.

Kelley, M. J., & Clausen-Grace, N. (2010). Guiding students through expository text with text feature walks. *The Reading Teacher, 64*: 191–195. doi: 10.1598/RT.64.3.4

Lipson, M. Y., & Wixson, K. K. (2010). *Successful approaches to RTI: Collaborative practices for improving K–12 literacy.* Newark, DE: International Reading Association.

Macon, F., Bewell, D. M., & Vogt, M. (1991). *Responses to literature.* Newark, DE: International Reading Association.

McCarrier, A., Pinnell, G. S., & Fountas, I. (2000). *Interactive writing: How language and literacy come together.* Portsmouth, NH: Heinemann.

Nag-Arulmani, S., Reddy, V., & Buckley, S. (2003). Targeting phonological representations can help in the early stages of reading in a non-dominant language. *Journal of Research on Reading, 26*(1), 49–68.

Nagy, W., Anderson, P., & Herman, R. (1987). Learning word meanings from context during normal reading. *American Educational Research Journal, 24,* 237–270.

Palinscar, A. S., & Brown, A. (1984). Reciprocal teaching of comprehension-fostering and comprehension-monitoring activities. *Cognition and Instruction, 1*(2), 117–175.

Pressley, M., Hilden, K., & Shankland, R. (2005). *An evaluation of end-grade-3 dynamic indicators of basic early literacy skills (DIBELS): Speed reading without comprehension, predicting little* (Technical Report). East Lansing, MI: Literacy Achievement Research Center.

Raphael, T. E. (1982). Question answering strategies for children. *The Reading Teacher, 36*(2), 186–190.

Reutzel, D. R. (2015). Findings primary teachers will want to know. *The Reading Teacher, 69*(1), 14–24.

Richardson, J. (2009). *Next step in guided reading: Focused assessments and targeted lessons for helping every student become a better reader.* New York: Scholastic.

Richardson, J., & Walther, M. P. (2013). *Next step guided reading assessment: Grades K–2.* New York: Scholastic.

Richardson, J., & Walther, M. P. (2013). *Next step guided reading assessment: Grades 3–6.* New York: Scholastic.

Schilling, S. G., Carlisle, J. F., Scott, S. E., & Zeng, J. (2007). Are fluency measures accurate predictors of reading achievement? *The Elementary School Journal, 107*(5), 429–448.

Shanahan, T. et al. (2008). Developing early literacy: Report of the National Literacy Panel. Retrieved from http://lincs.ed.gov/publications/pdf/NELPReport09.pdf

Sousa, D. (2014). *How the brain learns to read.* Thousand Oaks, CA: Corwin.

Vygotsky, L. (1978). *Mind in society.* Cambridge, MA: Harvard University Press.

Zutell, J., & Rasinski, T. (1989). Reading and spelling connections in third and fifth grade students. *Reading Psychology, 10,* 137–155.

APPENDICES

A	Strategies and Skills by Level	289
B	Word Lists by Level	300
C	Alphabet Chart	305
D	Letter/Sound Checklist	306
E	Lesson Plan Templates	307
F	Sight Word Charts for Monitoring Progress	317
G	Shared Retelling Cards	321
H	Sound Box Template	322
I	Sound Box and Analogy Chart Templates	323
J	Word Knowledge Inventory	324
K	My Word Wall	325
L	New Word List Template	326
M	Character Feelings and Traits	327
N	Comprehension Cards	328

All Appendix items can be downloaded from scholastic.com/NSFresources.

APPENDIX A
Strategies and Skills by Level

Summary of skill focus, word study activities, and guided writing

Level	Skill Focus	Sound Sorts	Magnetic Letters (Making Words)	Sound Boxes	Analogy Charts	Guided Writing
Pre-A	Letters, sounds, print concepts	Initial consonants	Match letters to alphabet chart. Make first name.	None	None	Interactive writing
A 1	Consonants	Initial consonants	Exchange initial consonants: *cat-fat-mat-bat*	2 or 3 boxes *me, go, he, so* *can, map, hat*	None	Dictated sentence 3–5 words
B 2	Consonants Short vowels (*a, o*)	Initial and final consonants Short *a* and *o*	Exchange initial and final consonants: *can-pan-pat-mat-man*	2 or 3 boxes *at, on, am, hop, fan, mom, dad*	None	Dictated or open-ended sentence 5–7 words
C 3/4	Short vowels (*a, e, i, o, u*) Hearing sounds in sequence (CVC)	Short *e, i, u*	Exchange initial, medial, and final letters; include all short vowels: *pot-hot-hop-mop-map-cap-lap-lad-lid*	3 boxes (CVC) *mat, bed, did, hop, fun*	None	Dictated or open-ended sentence 7–10 words
D 5/6	Digraphs (*sh, ch, th*) Endings (*-s, -ing*) Onset/rime	Initial and final digraphs	Exchange initial, medial, and final letters; include digraphs; break at onset and rime: *hop-shop-chop-chip-chin-thin*	3 boxes (words with digraphs) *chat, then, with, ship, such, much*	None	Dictated or open-ended sentences Include endings: *-ing, -s,*
E 7/8	Initial blends Onset/rime Endings (*-ed, -er*)	Initial blends	Add and delete initial clusters; break at onset and rime: *cap-clap-clip-grip-grin-spin*	4 boxes (initial blends, short vowels) *slip, clan, step*	None	2 or 3 sentences B-M-E Facts learned

Level	Skill Focus	Sound Sorts	Magnetic Letters (Making Words)	Sound Boxes	Analogy Charts	Guided Writing
F 9/10	Final blends Onset/rime	Final blends	Add and delete final clusters; break at onset and rime: *went-wept-west-lest-list-limp*	4 boxes final blends *lamp, last, test, went, milk, jump*	None	B-M-E (3 sentences) Facts learned Respond to a prompt
G 11/12	Initial and final blends Silent *e*	None	Silent-*e* feature: *mat-mate-mane-man*	5 boxes *stink, grunt, stomp*	**cat / make**; chat / shake; spat / snake; spam / grape	B-M-E (4 sentences) Somebody-Wanted-But-So (SWBS) Respond to a prompt
H–I 13–16	Vowel teams *ee, ar, ay, oa, or, all, ow (cow)* Endings	None	Vowel patterns: *cow-clown-crown-crowd* Break at onset and rime: *(cl-own)*	None	**eat / day**; beat / gray; seating / stayed; cheater / prayed	B-M-E (5 sentences) SWBS Problem-Solution Respond to a prompt
J+ 17+	Vowel teams *ou, ew, ight, aw, ai, oi, ow (low)* Make and break a big word	None	*de-light-ful* *e-nor-mous*	None	**rain / out**; stain / about; sprain / shouted; brainy / ground. **hop / hopping**; stop / stopping; clap / clapping; hug / hugging	Five-Finger Retell Character analysis Main idea/details Summary Compare/contrast Cause-effect Question-Answer Respond to a prompt

Use these charts to plan your lessons and guide acceleration decisions.

Strategies and Skills for Pre-A

Work With Letters and Names	Work With Sounds	Read and Discuss Books	Interactive Writing
• Learn letter names • Link letters to picture concepts • Learn letter sounds • Visual memory for first name • Visual scanning left to right • Letter formation	• Foundational skills • Hear syllables • Hear rhyming words • Hear initial consonants • Link sounds to letters	• Oral language • Vocabulary • Left-to-right directionality • One-to-one matching • Concept of letter and word • Concept of first and last letter/word • Attend to print • Period at the end of a sentence	• Hear sounds in words • Link sounds to letters • Form letters • Space between words • One-to-one matching

Strategies and Skills for Level A

Students learn to . . .	Picture Sorts	Making Words	Sound Boxes	Guided Writing
• maintain one-to-one on one line of print. • use meaning to predict, monitor, self-correct. • read and write about 10 words. • firm up letter knowledge. • hear and use initial consonant sounds in reading and writing.	Initial consonants Choose 2 (see pages 38–39; 81) Examples of pictures to sort for **Dd, Hh**: *desk, duck, horse, hand*	Change initial consonant: • *go-no-so* • *cat-hat-mat-pat* • *me-he-we-be* • *hop-mop-top-cop* • *pot-lot-hot-dot* • *pan-man-ran-fan* • *map-cap-tap-gap* • *mad-had-sad-pad* • *dog-fog-log-hog*	2 or 3 boxes | S | O | *me, we, he, go, no* | m | a | p | *map, can, dad*	Dictate a sentence with 3–5 words. **Examples:** *I like pizza.* *I see the turtle.* *My mom is nice.* *We can go fast.*

Use these charts to plan your lessons and guide acceleration decisions.

Strategies and Skills for Level B

Students learn to...	Picture Sorts	Making Words	Sound Boxes	Guided Writing
• maintain one-to-one on two lines of print. • use meaning, structure, and known words to predict, monitor, and correct. • cross-check meaning and first letters with prompting. • read and write about 20 words. • hear and use initial and final consonants. • hear and use short vowels (*a* and *o*).	Short vowels (*a* and *o*) Choose 2 (see page 82) Examples of pictures to sort for **a, o**: *hat, cat, mop, box*	Change final consonant: • *rat-rag-ram-ran-rap* • *cat-cap-can-cab* • *man-mat-map-mad* • *hat-ham-had-has* • *hot-hop-hog* Change initial and final consonant: • *mat-map-man-pan* • *sat-sad-mad-had* • *dog-hog-hot-dot* • *hot-cot-cop-hop*	2 or 3 boxes | a | t | *am, at, as, on, up, an* | c | a | t | *cap, dog, log, mat*	Dictate a sentence with 5–7 words. **Examples:** *The rat is in the cage.* *Look at the pig in the road.* *Look at the big cat.* *We go to the lake to swim.*

Strategies and Skills for Level C

Students learn to...	Picture Sorts	Making Words	Sound Boxes	Guided Writing
• use meaning, structure, known words, and initial consonants to predict, monitor, and self-correct. • cross-check meaning and first letters to solve unknown words without prompting. • read and write about 30 words. • hear and record CVC sounds in sequence with prompting.	Short vowels (*e, i, u*) Choose 2 or 3 (see page 82) Examples of pictures to sort for **e, i, u**: *bed, leg, pig, lip, cup, rug*	Change initial, medial, and final letters: • *can-cap-map-mop-top* • *sat-sad-mad-mud-bud* • *dog-dot-hot-hop-hip* • *ran-run-bun-bug-bag* • *lap-lip-lid-lad-mad* • *got-get-net-pet-peg* • *his-hit-pit-pot-hot-hop* • *had-hid-rid-rig-wig* • *run-bun-bin-bit-bet*	3 boxes | r | u | g | *bag sit* *hop gum* *rap big* *job wet* *cab hop* *vet tag* *cap mob* *rid fog* *can jog* *get nod*	Dictate a sentence with 7–10 words. **Examples:** *Come and look at my red car.* *We will catch the big fish in the lake.*

Use this chart to plan your lessons and guide acceleration decisions.

Strategies and Skills for Level D

Students learn to...	Picture Sorts	Making Words	Sound Boxes	Guided Writing
• maintain meaning while solving new words. • cross-check without prompting. • use known parts with prompting. • attend to endings with prompting. • blend the sounds in small words. • reread to access meaning. • read without pointing. • read in short phrases. • read and write about 40 words. • use digraphs and short vowels. • read dialogue with expression. • hear and record sounds in sequence without support. • retell the story with support.	Digraphs Choose 2 or 3 (see pages 132–133) Examples of pictures to sort for **sh**, **ch**, **th**: *ship, sheep, chick, cheese, thumb, think*	Change initial, medial, or final letters. Include digraphs. Break at onset and rime. *(ch-ip)* • *hip-chip-chop-shop-ship* • *bat-bath-math-mash* • *did-dish-dash-mash-mush-much-such* • *hat-chat-chap-chip-ship* • *cat-chat-that-than-thin* • *map-math-bath-bash* • *the-then-than-that*	3 boxes | m | a | sh | math shop chin this such dash chat dish chop thud such shot path hush with chip	Dictate two sentences. **Examples:** *Ben is looking for his bear. Mom said to check the chair.* *The man is going to the fire. He will get the cat to come to him.*

Use this chart to plan your lessons and guide acceleration decisions.

Strategies and Skills for Level E

Students learn to . . .	Picture Sorts	Making Words	Sound Boxes	Guided Writing
• maintain meaning while using known parts to solve words. • cover the endings to solve words. • monitor with meaning, blends, and endings. • read and write an increasing number of sight words. • read familiar text with fluency. • read new text with some phrasing. • read with expression. • understand simple contractions made from known words (e.g., *can't, didn't, I'm, I'll, you're, we're, isn't they're, he's, she's, it's*) • orally segment one-syllable words at the onset and rime (*st-ick*). • hear and write a CCVC word in sequence.	Initial Blends Select blends that begin with the same letter. Choose 2 or 3 (see pages 132–133) Examples of pictures to sort for **fl**, **fr**: *flower, flag, fruit, frog*	Change initial blend, medial vowel, or final letter. Break at onset and rime. (gr-ab) • bag-brag-brat-flat-flit • lip-clip-slip-slit-spit-spot • lap-clap-slap-slam-spam • rim-trim-trip-trap-strap • stub-stab-grab-gram-glam-glum • crab-slab-grab-grub-snub • skin-skip-trip-trap-clap-clip • plum-drum-drug-snug-snag • step-stop-slop-slip-blip • win-twin-twig-swig-swim	4 boxes | c | r | a | b | brag clip snug clam drop spun clap drip crab flip sled flop grin sped grip plot flap skid	Prompt students to write about the story. **Prompt:** Write a sentence about the beginning and another about the end of the story. Use the pictures if you need help. **Example:** Bella did not want to share her bone. She hid her bone in the snow. **Prompt:** What did you learn about fireflies? **Example:** They have two wings and two big eyes. They light up at night.

Use this chart to plan your lessons and guide acceleration decisions.

Strategies and Skills for Level F

Students learn to...	Picture Sorts	Making Words	Sound Boxes	Guided Writing
• maintain meaning while using known parts and endings to solve new words. • attend to the middle and end of words with prompting. • use onsets and rimes to solve words with prompting. • read new books with greater fluency and expression. • use punctuation to read with phrasing and expression. • understand more challenging contractions (e.g., couldn't, won't, we'll, we've, I've, who'll, they'll). • hear and record final blends in one-syllable words.	Final blends Choose 2 or 3 (see pages 132–133) Examples of pictures to sort: • **-mp** camp, lamp, jump • **-nd** band, land, sand • **-ng** sing, bang, lung • **-st** nest, rest, west • **-sk** mask, tusk, desk • **-nk** tank, bank, junk, pink, link • **-ft** raft, gift, lift • **-nt** ant, mint, bent • **-lt** felt, melt, belt, bolt • **-lk** milk, silk	Change initial letter, medial vowel, or final blend. Break at onset and rime. (s-ing) • ask-bask-bash-mash • bang-bank-band-land • camp-damp-dump-lump • gang-fang-pang-pant • fast-last-lest-left-lent • rang-sang-sank-tank • raft-rant-pant-past-pest • belt-bend-bent-best • desk-dusk-tusk-must • went-west-test-tend • lift-lint-list-last-cast • just-jest-rest-rust-runt • soft-sift-silt-hilt-hint • felt-belt-best-bent-went • milk-silk-silt-wilt	4 boxes | k | e | p | t | gust pink kept fang band desk lift bang film lend rung damp lung mend mist belt sang risk lump dusk mend sink land task	Prompt students to write about the story. **B-M-E** (3 sentences) **Prompts:** • Write three sentences about the story. Use your pictures if you need help. • What was the problem? How was it solved? • Write three facts about firefighters.

Use this chart to plan your lessons and guide acceleration decisions.

Strategies and Skills for Level G

Students learn to . . .	Making Words	Sound Boxes	Analogy Charts	Guided Writing
• maintain meaning while solving new words using known parts, endings, and familiar rimes. • read new books with greater fluency and expression. • break words apart. (Discourage letter-by-letter sounding!) • monitor by attending to the middle and end of words. • use analogies to problem-solve during writing with prompting (e.g., *If you know* like, *you can write* hike). • hear and record initial and final blends in one-syllable words. • apply the silent-*e* rule with prompting.	Initial and final blends • *cash-clash-clasp-clamp-cramp* • *band-brand-bland-blank-blink* • *lush-blush-brush-crush-crust-crest-chest* • *pit-spit-split-splint-sprint* • *think-chink-shrink-rink-risk* • *ran-ranch-branch-brunch* • *went-west-wept-swept-crept* **Silent-*e* rule** • *hat-hate-mate-mat-rat-rate* • *pal-pale-pane-pan-man-mane* • *slid-slide-slime-slim-dim-dime*	4 or 5 boxes | c | r | a | sh | | t | w | i | s | t | brand blank clank cramp crash flash grand grasp plant shaft smash stamp champ clamp clash plump skunk slump sling stump stung thump trunk trust crust grump grunt stunt blush brush crush flush munch lunch bunch crunch	**Silent-*e* rule** **Easy** (Rime is constant.) | hot | hope | |---|---| | spot | rope | | trot | slope | | slot | mope | **Harder** (Rime changes, but vowel sound is constant.) | cat | came | |---|---| | chat | shame | | flag | quake | | clam | brave | **Hardest** (Rime and vowel sounds change. Students sort words by short- and long-vowel sound.) | cat (short) | cake (long) | |---|---| | slap | grape | | twig | spoke | | shut | bride |	Prompt students to write about the story. **B-M-E** (3–5 sentences) **SWBS** *The lion wanted to eat the rabbit, but a deer came by, so the lion let the rabbit go.* **Problem-Solution** What was the problem? How was it solved? **Question-Answer** Write questions that were answered in the book and answer the questions. **Facts** What did you learn from reading this book? **Picture prompt** Choose your favorite picture and write three sentences about it. Include details.

Use this chart to plan your lessons and guide acceleration decisions.

Strategies and Skills for Levels H and I

Students learn to...	Making Words	Sound Boxes	Analogy Charts	Guided Writing
• maintain meaning while quickly solving new words using a variety of strategies. • read new books with greater fluency. • use analogies to problem-solve during reading with the teacher's support. • learn vowel patterns during reading and writing with support. *ee, ar, ay, oa, or, all, ow (cow)* • apply the silent-e rule in writing with a little prompting.	Silent-e rule • *came-same-shame-sham-ham* • *hop-hope-slope-slop-shop* • *rip-ripe-gripe-grip-grim-grime* Vowel patterns • *day-say-stay-slay-play-pray* • *car-cart-chart-charm-harm* • *see-seed-weed-week-cheek-creek-creep* • *boat-boast-coast-coach-roach-roast* • *for-fork-pork-porch-scorch* • *cow-clown-crown-crowd*	5 boxes | s | p | l | i | t | | s | c | r | u | b | See examples listed for Level G. When students can write a word phonetically, including blends, sound boxes are no longer necessary.	**Vowel teams** *ee, ar, ay, oa, or, all, ow (cow)* | car | cow | |---|---| | far | now | | card | plow | | started | crowd | | see | for | |---|---| | tree | fort | | sweep | sport | | sleeping | stormy | | boat | all | |---|---| | float | tall | | coach | stall | | toaster | smallest | To increase the challenge, include words with initial blends and endings.	Students write in response to the teacher's prompt. **B-M-E** (5 sentences) **Track a Character's Feelings** How did the character feel at the beginning, middle, and end? What events caused those feelings? *In the beginning Kenny was excited to help the farmer. In the middle Kenny was sad that the pig didn't want to be petted. At the end Kenny was happy he found a stick to scratch the pig.*

Use this chart to plan your lessons and guide acceleration decisions.

Strategies and Skills for Level J

Students learn to...	Making Words	Analogy Charts	Guided Writing
• increase reading stamina. • flexibly use a variety of strategies to solve new words. • read new books with fluency and expression, stopping only to problem-solve. • use vowel patterns in reading and writing with support. • use the silent-*e* feature in reading and writing with support. • write two-syllable words with support. • use illustrations to determine the meaning of unknown words. • respond to a story in writing with decreasing support. • retell a story independently. • read and respond to nonfiction.	Vowel Patterns • *out-ouch-pouch-pound-round-around* • *rain-train-strain-sprain-brain-brainy* • *snow-show-shown-grown-growth* • *night-right-fright-flight-slight-slightly* • *oil-coil-coin-join-joint-point-pointy* • *few-flew-blew-brew-crew-chew-chewy* • *saw-law-claw-draw-squaw-squawk*	**Vowel teams** *ew, ou, ight, aw, oi, ai, ow* Gradually increase the difficulty of the task by using words with digraphs, blends, prefixes, and suffixes. | out | snow | |---|---| | pout | know | | sprout | known | | about | blowing | | found | unknown | | night | oil | |---|---| | bright | soil | | lightly | moist | | mighty | unspoiled | | new | saw | |---|---| | flew | claw | | threw | thaw | | chewed | drawn | | unscrew | crawling |	Students write in response to the teacher's prompt. **Five-Finger Retell** **SWBS-Then** *Victor wanted to fly his kite, but it was too small so he built his own kite.* THEN *Victor wanted to fly his new kite, but it lifted him to the top of the roof so his dad had to get him down.* • Problem-solution • Character's actions (B-M-E) • Character's feelings (B-M-E) • Write facts about a nonfiction topic • Important event: Find the picture that shows the most important event in the story. Write about it.

Use this chart to plan your lessons and guide acceleration decisions.

Strategies and Skills for Levels K and Higher

Students learn to...	Making Words	Analogy Charts	Guided Writing
• increase reading stamina. • flexibly use a variety of strategies to solve new words. • read new books with fluency and expression, stopping only to problem-solve. • use vowel patterns in reading and writing. • use the silent-*e* feature in reading and writing. • write words with two and three syllables. • attend to prefixes and suffixes in reading and writing. • use vocabulary strategies to determine the meaning of unknown words with prompting. • respond to a story in writing with decreasing support. • use more complex comprehension strategies. • read and respond to nonfiction and poetry.	Make and Break a Big Word Select a multisyllabic word from the story. Make it (*understand*) Break it (*un-der-stand*) Say it (un/der/stand) Make it again	**Vowel teams** Continue to teach vowel teams students need to learn **e drop** Drop the silent *e* when adding a suffix that begins with a vowel. (-ed, -ing) | like | liked | | spike | spiked | | choke | choked | Add suffixes (-ly, -ful) | love | lovely | | real | really | | soft | softly | | care | careful | Double the consonant (when there is one letter after the vowel) | hop | hopping | | run | running | | shut | shutting | Do not double (when there is more than one letter after the vowel) | jump | jumping | | wish | wishing | | hold | holding |	Students write in response to the teacher's prompt. Connect the written response to the comprehension focus for the lesson. • Compare/contrast • Cause-effect • Character motivation • Chapter summaries • Character traits/evidence • Write facts about a nonfiction text using text features (glossary, index, illustrations, diagrams, etc.) • Reflections and wonderings • Opinion/evidence • Argument/evidence • Describe author's point of view • Compare/contrast characters, events, ideas from two texts

APPENDIX B
Word Lists by Level

Word lists for each skill and level to use with word study activities

Levels B & C CVC Words for Sound Boxes					Level D Digraphs
A	O	I	U	E	sc/ch/th
cab	hog	bin	hum	fed	mash
dad	jog	fin	gum	beg	dash
cat	fog	pin	bum	yet	cash
sad	log	tin	mug	led	wish
cap	top	dip	tub	wed	dish
can	dot	win	cub	red	fish
had	got	did	fun	jet	ship
ham	cot	hid	sun	let	shop
hat	lot	bid	yum	pet	shot
mad	not	kid	gun	met	shed
man	hot	lid	mud	wet	rush
zap	pot	big	rug	set	mush
map	hop	dig	rut	net	hush
ram	mob	pig	gut	get	shut
rag	mop	rig	run	leg	
rap	pop	wig	nut	ten	chat
van	bob	dim	hut	hen	chin
rat	job	him	rub	peg	chop
bad	rob	rid	sub	bet	such
ran	sob		bus	pen	much
wag	dog			den	
tab	cob			bed	that
mat				bet	this
jam					then
pat					them
pan					thud
pad					path
yam					math
has					bath
					with

Word lists for each skill and level to use with word study activities

Level E Initial Blends for Sound Boxes		Level F Final Blends for Sound Boxes *endings may be added*		
brag	skip	and	elf	limp*
clam	slid	ant	end*	link*
clap	slim	ask*	felt	list*
crab	slit	band	held	milk*
drag	spin	bang*	help*	mint
flag	spit	bank*	kept	mist*
flap	trim	camp*	left	pink
flat	trip	damp	lend*	risk*
flash	twig	fang	lent	sift*
crash	twin	fast*	melt*	pond
clash	swim	hand*	mend*	romp*
smash	blob	hang*	next	chomp*
trash	crop	lamp	nest*	dusk
glad	drop	land*	pest	dust*
grab	flop	last*	rent*	gust*
plan	plop	mask*	rest*	hump*
slam	plot	pant*	self	thump*
slap	slot	thank*	send*	hunk
snap	spot	past	sent	jump*
stab	stop	rang	tend*	junk
swam	trot	raft	test*	just
trap	club	sand*	went	lump*
sled	drug	tank	west	lung
sped	drum	task	film	must
stem	plug	champ	fist	pump*
step	slush	shaft	gift	rung
clip	blush	belt	hint*	rust*
crib	crush	bend*	lift*	sung
drip	brush	bent	chest	sunk
flip	flush	best	shelf	tusk
grin	plum	desk	bench	
grip	plus		chimp	
skid	snug		shift*	
skin	spun		think*	
shrug	stud			

Word lists for teaching blends and the silent-e feature.

Levels F and G	
Initial and Final Blends for Sound Boxes	**Silent-e Feature**

short a	shrink	at-ate
brand	sling	can-cane
blank	split	cap-cape
clang	twist	hat-hate
clank	strip	mad-made
grand		man-mane
grasp	**short o**	mat-mate
plank	stomp	plan-plane
plant	strong	rag-rage
stamp		rat-rate
clamp	**short u**	tap-tape
drank	plump	scrap-scrape
stand	skunk	bit-bite
strap	slump	dim-dime
scrap	slung	fin-fine
shrink	stump	hid-hide
ranch	stung	kit-kite
draft	trunk	pin-pine
splash	trust	rid-ride
	crust	rip-ripe
short e	grump	slid-slide
spent	grunt	spin-spine
swept	stunt	strip-stripe
blend	crunch	twin-twine
spend	scrub	hop-hope
shred	shrunk	not-note
	scrunch	rob-robe
short i		rod-rode
blink		slop-slope
crisp		cub-cube
drift		cut- cute
drink		hug-huge
print		us-use
stink		tub-tube
swift		
shrimp		

Word lists for teaching complex vowels

_____ Levels H and Higher _____								
-ay	-all	-ar	-or	-ee		-oo		-er, -ir, -ur	-ow
day	**ball**	**car**	**for**	**see**	**see**	**look**	**zoo**	**her**	**how**
bay	call	bar	born	bee	seem	book	boom	germ	now
hay	fall	far	cord	tree	seen	brook	bloom	fern	cow
jay	hall	jar	cork	beef	seep	cook	boost	stern	pow
lay	mall	tar	corn	beep	sheep	crook	boot	term	wow
may	tall	arm	fork	beet	sheet	foot	broom	clerk	town
pay	wall	arch	fort	deed	sleet	good	cool		plow
ray	small	art	forth	deep	speech	hood	food	**girl**	gown
say	stall	bark	horn	feed	speed	hoof	loop	sir	down
way		card	north	feel	steep	hook	moo	bird	drown
gray		cart	pork	feet	sweep	shook	moon	chirp	crowd
play		charm	porch	heel	sweet	stood	noon	dirt	crown
pray		chart	port	jeep	street	took	pool	firm	clown
stay		dark	scorch	keep	teeth	wood	proof	first	brown
tray		dart	scorn	meet	three	wool	roof	shirt	
spray		harm	short	need	knee		root	skirt	**show**
		farm	sort	peel	kneel		school	stir	blow
		hard	sport	peep	queen		scoop	third	blown
		march	stork	reed	screen		scoot	thirst	bowl
		park	storm	reef	cheek		shoot	whirl	crow
		part	sworn	seed	creek		smooth		flow
		scar	thorn	seek			snoop	**fur**	flown
		scarf	torch				soon	burn	glow
		shark	torn				spoon	burp	grow
		smart	worn				stool	curl	grown
		spark					swoop	hurt	know
		star					too	nurse	known
		start					tool	burp	low
		yard					toot	church	own
		yarn						turn	shown
								spurt	slow
									snow
									stow
									throw
									thrown

Word lists for each skill and level to use with word study activities

Levels H and Higher

-oa	-ai	-ea		-ou	-ew/-ue	-oy/-oi	-aw/-au	-igh/-eigh
boat	**rain**	**eat**	**eat**	**out**	**-ew**	**-oy**	**-aw**	**-igh**
coat	aid	bead	meal	loud	new	boy	saw	night
loaf	aim	beak	mean	ouch	blew	toy	claw	bright
loan	bait	beam	meat	pouch	chew	coy	crawl	fight
oak	fail	bean	neat	shout	crew	annoy	dawn	flight
oat	jail	beat	peach	south	dew	destroy	draw	high
road	faith	cheat	peak	spout	drew	enjoy	drawn	knight
boast	laid	clean	real	sound	few	joy	fawn	light
coach	maid	cream	reach	proud	flew	joyful	hawk	might
coast	nail	deal	teach	mouth	grew	loyal	jaw	right
croak	paid	dream	read	count	knew	oyster	law	sigh
float	pain	each	seal	cloud	screw	royal	lawn	sight
foam	paint	east	seam	round	stew	voyage	paw	slight
goal	rail	feast	seat	around	threw		raw	thigh
goat	sail	beast	sneak	ground		**-oi**	shawl	tight
groan	tail	heat	speak	pound	**-ue**	oil	slaw	
load	wait	lead	squeak	found	blue	boil	sprawl	**-eigh**
moan	braid	leaf	steal	sprout	glue	broil	squawk	eight
oath	brain	leak	stream	grouch	hue	coil	straw	weight
roam	chain	lean	team	crouch	clue	foil	thaw	freight
roast	claim	leash	treat		true	join	yawn	neigh
soak	drain	least			cue	joint	bawl	neighbor
soap	faint					moist		eighty
toad	grain					point	**-au**	weightless
toast	plain					soil	because	
throat	saint					spoil	caught	
	snail					poison	cause	
	sprain					moisture	fault	
	stain					avoid	haul	
	strain					toilet	haunt	
	trail						launch	
	train						sauce	
	waist						taught	

APPENDIX C
Alphabet Chart

A a	B b	C c	D d	E e
F f	G g	H h	I i	J j
K k	L l	M m	N n	O o
P p	Q q	R r	S s	T t
U u	V v	W w	X x	Y y
Z z				

APPENDIX D
Letter/Sound Checklist

Directions: Highlight the letters and sounds each student knows.

Student: _____

Letters

A	B	C	D	E	F	G	H	I	J	K	L	M	N	O	P	Q	R	S	T	U	V	W	X	Y	Z
a	b	c	d	e	f	g	h	i	j	k	l	m	n	o	p	q	r	s	t	u	v	w	x	y	z

Sounds

a	b	c	d	e	f	g	h	i	j	k	l	m	n	o	p	q	r	s	t	u	v	w	x	y	z

Student: _____

Letters

A	B	C	D	E	F	G	H	I	J	K	L	M	N	O	P	Q	R	S	T	U	V	W	X	Y	Z
a	b	c	d	e	f	g	h	i	j	k	l	m	n	o	p	q	r	s	t	u	v	w	x	y	z

Sounds

a	b	c	d	e	f	g	h	i	j	k	l	m	n	o	p	q	r	s	t	u	v	w	x	y	z

Student: _____

Letters

A	B	C	D	E	F	G	H	I	J	K	L	M	N	O	P	Q	R	S	T	U	V	W	X	Y	Z
a	b	c	d	e	f	g	h	i	j	k	l	m	n	o	p	q	r	s	t	u	v	w	x	y	z

Sounds

a	b	c	d	e	f	g	h	i	j	k	l	m	n	o	p	q	r	s	t	u	v	w	x	y	z

Student: _____

Letters

A	B	C	D	E	F	G	H	I	J	K	L	M	N	O	P	Q	R	S	T	U	V	W	X	Y	Z
a	b	c	d	e	f	g	h	i	j	k	l	m	n	o	p	q	r	s	t	u	v	w	x	y	z

Sounds

a	b	c	d	e	f	g	h	i	j	k	l	m	n	o	p	q	r	s	t	u	v	w	x	y	z

APPENDIX E Lesson Plan Templates

Pre-A Lesson Plan (< 40 letters)

Students: _____ Date: _____

COMPONENTS AND ACTIVITIES	OBSERVATIONS/NOTES
Working With Names (2–3 minutes) Choose one. Omit once child can write first name without a model (using correct letter formation).	
☐ Name puzzle ☐ Magnetic letters ☐ Rainbow writing	
Working With Letters (2–3 minutes) Choose one per day. Activities 5, 6, and 7 are for children who know at least 30 letters.	
☐ 1. Match the letters in the bag ☐ 2. Match letters to an ABC chart ☐ 3. Name letters left to right ☐ 4. Find the letter on an ABC chart ☐ 5. Name a word that begins with that letter ☐ 6. Find the letter that makes that sound ☐ 7. Name the letter that begins that word	
Working With Sounds (2–3 minutes) Choose one per day.	
☐ Clapping syllables 1 2 3 ☐ Hearing rhymes ☐ Sorting pictures	
Working With Books (5 minutes) Shared reading with Level A book; teach print concepts.	
Title: Choose one or two: ☐ One-to-one matching ☐ Concept of a word ☐ Identify first/last word ☐ Concept of a letter ☐ Identify first/last letter ☐ Identify period ☐ Locate upper/lowercase letters	
Interactive Writing and Cut-Up Sentence (5 minutes)	

Dictated sentence:

Letter formation:

Letters and Names Next Steps:	Sounds Next Steps:	Books Next Steps:	Writing Next Steps:

Teacher Notes—Pre-A Readers

Dates:	Observations	Next Steps
Student _____		Clap syllables Hear rhymes Hear initial sounds Attend to print One-to-one matching Use pictures Oral language Other: _____
Student _____		Clap syllables Hear rhymes Hear initial sounds Attend to print One-to-one matching Use pictures Oral language Other: _____
Student _____		Clap syllables Hear rhymes Hear initial sounds Attend to print One-to-one matching Use pictures Oral language Other: _____
Student _____		Clap syllables Hear rhymes Hear initial sounds Attend to print One-to-one matching Use pictures Oral language Other: _____

Emergent Guided Reading Plan (Levels A–C)

Students: _____ Dates: _____

Title/Level	Strategy Focus	Comprehension Focus

DAY 1

1. Sight Word Review
(write three familiar words) *1–2 minutes*

2. Book Introduction *3–5 minutes*

Synopsis:

New Vocabulary or Language Structures:

DAY 2

1. Sight Word Review
(write three familiar words) *1–2 minutes*

New SW from Day 1		

2. Reread Yesterday's Book
(and other familiar books)

Observations or take a running record on one student.

3. Read With Prompting *8–10 minutes*

Monitoring and Word-Solving Prompts
- ☐ Point to each word. (Levels A & B)
- ☐ Try it. Check the picture. What would make sense?
- ☐ Reread the sentence and make the first sound.
- ☐ What would make sense and look right?
- ☐ Show me the word ____. (Locate a sight word.)
- ☐ Check the word with your finger.
- ☐ Could it be ____ or ____?
- ☐ How do you know it is ____ and not ____?

Fluency and Comprehension Prompts
- ☐ Don't point. (Discourage pointing at Level C.)
- ☐ Read it the way the character would say it.
- ☐ What did you read? Tell me about the story.
- ☐ Does this book remind you of something you have done?
- ☐ How is this book like another book you have read?
- ☐ Have you ever felt the way the character feels? When? Why?
- ☐ What is your favorite part? Why?
- ☐ What was the problem? How was it solved?

4. Discussion Prompt *2–3 minutes*

5. Teaching Points for Emergent Readers (choose 1 or 2 each day) *1–2 minutes*

- ☐ One-to-one matching (discourage pointing at Level C)
- ☐ Use picture clues (meaning)
- ☐ Monitor for meaning
- ☐ Monitor with letters and sounds
- ☐ Cross-check letters and sounds with pictures
- ☐ Locate known words
- ☐ Visually scan left to right
- ☐ Reread to problem-solve

6. Teach One Sight Word *2–3 minutes*

Word: _____   1. What's Missing?   2. Mix & Fix   3. Table Writing   4. Write It (and Retrieve It)

6. Reteach Same Sight Word *2–3 minutes*

7. Word Study (choose one) *3–4 minutes*
- ☐ Picture sorting
- ☐ Making words
- ☐ Sound boxes

7. Guided Writing *5–8 minutes*
A: 3–5 words
B: 5–7 words
C: 7–10 words

8. Next Steps

Text was: Hard   Appropriate   Easy

Next book: _____

Next Focus:

Students to assess and analyze:

Complete the shaded boxes before you meet with the group. Add observations and notes during the lesson.

Teacher Notes—Emergent Readers (Levels A–C)

Dates:	Observations	Next Steps
Student _____		One-to-one matching Use pictures Use first letters Cross-check M, S, and V Hear and record sounds Other: _____
Student _____		One-to-one matching Use pictures Use first letters Cross-check M, S, and V Hear and record sounds Other: _____
Student _____		One-to-one matching Use pictures Use first letters Cross-check M, S, and V Hear and record sounds Other: _____
Student _____		One-to-one matching Use pictures Use first letters Cross-check M, S, and V Hear and record sounds Other: _____
Student _____		One-to-one matching Use pictures Use first letters Cross-check M, S, and V Hear and record sounds Other: _____

Early Guided Reading Plan (Levels D–I)

Students:	Dates:

Title/Level	Strategy Focus	Comprehension Focus

DAY 1

1. Sight Word Review — 1–2 minutes

2. Book Introduction — 3–4 minutes

Synopsis:

New Vocabulary or Language Structures		

3. Read With Prompting — 8–10 minutes

Monitoring and Word-Solving Prompts
- ☐ Reread and make the first sound.
- ☐ What would make sense and look right?
- ☐ Check the middle (or end) of the word.
- ☐ Cover the ending. Find a part you know.
- ☐ Do you know another word that looks like this one?
- ☐ Try the other vowel sound.

Fluency and Comprehension Prompts
- ☐ Don't point. Read it faster.
- ☐ Read it the way the character would say it.
- ☐ Teacher frames 2–3 words or slides finger to support phrasing.
- ☐ What did you just read? What happened at the beginning?
- ☐ Why did the character do (or say) that? What are you thinking?
- ☐ What have you learned?

4. Discussion Prompt — 2–4 minutes

5. Teaching Points for Early Readers (choose 1 or 2 each day) — 1–2 minutes

Word-Solving Strategies
- ☐ Monitor for M, S, V
- ☐ Reread at difficulty
- ☐ Attend to endings
- ☐ Use known parts
- ☐ Contractions
- ☐ Use analogies
- ☐ Break words

Examples:

Fluency & Expression
- ☐ Attend to bold words
- ☐ Reread page ____ for expression
- ☐ Read it like the character
- ☐ Attend to punctuation

6. Teach One Sight Word — 1–2 minutes

Word:

DAY 2

1. Sight Word Review — 1–2 minutes

New SW from Day 1		

2. Reread Yesterday's Book (and other familiar books)

Observations or take a running record on one student.

6. Reteach Same Sight Word — 1–2 minutes

1. What's Missing?   2. Mix & Fix   3. Table Writing   4. Write It (and Retrieve It)

7. Word Study (choose one) — 3–5 minutes

- ☐ Picture sorting
- ☐ Making words
- ☐ Sound boxes
- ☐ Analogy charts

7. Guided Writing — 8–10 minutes

- ☐ Dictated sentences
- ☐ B-M-E
- ☐ Problem-Solution
- ☐ SWBS
- ☐ New facts you learned
- ☐ Other: ____

8. Next Steps

Text was: Hard   Appropriate   Easy

Next Focus:

Students to assess and analyze:

Complete the shaded boxes before you meet with the group. Add observations and notes during the lesson.

Teacher Notes—Early Readers (Levels D–I)

Dates:	Observations	Next Steps
Student _____		Monitor for Meaning Word Solving Fluency Retell Other: _____
Student _____		Monitor for Meaning Word Solving Fluency Retell Other: _____
Student _____		Monitor for Meaning Word Solving Fluency Retell Other: _____
Student _____		Monitor for Meaning Word Solving Fluency Retell Other: _____
Student _____		Monitor for Meaning Word Solving Fluency Retell Other: _____

Transitional Guided Reading Plan (Levels J–P)

Students: _____ Dates: _____

Title/Level	Strategy Focus	Comprehension Focus

DAY 1	DAY 2	DAY 3

DAY 1

1. Book Introduction *3–4 minutes*

Synopsis:

New Vocabulary
1. Define
2. Connect
3. Relate to Book
4. Turn & Talk

Model Strategy:

2. Read With Prompting *10–15 minutes*

Monitoring and Word-Solving Prompts
- ☐ Does that make sense?
- ☐ Reread and sound the first part.
- ☐ Read on. What would make sense?
- ☐ Check the middle (or end) of the word.
- ☐ Break the word apart.
- ☐ Do you know a word with this part in it?
- ☐ How can you figure out that word?

Fluency Prompt
- ☐ Read it like the character would say it.

Comprehension Prompts
- ☐ What did you read?
- ☐ Why did the character say (or do) that?
- ☐ What was important on this page? Why?
- ☐ What caused _____?
- ☐ What are you thinking?
- ☐ What question do you have?

3. Discussion Prompt *3–5 minutes*

4. Teaching Points for Transitional Readers *1–2 minutes*

Word-Solving Strategies
- ☐ Sound 1st part
- ☐ Endings
- ☐ Use known part
- ☐ Use analogies
- ☐ Break big word

Vocabulary Strategies
- ☐ Look for clues
- ☐ Check the picture
- ☐ Use a known part
- ☐ Make a connection
- ☐ Substitute a word
- ☐ Use the glossary

Fluency
- ☐ Phrasing
- ☐ Expression
- ☐ Dialogue
- ☐ Punctuation
- ☐ Bold words

Examples:

5. Word Study for Day 2 *3–5 minutes* (optional on Day 1 if time allows)
- ☐ Sound boxes
- ☐ Analogy charts
- ☐ Make a big word

6. Next Steps
Text was: Hard Appropriate Easy   Next Focus:

DAY 2

1. Introduce Next Section *1–2 minutes*

New Vocabulary (4 steps)

Observation/Assessments:

DAY 3

1. Writing Prompt
- ☐ B-M-E
- ☐ Problem-Solution
- ☐ Five-Finger Retell
- ☐ SWBS
- ☐ Character Analysis
- ☐ Ask and answer questions
- ☐ Event—details
- ☐ Key word summary
- ☐ Compare/Contrast
- ☐ Cause-effect
- ☐ V.I.P.
- ☐ New facts you learned
- ☐ Other: _____

2. Plan *3–5 minutes*

3. Write *15–17 minutes*

Observations and Teaching Points:

Students to assess and analyze:

Complete the shaded boxes before you meet with the group. Add observations and notes during the lesson.

Teacher Notes—Transitional Readers (Levels J–P)

Dates:	Observations	Next Steps
Student _____		Monitor for Meaning Word Solving Fluency Vocabulary Retell Comprehension
Student _____		Monitor for Meaning Word Solving Fluency Vocabulary Retell Comprehension
Student _____		Monitor for Meaning Word Solving Fluency Vocabulary Retell Comprehension
Student _____		Monitor for Meaning Word Solving Fluency Vocabulary Retell Comprehension
Student _____		Monitor for Meaning Word Solving Fluency Vocabulary Retell Comprehension

Fluent Guided Reading Plan (Levels N and Higher)

Dates	Title/Level	Comprehension Focus

DAY 1	DAY 2	DAY 3	DAY 4
1. Introduce New Book *2–3 minutes*	**1. Before Reading** *1 minute*		**1. Writing Prompt**
Synopsis:	Review strategy:	Review strategy:	

2. New Vocabulary *1–2 minutes* | **2. Plan** *3–5 minutes*

Steps: 1. Define   2. Connect   3. Relate to Book   4. Turn and Talk

p.	Word-Synonym	p.	Word-Synonym	p.	Word-Synonym

3. Read and Respond *10–12 minutes* | **3. Write With Prompting** *15–17 minutes*

Model Strategy *(if necessary)*

Prompts for Fluent Readers
Explain what you just read.
Were there any confusing parts (words, sentences)?
How can you help yourself?
What are you thinking? Why do you think that?
What questions do you have? What are you wondering?
Summarize what you read. What's most important?
What motivated the character to do (or say) that?
How is the character feeling (changing)?
What caused _____? What was the effect of _____?
What is the theme/author's message?
Why did the author include this text feature? Explain it.

Observations and Teaching Points:

4. Discuss and Teach *4–5 minutes*

5. New Word List *1–2 minutes*

Word	Definition	Word	Definition	Word	Definition

6. Next Steps — Text was: Hard   Appropriate   Easy | Next Focus: | *Students to assess and analyze:*

Complete the shaded boxes before you meet with the group. Add observations and notes during the lesson.

Teacher Notes—Fluent Readers (N and Higher)

Dates:	Observations	Next Steps
Student _____		
Student _____		
Student _____		
Student _____		
Student _____		

APPENDIX F Sight Word Charts for Monitoring Progress

Sight Word Chart for Monitoring Progress—Level A

	Student 1	Student 2	Student 3	Student 4	Student 5	Student 6
am						
at						
can						
go						
is						
like						
me						
see						
the						
to						

Sight Word Chart for Monitoring Progress—Level B

	Student 1	Student 2	Student 3	Student 4	Student 5	Student 6
dad						
he						
in						
it						
look						
mom						
my						
on						
up						
we						

Sight Word Chart for Monitoring Progress—Level C

	Student 1	Student 2	Student 3	Student 4	Student 5	Student 6
and						
are						
come						
for						
got						
here						
not						
play						
said						
you						

Sight Word Chart for Monitoring Progress—Level D

	Student 1	Student 2	Student 3	Student 4	Student 5	Student 6
day						
down						
into						
looking						
she						
they						
went						
where						
will						
your						

Sight Word Chart for Monitoring Progress—Level E

	Student 1	Student 2	Student 3	Student 4	Student 5	Student 6
all						
away						
back						
big						
her						
over						
this						
want						
who						
with						

Sight Word Chart for Monitoring Progress—Level F

	Student 1	Student 2	Student 3	Student 4	Student 5	Student 6
came						
have						
help						
next						
now						
one						
some						
then						
was						
what						

Sight Word Chart for Monitoring Progress—Levels G, H, and I

	Student 1	Student 2	Student 3	Student 4	Student 5	Student 6
Set 1						
didn't						
don't						
eat						
from						
give						
good						
make						
of						
out						
saw						
were						
when						
Set 2 (more challenging)						
again						
because						
could						
does						
every						
laugh						
many						
new						
night						
very						
walk						
why						

APPENDIX G **Shared Retelling Cards**

In the beginning . . .	Next . . .
The problem is . . .	After that . . .
Then . . .	Finally . . .

APPENDIX H
Sound Box Template

APPENDIX I

Sound Box and Analogy Chart Templates

Sound Box

Analogy Chart

APPENDIX J Word Knowledge Inventory

Student _____ Date _____

Directions: Dictate the following words as the student writes them on a blank sheet of paper. Then circle the skills that need further instruction.

	Short Vowel	Digraph	Initial Blend	Final Blend	Long Vowel VCe	Vowel Team Diphthong	R-controlled vowel	Inflectional ending
Word Knowledge Inventory for Transitional Readers								
1. grab	a		gr					
2. sled	e		sl					
3. chin	i	ch						
4. shot	o	sh						
5. thud	u	th						
6. brick			br	-ck				
7. plump			pl	-mp				
8. skunk			sk	-nk				
9. clasp			cl	-sp				
10. stroke			str		o-e			
11. twine			tw		i-e			
12. quake			qu		a-e			
13. stark			st				ar	
14. thorn			th				or	
15. squirt			squ				ir	
16. snare			sn		-are			
17. drain			dr			ai		
18. gleam			gl			ea		
19. croak			cr			oa		
20. fright			fr			igh		
21. blowing			bl			ow		ing
22. talked						alk		ed (/t/)
23. sprouted			spr			ou		ed (/ed/)
24. spoil			sp			oi		
25. prowled			pr			ow		ed (/d/)
26. flapped			fl					-pped doubling feature
27. tries			tr					y to i add -es
28. hiking								e drop
Activities	picture sorts, making words, and sound boxes			analogy charts				

APPENDIX K
My Word Wall

A
about, animals
afraid, another
after, around
again, asked
always

B
beautiful, believe
because, between
before, bought
beginning

C
called, coming
care, could
caught, course
children, cried

D
decided, doesn't
didn't, don't
different, dropped
does

E
even
ever
every
excited
exciting

F
favorite
first
found
friend
frightened
from

G
getting
girl
give
goes
gone
good

H
happy
happened
hear
heard
house
how

I
if
I'll
interesting
it's (it is)

J
jumped
just

K
kept
knew
know

L
laughed
learned
little
looked

M
made
many
middle
more
mother

N
named
need
new
night
now

O
of, only
off, other
once, our
one

P
people
perfect
place
pretty
put

Q
quick
quiet

R
ready
really
right
running

S
said
saw
scared
special
stopped
surprised

T
their, thought
then, threw
there, too
they, touch
things, tried

U
until
upon
use

V
very

W
walk, went
wanted, were
was, with
water, would

Wh
what, while
when, who
where, why
which

Y
year
young
your
you're (you are)

APPENDIX L

New Word List Template

New Word	Definition

APPENDIX M

Character Feelings and Traits

Feeling: How does the character feel now? **Trait:** How does the character act most of the time?
(Shaded words are more challenging.)

Happy	Sad	Mad	Good
glad	unhappy	angry	kind
joyful	sorry	upset	helpful
proud	hurt	cross	safe
merry	gloomy	grumpy	friendly
thrilled	lonely	grouchy	thankful
pleasant	hopeless	moody	caring
excited	ashamed	cranky	polite
overjoyed	disappointed	furious	respectful
delighted	discouraged	irritated	thoughtful
terrific	depressed	displeased	patient
cheerful	sorrowful	touchy	generous
optimistic	miserable	annoyed	gracious
elated	melancholy	aggravated	faithful

Scared	Mean	Brave	Other
afraid	selfish	unafraid	lazy
frightened	rude	bold	clever
nervous	cruel	fearless	hopeful
shy	greedy	daring	bored
worried	nasty	confident	curious
terrified	hateful	courageous	responsible
anxious	unfair	determined	impatient
confused	ungrateful	adventurous	embarrassed
panicked	dishonest	plucky	concerned
petrified	uncharitable	heroic	frustrated

_____ felt _____ because _____ .

_____ was _____ because _____ .

The character is _____ . The evidence in the text is _____ .

APPENDIX N # Comprehension Cards

Make six copies of these cards and store them in a file box. Students can use the cards during guided reading and guided writing to (1) write short responses as they read, (2) discuss the text, and (3) write about the text.

Fix-Up Strategies

When you are confused . . .
- Reread or read on.
- Ask yourself a question.
- Use text features.
- Make a connection.
- Replace words you don't know with words that make sense.

STP

Stop—Stop reading; cover the text.

Think—What did I read?

Paraphrase—Put in your own words.

B-M-E

What happened at the beginning, middle, and end?

At the beginning _____.

In the middle _____.

At the end _____.

Five-Finger Retell

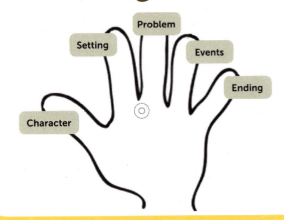

Key Word Summary

What were the most important words?

_____
_____
_____
_____

Use the key words to write a summary.

Who-What

Who is the most important character?

What did he or she do?

Vocabulary Strategies

1. Reread (or read on) and look for clues.
2. Use the picture to explain the word.
3. Use a known part.
4. Make a connection.
5. Substitute a word that makes sense.
6. Use the glossary.

Green Questions

I must go to the text and find the answer.

Who . . . ?   When . . . ?

What . . . ?   How . . . ?

Where . . . ?   Which . . . ?

Red Questions

I must stop and think about the answer.

Why . . . ?

Why do you think . . . ?

How . . . ?

What if . . . ?

V.I.P.
Fiction

Action—What is the most important thing the character did?

Feeling—What is the most important feeling the character had?

V.I.P.
Nonfiction

1. Flag an important fact or sentence.
2. Write a few key words.
3. Use the key words to write a main idea statement.

Main Idea/Details

1. Turn the heading into a question.
2. Bullet key words that answer the question.
3. Use the question and key words to identify the main idea of the passage.

Track the Character's Feelings

How did the character feel at the beginning, middle, and end?

The character felt _____ because _____.

Character—Trait—Evidence

What trait describes the character? What is your evidence?

Character	Trait	Evidence

The character is _____. In the story she (or he) _____.

Who-What-Why

Who is the most important character?

What did he or she do?

Why did he or she do that?

Create a Sociogram

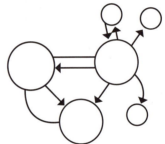

1. Identify characters.
2. Draw circles and lines.
3. Describe relationships.

Yellow Questions

I must slow down and look for the answer.

How are _____ and _____ similar?

How are _____ and _____ different?

What caused . . . ?

What was the effect of . . . ?

Cause-Effect

1. Find an important event.
2. Write a "what caused" or "why" question.

   What caused _____?

   Why _____?

3. Answer your question.

Make an Inference
Fiction

1. Find an important or surprising dialogue or action.
2. Why did the character say or do that?
3. What is the character thinking?
4. What are you thinking?

I'm thinking _____ because the character _____.

Make an Inference
Nonfiction

1. Find an important sentence.
2. Ask a "why" question about the sentence.
3. Answer your "why" question.

Draw Conclusions

Use clues from the text and what you know to make an inference.

I read . . . . I know . . . . I conclude . . . .

If . . . then . . . .

SWBS

_____ wanted _____
(somebody)

but _____ so _____.

Then _____.

Thesis-Proof

Thesis Statement	
Support	Oppose
Summary	

Reciprocal Teaching

Predict: What will you read next?
I predict I will learn . . . because . . . .

Clarify: What confused you?
At first, I didn't understand . . . so I . . . .

Question: What were you wondering?
I wonder . . . . How . . . ? What would happen if . . . ?

Summarize: Summarize what you read.
This passage is about . . . .

Evaluative Questions

1. Why did the author write this?
2. What are the facts and opinions?
3. Do you agree or disagree?
4. What is your evidence?

Problem-Solution

Record key words.

Problem	Solution

The problem was _____.

The problem was solved _____.

Shared Retelling
(with transitional words)

At the beginning _____.
Then _____.
Next _____.
After that _____.
Finally _____.

Write an Opinion—SOAR

S—State opinion
O—Offer reasons
A—Add examples
R—Restate opinion

Word-Solving Strategies

1. Reread (or read on) and think. What would make sense?
2. Sound the first part.
3. Check the picture.
4. Cover the ending.
5. Break the word apart. (*pre-tend*)
6. Connect to parts you know. (*rain-raised*)

Compare & Contrast

Same	Different
They both _____.	One is _____ but the other _____.

Index

A
advanced readers, 250–251
alphabet book, 19, 28,
    tracing activity, 29–32, 34, 43, 48–49, 52, 54
analogy charts, 136–137
    silent e, 137, 183–188, 296–299, 302
    vowel patterns, 132, 134, 136–137, 183–184, 191–192, 290, 297–299, 302
Assessment Summary Charts
    emergent, 59–61
    early, 112–114
    transitional, 166–168
    fluent, 227–229
assessments
    pre-A, 25
    emergent, 54–61
    early, 107–114
    transitional, 161–168
    fluent, 221–229

B
balanced reading approaches, 14–16
Beginning-Middle-End (B-M-E), 260, 328
    use of, 21–22, 141, 157, 173, 178, 195–196, 244, 270, 289–290, 295–298
buddy reading, 20, 99, 150, 152, 214, 259, 261, 263, 272

C
cause-and-effect relationships, 244, 276, 290, 299, 330
    in transitional guided reading plan, 175, 202, 313
character analysis, 175, 202, 224, 290, 313
character feelings, 270, 327, 330
    use of, 12, 118, 127–128, 141, 173, 179–182, 196, 224, 246, 267, 290, 297
character motivation, 249, 273, 299
character traits, 271, 327
    use of, 12, 173, 179–180, 196, 224, 232, 249, 256, 267, 270,
compare and contrast, 275, 332
    use of, 22, 66, 118, 128, 141, 174, 175, 182, 197, 202, 226, 229, 240, 244–245, 249, 251, 256, 284, 285, 290, 299, 313
comprehension cards, 328–332
comprehension interview, 221–226
comprehension lessons/strategies, 256
    analyze relationships, 274–276
    asking and answering questions, 265–266
    character analysis, 270–273
    comprehension monitoring, 258
    evaluating, 283
    inferring, 277–280
    main idea/details, 267–269
    retelling, 259–263
    summarizing, 281–282
    text features, 284
    text structure, 285
    vocabulary, 264
comprehension monitoring, 56, 108, 110
comprehension teaching, 66–68, 94, 118–120, 125,

D
decoding strategies, 110, 116, 123, 129, 134, 148, 161–162, 166, 176–177, 180, 183, 188, 203, 206, 211, 216–217
draw conclusions, 230, 232, 280, 329

E
early guided reading, 106–158
    Assessment Summary Chart, 112–114
    comprehension, teaching for, 118–120
    fluency, teaching for, 125, 152
    guided writing, 139–144, 156, 158
    lesson description, 117–149
    lesson plan, 120, 146, 311
    making words, 133–134
    materials for, 116
    picture sorting, 133
    prompts for reading, 124–128, 138
    retelling, teaching for, 108, 118–119, 120, 125, 126–128, 140–141, 152
    selecting texts, 115–116
    Sight Word Chart, 111, 122
    sight word instruction, 130–131, 152
    sight word review, 121
    sound boxes, 135–136
    sound box template, 322
    teaching points for reading, 129
    teaching points for writing, 144
    ten-minute lesson, 115, 154
    word solving, teaching for, 129
    word study, 131–137, 157
emergent guided reading, 53–105
    Assessment Summary Chart, 59–61
    comprehension, teaching for, 66
    guided writing, 88–92
    lesson description, 65–92
    lesson plan, 68, 94, 309
    materials for, 64

making words procedures, 82–83
picture sorting procedures, 81–82
prompts for reading, 75–77
selecting texts, 63–64
Sight Word Chart, 58
sight word instruction, 57–58, 76–80, 88
sight word review, 69–72
sound box template, 322
sound box procedures, 84–86
teaching points for reading, 77
teaching points for writing, 92
ten-minute lesson for individuals, 102–103
evaluating text, 232, 256, 283
evaluative questions, card, 332

F
Five-Finger Retell, 179, 261, 328
    use of, 22, 152, 157, 175, 195, 202, 245, 309, 313
fix-up strategies card, 332
fluency, teaching for, 105, 117, 119, 130, 132, 138, 143, 152, 157, 163–165, 170, 172, 174, 177–179, 212, 216–217, 219–220, 246, 252–254
fluent guided reading, 219–254
    Assessment Summary Chart, 227–229
    guided writing, 242–249
    lesson description, 233–247
    lesson plan, 233, 249, 315
    materials for, 233
    new word list, 220, 241, 253, 326
    prompts and teaching points, 239, 246–247
    selecting a focus strategy, 230
    selecting texts, 231–232

G
green questions, 265, 329
guided reading, definition, 13
guided writing prompts
    early, 144
    emergent, 92
    fluent, 246–247
    transitional, 199–200

I
independence, six weeks to, 16–18
independent literacy activities, 18–22
independent reading, 15–19, 23–25
infer from action, 278
infer from dialogue, 277
infer from inner thoughts, 279
inference cards, fiction, 331
inference cards, nonfiction, 331

K
key word summary, 282, 328

L
lesson plans
    pre-A, 33, 44, 307
    emergent, 68, 94, 309
    early, 120, 146, 311
    transitional, 175, 202, 313
    fluent, 233, 249, 315
letter formation, 43–44
    use of, 30, 34, 36, 41–42, 49, 57, 69–70, 90, 144, 194, 199, 291
Letter/Sound Checklist, 306
    use of, 27, 31, 38, 40, 41, 50, 55, 59, 64, 81
literacy activities, 18–22
    ABC word study/spelling, 21
    book boxes, 19, 24,
    buddy reading, 20–21, 99, 150, 152, 214, 259, 261, 263, 272,
    computer, 22
    listening, 21
    Readers Theater, 20, 212, 214,
    research, 22, 265, 266, 283
    oral retelling, 22
    poems and songs, 21
    word wall, 21, 171, 194, 199, 217, 246, 325
    writing, 20
    ideas for intermediate grades, 22

M
main idea and details, 220, 223, 225, 229, 232, 239–240, 244–245, 256, 267–269, 285, 290, 329
make and break a big word, 183–184, 188

N
neurological impress, 212
New Word List, 12, 25, 220, 241–242, 249, 253, 315, 326

O
opinion writing plan (SOAR), 245, 332

P
personal word wall, 21, 171, 193, 194, 199, 217, 246
picture sorting, 28, 29, 33, 34, 38–39, 41, 44, 50, 64, 68, 80–82, 86, 94, 107, 116, 120, 131–133, 146, 152, 157, 211, 291–295, 307, 309, 311, 324
pre-A reading, 26–52
    alphabet chart, 21, 27–29, 34, 37–38, 41–42
    assess, 27
    concepts of print, 40
    grouping, 27
    interactive writing, 33, 41–42, 44, 50
    lesson procedures and purposes, 34
    lesson plan, 44, 307
    lesson description, 35–42
    letter activities, 36–37
    letter bags, 37

letter formation, 43–44
Letter/Sound Checklist, 27, 31, 38, 41, 306
materials for, 27–28
name activities, 35–36
name puzzle, 28, 33, 34, 35–36, 44, 307
picture sorting, 28, 29, 33, 38–39, 44, 307
rainbow writing, 36
trace an alphabet book, 29–32
working with books, 39–40
working with names and letters, 35–37
working with sounds, 38–39
Problem–Solution, card, 332
procedures and purposes
    pre-A lesson, 34
    emergent lesson, 67
    early lesson, 119
    transitional lesson, 174
prompts for guided reading
    emergent readers, 76
    early readers, 125
    transitional readers, 178, 313
    fluent readers, 239, 315

Q
questions, asking, 221, 223, 225, 232, 237–239, 265–266, 275
question cards, 329, 332

R
read-aloud, interactive, 14–15
reading stages, 8
reading workshop, 17–18
reciprocal teaching, 286
reciprocal teaching card, 331
red questions, 266, 329
retelling, 259–263, 332
rubrics
    emergent lesson, 59–60
    early lesson, 113
    transitional lesson, 166–167
    fluent lesson, 222–226, 253
retell, 108, 118–120, 125, 127–128, 138, 141, 148, 152, 179, 200, 213, 259–263
running records, 55–56, 108–110, 163–164, 204

S
schedules, 17–18, 23
shared reading, 15, 39–40, 48, 50, 99, 271
shared retelling, 120, 128, 138, 152, 175, 179, 200, 213, 321
skills, by level, 289–299
SOAR writing plan, 245, 332
sociogram, 274, 330
Somebody-Wanted-But-So (SWBS), 141, 157, 195, 239, 281, 331
sound box template, 322
STP (Stop, Think, Paraphrase), 173, 259, 328
struggling readers
    pre-A, 48–50
    emergent, 98–102
    early, 150–154
    transitional, 203–207, 210–215
summarize, 195–197, 223, 226, 232, 238–239, 244, 281–282, 286, 331

T
teaching independence, first six weeks, 16–18
ten-minute lessons
    emergent, 102
    early, 154
thesis-proof, 283, 331
trace an alphabet book, 29–32, 34, 43, 48–49, 52, 54
track the character's feelings, 270, 327, 330
transitional guided reading, 159–218
    analogy charts, 174, 175, 183–192, 202, 211
    Assessment Summary Chart, 166–168
    assessments for, 161–164
    grouping, 167
    guided writing, 174, 194–200
    introducing new vocabulary, 176–177, 206–207, 213
    lesson description, 172–198
    lesson plan, 175, 202
    making a big word, 188
    materials for, 171
    personal word wall, 194, 199, 217
    prompts for reading, 177–182
    prompts for writing, 199–200
    selecting texts, 170–171
    sound boxes, 175, 183–184, 199, 202, 211
    word knowledge inventory, 161–162
    word study, 183–188

V
V.I.P. (Very Important Part), fiction, 267
V.I.P. (Very Important Part), nonfiction, 268
vocabulary instruction, 74, 123, 176–177, 206–207, 213, 235–241, 264, 300–304, 325
vocabulary strategies card, 329

W
who-what strategy, 173, 213, 263, 328
who-what-why, 272, 330
word knowledge inventory, 161–162
word-solving strategies card, 332
writing an opinion, 245, 283, 332

Y
yellow questions, 275, 330

Jan Richardson's Next Step Collection

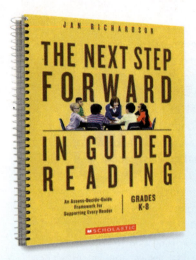

The Next Step Forward in Guided Reading
The essential resource for teaching guided reading—with over 50 videos and dozens of downloadable resources
978-1-338-16111-3 | $51.99

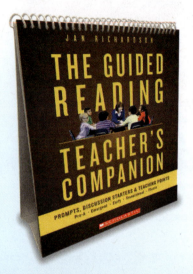

The Guided Reading Teacher's Companion: Prompts, Discussion Starters & Teaching Points
A handy desktop reference with just-right language to use at every step of a guided reading lesson, pre-A to fluent
978-1-338-16345-2 | $19.99

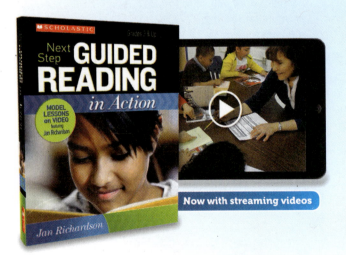

Next Step Guided Reading in Action, Grades K–2 and Grades 3 & Up
Complete model lessons with Jan teaching students at every reading stage
Grades K–2: 978-0-545-39704-9 | $59.99
Grades 3 & Up: 978-0-545-39706-3 | $59.99

The Next Step Forward in Guided Reading Companion Pack
978-1-338-16368-1 | $71.98